SNOW AND SAND

Vicka Markov Surovtsov

iUniverse, Inc.
New York   Bloomington

Snow and Sand

iUniverse books may be ordered through booksellers or by contacting:

iUniverse
1663 Liberty Drive
Bloomington, IN 47403
www.iuniverse.com
1-800-Authors (1-800-288-4677)

ISBN: 978-1-4502-5057-3 (sc)
ISBN: 978-1-4502-5058-0 (ebook)

Library of Congress Control Number: 2010911823

Printed in the United States of America

iUniverse rev. date: 8/31/2010

Dedication

To my father, Anatole Markov

Acknowledgments

I wish to thank my editor and friend Arlene Uslander, for her suggestions and meticulous editing and support during the progress of this work.

I also want to express my gratitude to my friend Alla Crone, for her constant support, and to Ellen Boneparth, Carol A. Collier, and Cynthia Weissbein for their suggestions and encouragement at all times.

My sincere gratitude goes to to Patty Shannon, for her excellent work and patience and to Jonathan Tamal for his technical support in keeping my computer healthy.

Introduction

This is a story about a promise made fifty years ago.

In 1961, shortly before my father passed away, I promised him to visit Russia when its citizens would have the good sense to get rid of the Communist tyranny, which had held that vast country under its heavy hand for so many years.

I promised, although I had serious doubts about Communism collapsing in Russia—ever.

Father was certain the day would come. He was waiting in exile for over forty years, ready to go back to his beloved country, but alas, he was not given the chance to ever see the white, blue and red flag fly over the Kremlin.

In reading my father's diary, and talking to my mother about those tragic years, I was shocked to hear my gentle, loving mother describe to me how she had summoned the courage to shoot and kill a Communist soldier who had found her hiding place and was threatening her. After learning of my parents' tragic experiences, and fulfilling my promise to my father to visit Russia, I knew I had to write this book.

My memoir is in three parts, because I would do an injustice to my father's memory were I to speak only about my very first, but extraordinary pilgrimage to our ancestral nest in 2005.

Part I (1894–1920), which depicts my parents' background and subsequent odyssey during the terrible years of the Revolution, is a sober account of events based on Father's diaries and Mother's recollections. Part II (1920–1958) is about our life in Egypt, and my own life in particular.

Part III (2005) is an account of my visit to Russia, where, being true to my lighthearted approach to life, I found myself occasionally in some deliciously funny situations. Although written rather tongue in cheek, it has not, in any way, affected my tentative respect for the new Russian democracy.

Father left Russia as a young man in his twenties, but the rest of his fruitful and talented life as a writer was spent in Egypt. An important part of this memoir is my account of how a Russian community was established in Alexandria in 1920, when several ships overloaded with members of the Russian White Army landed there. They were immediately quarantined because of the raging typhus fever. Some died and many left after a while, but a nucleus of about a thousand stayed in the country, which welcomed them with open arms.

Father kept a detailed diary all his life, and shared with his family his experiences and thoughts, which I have tried to describe as well as I could.. Set in the first decades of the twentieth century, I followed my parents' lives as faithfully as I could, ending in the historical toppling of the Russian Empire by the Communist regime.

I grew up with stories of life in Russia, and our family's struggle against the destruction of their values. Before I was old enough to know there was a Soviet Union, I knew there was our estate of Pokrovskoye, in the Kursk region, where Father collected mushrooms together with the village boys, where Grandfather Leo raised racehorses, and where my beautiful grandmother, Victoria, whose photograph always graced my father's desk, gave fabulous parties.

Father and Mother's first difficult years were documented in his diaries, and they are still part of my recollection. The events are etched in my mind as told and retold by both my parents to the child that I was, absorbing and enjoying the stories as fascinating fairy tales.

I have dedicated this memoir to my dear father, who instilled in me the importance of keeping the faith of my forefathers, the pride of my origins, and above all, the ability to look at myself in the mirror without a sense of shame.

Father loved the fertile black soil of Russia, which my ancestors enriched with their blood on countless battlefields to preserve it from enemies.

Father believed that Russia would rise again, free from enemies, domestic and foreign. He trusted the Russian people, who loved their country more than their government. "Governments come and go," he frequently pointed out. "But the Russian soil, where our roots go so deep, has never been conquered by anyone," although Napoleon and Hitler did their best, and even the Tartars could not resist the opposition of the people who called their country "Mother Russia."

Father died at the age of sixty-seven, but when I visit him in Colma, California, south of San Francisco, known as the "City of Souls," where he is resting beside my mother, his beloved Zhenia, I tell them about my visit to Russia: about the changes, hopes and disappointments, as well as of Moscow and St. Petersburg, where I walked on cobbled streets familiar to them both. But, most important of all, I share with him the view from the hill where once stood the white house with columns. Pokrovskoye.

PART I
1884-1920

One

My father, Anatoli Markov, was born in 1894 at the Pokrovskoye Estate into an old established family of Russian gentry, in the fertile province of Kursk, located southeast of Moscow. His grandfather, Evgeni Markov, was a wealthy man. Besides being a well-known writer, he was a banker and the elected Marshal of the Noblemen's Association of Kursk. Evgeni believed that since he gave his four sons an excellent education, they should do very well on their own. And, with that thought in mind, he divided his land equally between them, with instructions to work hard. He left everything else to his wife, his beloved companion.

Leo, my grandfather, was Evgeni's eldest son. He married Victoria Rishkova, my grandmother, in 1888. They had known each other since childhood, as only three miles separated their two estates, which, at that time, qualified them as close neighbors.

Victoria was five years younger than Leo. During summer vacations they were part of a large group of friends who spent a lot of time together. When Victoria was eighteen Leo noticed that she was no longer the awkward teenager he had known, but had blossomed into a dark-eyed beauty. He was in his third year at the engineering school when he fell in love with her the summer she graduated from the Institute for Noble Young Women, in Voronezh.

Leo was not the only one who was attracted to Victoria. Soon he found out that he faced tough competition, for Victoria had already mastered the art of keeping a devoted following of young admirers to do her bidding. At first, she did not take his blushing declarations seriously, but Leo was persistent. He patiently courted her and eventually mustered the courage to ask her to marry him. She laughed at him, but, swayed by Leo's perseverance, gradually started to think about him differently, endowing him with qualities of romantic heroes of her French novels, and finally accepted his proposal. Her mother, who saw Leo Markov as a suitable match for her daughter, encouraged her. Leo wanted to get married right away, but his father insisted that he first finish engineering school.

The Rishkins were a prosperous family of Russian nobility. (In Russian, the masculine and feminine names have to agree, therefore Victoria [fem.] is Rishkova, and the family name [masc.] is Rishkin.) They were related to the Tsar's family through their great-grandmother, the daughter of King Nicholas I of Montenegro. Montenegro was then a tiny kingdom with a very democratic king, chosen to rule by his devoted citizens. He had a slew of daughters whom he was anxious to marry off to Orthodox princes, and Russia, a historic protector of Serbia and Montenegro, was frequently seeking alliances through marriages to suitable princes of foreign-reigning families. Thus, several exotic-looking daughters of King Nicolas I of Montenegro married into the Russian royal family, injecting new turbulent blood into their family line. The Rishkins were influential in Kursk and even today, the Moscow-Kursk train stops at the Rishkino station.

Victoria's education at the prestigious Institute for Noble Young Ladies had prepared her for the typical life of a well-born girl. She was proficient in French and German, played piano quite well, and had read all the novels by Georges Sand. However, while Victoria was indulging in fantasies of her future married life, Leo was faced with a problem of how to earn his living. Russia, at that time, had just completed the occupation of Turkestan, whose reluctant natives were not disposed too favorably towards the Russian forces, who were bent on civilizing them, Russian style. One of the most pressing problems of the Russian authorities was the absence of organized communication between Russia and the newly-acquired territory. A bold project of a network of railways was planned, and Leo applied for the job as railway engineer, rashly promising his bride that a honeymoon in Turkestan was a romantic getaway.

After the wedding, Victoria packed her elegant wardrobe, said good-bye to her family and friends, and off they went to Turkestan, traveling by horse-drawn carriage through the mountain roads. After an exhausting trip of several days, the couple reached a small frontier town in Turkestan, where they were billeted in a native house, conveniently abandoned by its owners. The military barracks were in place when Leo reported for duty, and an orderly was assigned to him to help with household chores. To Victoria's consternation, he was to be the only help around their new home. He was recently conscripted, a lad from a remote Russian village, who had just arrived with his regiment in the newly-occupied territory. No female help was available, as the natives did not allow their womenfolk to have any contact with the Russians.

Leo spent the day in a frustrating effort to learn what he was supposed to do. He arrived home that evening hungry and upset, to find his bride in tears—no food in the house, and a panicky young orderly wondering whether to desert or lie down and die. The newlyweds hadn't thought of taking along any household items, such as pots and pans for cooking. All the rosy stories of the natives welcoming the occupying forces with open arms vanished as the couple contemplated the harsh reality. Neither Leo nor Victoria was prepared for the new life. However, the problem of food took second place to the following events.

After a few months, Victoria realized she was pregnant. She wanted to return home, but winter had already set in and the mountain roads were impassable, so she had to face the fact that she must remain in the Turkestan village. There was no doctor and no women to advise her, and Victoria went through a difficult pregnancy. Alone, with the help of a military male nurse, she gave birth to a stillborn boy, whom she and Leo named Eugene. They buried him under a shady tree in their yard. Leo had been doing some serious thinking for the first time in his life. He came to the conclusion that since he was not about to get any financial help from his wealthy father, he might as well use his brains and think of a way to take care of his family.

Victoria, grieving for her lost child, was about to give up on life when Leo told her that he was going to resign from his job and that they would return to Russia. She was delighted to hear that their ordeal was over and she would be returning to her family and friends. Although still mourning for her son, her natural optimism took over and she was looking forward to their departure. A month later, Leo and Victoria traveled back to Russia. The return journey was as difficult as the arrival, but this time, Victoria was immersed in thoughts of happy reunions, while Leo was weighing the possibilities of developing the Pokrovskoye Estate, where Eugene had retired. He hoped to convince his father to let him have a free hand in modernizing the family estate.

Upon their return, Victoria's indifference to all that pertained to the practical aspects of living only increased as time passed. It was not unusual for girls of her class to be mainly interested in the lighter facets of life, such as giving parties, hunts and picnics. Leo secretly hoped that she would show more interest in the running of their household, which she left to the servants. (In those almost feudal days, both Leo's and Victoria's families being very wealthy, it was not uncommon for in-laws to share their peasants with newlyweds. It was considered part of the dowry.) Leo only confided in his brother, Nicholas, who argued that Victoria was as yet too young. So he held his peace and watched indulgently as Victoria plunged into the social life that she had missed so much.

Leo was able to persuade his father to go along with his proposal and Evgeni Markov moved with his wife to his Alexandrovka Estate, abandoning the Pokrovskoye to Leo, on condition that he develop the adjoining land owned by his widowed Aunt Sophia. As far as ideas were concerned, Leo was the worthy son of his father. Within five years, he not only increased his yearly income from the sale of rye and wheat crops, but also added a dairy farm, which proved to be a thriving enterprise. He was able to repay his debt to his father, and even purchased a stable of Arabian horses that won prizes at the local fairs.

* * *

After a troublesome start, Leo and Victoria did enjoy a happy married life. They had three children before the turn of the century: Nicholas, Anatoli (my father), and Sonia. According to my father, Victoria was a devoted and loving mother. The young children enjoyed the freedom of country life, playing with neighbors and cousins. Both Nicholas and

Anatoli were encouraged to play with peasant boys, with whom they bonded for life. Both boys attended cadet schools in Voronezh, while Sonia was a student at the Smolensk Institute in Moscow. When the children were home from school, they had governesses who taught them German and French. But to my father, nothing could equal the joy of returning to his home during the school breaks. Since his early years, he was irresistibly drawn to the beautiful countryside surrounding their estate. He never forgot the lessons he learned from his peasant friend Yasha. Yasha taught him how to recognize the call of different birds and the best places to fish along the shores of the River Tim. It was Yasha, also, who instilled in him a deep love of nature, which stayed with Father to the end of his days. Nicholas, too, was always welcome among the peasant families and often helped them at harvest time. At seventeen, he fell in love with the beautiful Anfisa, Yasha's sister. This was the first and last love of his tragically short life.

* * *

At Pokrovskoye, the twentieth century began ominously, with the death of my great-grandfather, Evgeni Markov. Although expected for some time, this sad event shook the foundations of the Markov clan, from which they never recovered.

During his lifetime, Evgeni Markov, due to his boundless energy and diplomacy, was able to advise and counsel his sons, inspiring them to use their talents constructively. His son Rostislav was an aspiring writer, while Nicholas was just beginning to be well known in the Russian Duma (Parliament) as the conservative member for Kursk, whose radical ideas earned him many enemies among the liberal members of the Duma. The sons and their families were at the center of the Kursk society, enjoying well-deserved reputations untouched by scandals. After Evgeni's death, this started to change.

While the foundations of Russia started to shake, the moral standards of its society deteriorated. In the small world of Leo Markov's family, rumbling echoes of impending doom seemed to reflect the political climate.

Victoria discovered, with some surprise, that she was pregnant again. Nicholas and Anatoli were already in the cadet school at Voronezh while

Sonia was in her first year at the Institute for Young Ladies at Voronezh. . Although she never had any difficulties during her earlier pregnancies, she felt this one was different. She had several fainting spells and a specialist was summoned. To everybody's surprise, she was diagnosed with a chronic heart condition. The physician advised her to rest as much as possible, and Leo decided to hire a woman who would take care of his wife and also help her after the birth of the child.

Two

Thus Maria Vassilivna became part of the Markov family. In his diary, Father described the scene when he first saw her.

During our Easter vacation, Mother called the three of us into her room and said, "Children, I want you to meet Maria Vassilivna. She will live with us as my companion and as my friend, I hope. In addition to that, she will assist the three of you with your lessons when you will be here on holidays."

A tall young lady in her twenties rose from her seat near Mother and said, "What beautiful children! Hello, I hope we soon will be good friends." She shook Nick's and my hand, and embraced Sonia.

Maria Vassilivna was in her late twenties. Tall and slender, she held herself very erect. Blond tresses crowned her head and I thought she was very beautiful.

Father was twelve years old at that time.

Maria proved to be a jewel. She helped Victoria in every possible way and soon they became very close. When friends visited Victoria, Maria would always stay and participate in the conversations, as part of the family.

The new companion came from an impoverished family of small gentry from Voronezh. Having finished the city gymnasium, she studied accounting; these skills enabled her to help Leo in the evenings after Victoria retired for the night.

Maria was invaluable when Victoria's son, Evgeni, was born. Still frail after giving birth, Victoria asked Maria Vassilivna to take over the care and feeding of the baby, for whom a wet nurse was soon found from the neighboring village.

When Victoria recovered, her natural good disposition returned and she resumed her former role of social hostess. By that time, everybody knew that Maria Vassilivna was more than a companion to Victoria. In fact, she was now introduced to friends as Victoria's "best friend." When little Evgeni started to talk, he referred to Maria as "blond mama" and "dark mama" to his mother. Everyone thought it was very cute.

No one was surprised when at Christmas and Easter, Leo would give equal gifts to both Victoria and Maria Vassilivna. Father remembered in his diary when Leo gave both Victoria and Maria similar expensive saddles for their horses. He also mentioned that Nick thought that it was quite unnecessary.

Father never spoke to me about the tragic day when everything started to unravel. After his death I read his diary, where he described what happened.

I was fourteen years old and we were all home for the summer holidays. It was noon and as I made my way to the dining room, I heard loud voices. All the family was already seated at the table with the exception of Mother, who was standing. Father was sitting with his gaze fixed upon Mother, with an expression of surprise and anguish. Her face was in tears. I did not recognize her usually soft voice. She pointed her finger at Maria Vassilivna, whose head was bowed. She was crying softly.

"So you have been his mistress for three long years," cried Mother. "You! My best friend! I trusted you with my life. I practically gave you my child and you deceived me with this weak man, whom I despise. Whose love you have taken away from me. Whom you stole from me as a thief in the night. And you!" She then whirled around to face Father, her black eyes raging. "And you! Have I been a bad wife to you? I gave you four beautiful children. How can you face them after what you have done to me? Oh my God! Oh my God, help me!"

She rushed from the dining room and ran up the stairs. I could hear her slam the door to her room. The servants, frightened by the commotion, crowded in the corridor, chattering among themselves. Father approached Nastia, Victoria's old nurse.

"Go to her, Nastia," he said. "Try to talk to her. Calm her down."

Nastia gave him a hard look and pushed him away from her.

"I'll go to her, Barin, but you just stay away from her for now. My poor *golubka* [dove], my poor angel."

Nastia, who was Mother's old nanny, knocked at Mother's door and spoke softly, while Nick, Sonia, and I huddled in a corner. After a while Mother opened her door and Nastia went in.

In the meantime, Maria Vassilivna and Father disappeared from the dining room. An hour later, a hired carriage arrived at our front door and Maria Vassilivna, her valise in hand, hurriedly got in.

Nastia opened the door to Mother's room.

"You can go in, children," she said. "She needs you with her."

We all went in. Mother was sitting on the couch. She put her arms around us and sobbed. "My poor little darlings," she said. Evgeni, who was frightened by the events, started to cry and soon fell asleep on her knees.

"She left," said Nick. His voice sounded like a growl and as I looked at him, I saw not a boy of sixteen, but a man. An angry man. He embraced Mother. "She is gone, that bitch," he said. "I hate her and I hate him, too. You don't need him, Mother, I will protect you."

"I hate her too," said Sonia, "but I don't understand. What happened, Mother? Tell me, please. Why are you crying?"

This page in Father's diary had many lines crossed out, and then there was more writing, obviously much later, as the ink was fresher and blue instead of black. I read on.

I did not say anything. I had a murderous rage in my heart and I started to hate my father. It is funny that five years have passed since that day, and I did not stop hating him.

Next morning my mother ordered the carriage and went to town. She came back in the afternoon. Father was still locked in his study. She called us to her bedroom and spoke seriously.

"Children, I want you to love me always, even when I am not here. I do not want you to hate your father, for no matter what he does, he is your father and you must remember that."

We cried, kissed her and promised to love her always, but we did not say anything about Father, at least I did not. And neither did Nicholas.

Mother smiled and said, "Go and play now. I love you."

She pushed us out of the room and we went outside. Some time later, we heard a loud bang from the upper landing. We rushed upstairs, pushing against each other. Mother was lying half on her side. Her left shoulder was covered in blood and she appeared dead. A small handgun was clutched in her hand.

Father was the first to reach her. He knelt by her side and tried to revive her. She moaned. He quickly picked her up and shouted to have the carriage brought to the door. There was a small clinic at the nearby village and the surgeon, after examining her, was able to extract the bullet from Mother's shoulder. There was not a great loss of blood and she recovered rapidly.

Later, my parents spent long hours talking behind closed doors. They finally reappeared, wet-eyed. Mother looked happy and Father had that guilty look every time he looked at her, and avoided our eyes.

Although Mother asked us to, I could not bring myself to love or respect him. I know Nicholas felt the same, but he never wanted to talk about what happened. Sonia did not really understand what it was all about, and kept asking us. She also asked the servants, who were only too eager to tell her what they thought had happened, with many embellishments.

Little Evgeni kept asking when his Blond Mama would come back, not aware that Mother was biting her lips when he said that.

Three

The diary continued:

As summer turned into fall and winter, the three of us were back in our respective schools. Mother wrote cheerful letters, but Father no longer wrote his usual half page of instructions to remind us to behave and to study.

When we were driven home for the Christmas holiday, Nicholas and I asked our coachman, Avsey, how everything was at home. Avsey was a new addition at the stables and probably was not instructed by the other servants to keep his mouth shut. So he was eager to repeat the gossip he heard from the maids.

"Everything is as usual, Barchuki," he said, grinning. "Barin is never at home, but he never asks me to drive. Old Ivan drives him, probably to Voronezh, so they say. That's none of my business what the Barin does. Ivan keeps his mouth shut and he knows why. Barina always stays at home and I do not see her often."

When we arrived Father was not home. Mother met us at the door and we could see that she was not well. She was pale with dark circles around her eyes. She hugged us a long time and pretended to be happy. Father arrived late in the evening, loaded with gifts for us. He spoke loudly and cheerfully, while we looked away.

At Christmas, many friends came, but it was not the same as before. Mother's friends would go straight to her room, where they spoke in whispers. Father was at home, but he was distant and moody.

Two days later, Mother took the four of us to Tula, where my uncle had a large town house. We went by train. Father was going to join us in the evening. When he arrived Mother decided to take us to a cinema where they were giving some American movies. It was held in an ancient concert hall, and we sat in the middle aisle, marveling at the moving pictures, projected by a strong light from the back wall.

What happened next is a blur in my memory. A sudden explosion of light, then screams and panic. "Fire! Fire! Where's the exit? Help, oh my God, Holy Virgin of Kursk, help me!!" People scrambled towards

11

the back door, pushing us from all sides. We were right in the middle and then the chairs overturned and we tumbled down. Mother was screaming for us and we tried to hold on to her, but the rushing crowd separated us. A thick smoke filled the hall and I started coughing. Nick was holding Evgeni. Sonia was clinging to me as we made it to the door, nearly suffocating. We couldn't see Mother in the sudden darkness and we emerged outside, pushed by the people behind us. Many had fallen and we heard screams and groans. Once outside, the noise was deafening. A fire engine, drawn by four horses, blocked the narrow street, and coils of hoses were snaking around, dragged by firefighters. Nicholas found us and dragged Sonia to where Evgeni stood, sobbing.

"Where's Mother?" Nicholas cried. "Where did you leave her? I have to find her. You wait here, don't move and I will go and get her."

He rushed off, but was prevented from going in by the firefighters.

"Let me go," he cried, "let me go. I have to find my mother. She is sick and she will die in there if I don't get her out."

"Careful now, Barchuk," said the bearded firefighter, restraining my brother. "You can't go in there. We'll find your lady. Let us do our job, and wait there with the others."

Nick ran to where we were standing.

"Tolia," he said, "hurry and find a carriage to take you home. Tell Father and Uncle to get here at once. They will be able to find her. Hurry, hurry." He pushed me and I flew down the street in search of a carriage. The streets, blocked by people eager to see the fire, were impassable and it was some time before I finally reached home. Father and Uncle rushed to find Mother while, stuck to the window, I tried to pray.

At last, a carriage stopped in front of our house. I rushed to the front door. It was already opened and Uncle was holding my mother in his arms. Father hovered around him. I stood transfixed as they went past me. Mother's head was lolling against his shoulder and she appeared to be asleep. They laid her tenderly on the couch in the hall.

Nicholas and Sonia walked in. Their arms were around each other, and the coachman carried Evgeni in his arms. The servants rushed towards them, taking Evgeni from them. He appeared dazed.

"Mother! You found Mother? Is she hurt? Why is she asleep?" I kept asking. Then I heard a sound I shall never forget. It was my father. He was crying, loudly, unashamedly, and that sound filled me with dread, for I knew that something unthinkable had happened. Our mother was not asleep. She was dead.

Nick, Sonia and I knelt in front of the couch. Mother's beautiful face was calm. Her eyes were closed, her mouth slightly open, and a sudden knowledge pierced my heart. Whatever happened to us now, she would never again be able to put her arms around us and protect us. She was indifferent to our tears and pain. She had just left us and we were now alone for the rest of our lives. My heart swelled with pain and anguish.

Nick kissed her hands. He did not cry. He looked tenderly at Mother, and softly rubbed the dark smudge on her cheek. Then he stood up and looked into my father's face. Really looked as if he saw him for the first time. Then he turned around on his heels and left the room.

Nick never returned home after that.

Four

There were no more entries in my father's diary about events that surrounded Grandmother's death. When I grew up, he spoke often about the tumultuous events at Pokrovskoye, and my mother completed the picture with what she knew.

After the funeral, my father continued his military schooling. He returned to Pokrovskoye for very short visits. He never forgave his father, either, but felt it was his duty as a son not to turn away from him.

Leo was probably quite sincere in grieving for Victoria. However, his passion for Maria Vassilivna never waned and he continued seeing her. He had set her up in an apartment near Voronezh and some months after his wife's death, he brought Maria back to Pokrovskoye. He said young Evgeni needed a mother, which was true, of course. Maria Vassilivna promptly moved into Victoria's room, much to Sonia's disgust. Father's sister seemed to change overnight into a serious young lady. On her sixteenth birthday she moved from Pokrovskoye to Rishkovo, as she could not stand the sight of Maria Vassilivna.

Nicholas continued his studies at the cadet academy and later at the officers' school, spending holidays with his Rishkin cousins. He participated in World War I, and during the Revolution, married his sweetheart, a peasant girl. They had no children. Nicholas Markov died in 1917 of pneumonia. He was twenty-three years old.

Five

My mother, Evgenia (Zhenia) Constantinovna Eggert von Ehofen, was born in Vladivostok in the year 1893, into a family whose German roots were buried in Danzig, Germany, but lived in Russia for many generations. Zhenia's father followed the example of his forefathers, and served the Russian Army as a colonel in a frontier regiment in Siberia. Grandmother Julia came from a Polish family.

My mother was the youngest of five daughters. There was a considerable age difference between my mother and her older sisters, but she was very close to her sister Mania, who was a year older. The only brother, Alexander, was away most of the time at the cadet school and was destined to eventually enter an officer academy from which he graduated into the prestigious Preobrazhenski Regiment, the Tsar's personal regiment.

According to my mother, she was her father's favorite and he spent much time with her on his visits. Zhenia was riding horses before she was six years old. She developed an independent character and liked to dress as a boy, much to her father's delight, and to the manifested disapproval of her older sisters, who thought that she was far too willful for a child her age. Zhenia adored her father, and when he died of an intestinal fever during one of his absences away from home, she was inconsolable. She was just twelve years old at the time. Her sisters, who were some ten years older, decided to take a hand in Zhenia's upbringing. They put pressure on Grandmother Julia, who was an indulgent and kind person, to turn Zhenia from the unruly tomboy into a young lady. Much to Zhenia's disgust, they sent her to a new high school, where she had to wear a dress and abandon her short haircut for long plaits, suitable for a young lady of her standing. I always smiled, hearing the resentment in Mother's voice against her older sisters when she told me about her battle with them, as I recognized what a brat she must have been. Even in later life, Mother retained that spark of independence of spirit as she sparred with Father on issues close to her heart.

To her own surprise, Zhenia enjoyed the new school and showed that she was capable of achieving anything she wanted to by graduating from the Vladivostok high school at sixteen. She announced to her mother and sisters that she wanted to be a doctor and after some noisy negotiations, they agreed to let her apply to the St. Petersburg Medical School. Because of her young age she had to have a special dispensation to take university courses, as usually the students graduated from high school at eighteen years of age. She was duly accepted, and probably her sisters heaved a sigh of relief to have her out of the house.

Aunt Mania decided to study social studies, and the two sisters traveled to St. Peterburg, where they rented an apartment. They soon joined the happy crowd of students, enjoying the rich culture of the city. Hard hours of studying alternated with outings to the opera, ballet and theater. St. Petersburg was the center of culture, where literary discussion groups flourished. Young people learned to question and discuss the political situation in their country. Socialist ideas sprouted readily and challenged young minds, imbuing them with ideas of freedom and equality, but Zhenia had no interest in politics. She devoted her days to studying medicine, often working late into the night, while Aunt Mania wholeheartedly adopted socialist ideas and joined an underground socialist group known as the "SR" (Social Revolutionaries).

These were troublesome times. After the suppressed revolutionary incidents of 1905, the police had increased their surveillance of illegal political societies, and arrests were made. Aunt Mania and her boyfriend were arrested. They were indicted with crimes against the monarchy and condemned to ten years imprisonment.

This was a terrible blow to my mother and to the conservative family, but there was nothing they could do.

When World War I broke out, Zhenia had just graduated from medical school. Heart afire with patriotic zeal, she volunteered as a doctor, and was posted to a field hospital in the town of Abbas Touman on the Russian Eastern Front in the Caucasus. This hospital was attached to a regiment fighting Austrian and Turkish forces, who were kept at bay by Russian and native forces of the area.

* * *

It so happened that at the same time, my father, Anatoli Markov, graduated from the Nicholas Cavalry School and immediately joined the prestigious Starodubski Regiment headed for the front lines. Unfortunately, he was not able to link up with his companions due to transportation problems.

Eager to fight for his country, rather than wait for the next orders, he impulsively volunteered for the Eastern Front. He was accepted into the Native Eastern Regiment, known as the "Savage Regiment."

At that time, in the remote territories of Caucasus, tribes from Georgia, Abhazia, Ossetia and Cherkessia, led by fundamentalists, were still trying to overthrow the Russian dominion. These were mostly outlaws, for most of the conquered lords of these regions lived in peace with the Russians. Several leading native families were granted Russian nobility titles. Many military schools included among their graduates a number of Eastern princes, who went on to faithfully serve the Russian Tsar. Railway communications were frequently interrupted and Father had many delays as he tried to reach the front. Patience not being his best quality, Father decided to make his own way, traveling with his stallion, which was accommodated in the special wagons for horses. He traveled south through Odessa, Kiev and Tiflis to Abhazia, where he finally was able to join his regiment. There he fought in several sorties and was seriously wounded by a bullet in the chest. He also tore up his knee in the skirmish, which killed his horse. Shell-shocked and depressed, he was ordered to recuperate in a sanatorium in Abbas Touman. He slept and rested for the first two weeks, and then boredom took over. He inquired whether there were any friends or acquaintances in that small town, and was pleasantly surprised to find that a Lieutenant Cazimir Chengeri was also a patient in the hospital. Father had met Cazimir briefly in Voronezh a couple of years before, and now he was happy to find someone whom he had known. He was given an address and they arranged for a meeting.

Six

When my mother arrived in Abbas Touman, there was no serious fighting as yet, though at night both sides would exchange occasional fire, without much damage. This situation soon changed when the Austrian and Turkish forces started shelling the Russian positions in real earnest. The number of wounded and dead steadily increased, and the small hospital soon filled with patients.

Besides my mother, there was Dr. Fomin, a bearded giant of a man, who at once took her under his wing. She told me that in spite of his size, he was very gentle with young wounded soldiers, and was loved by all the personnel. The medical supplies at the hospital were often running low, as deliveries were slow in arriving. They worked night and day under poor conditions. The serious cases were sent off to larger field hospitals to make room for more.

My mother was billeted in a small tent with two nurses, but they had little time for girl talk. They were exhausted most of the time and had to snatch a few hours' sleep when they could.

Sporadically, the shooting would stop and periods of inaction followed. Then they caught up on sleep and spent some more time talking to the convalescent soldiers. This was when Mother fell in love for the first time in her life.

Lieutenant Boris Vinogradov was twenty-two years old. Mother treasured his photograph all her life. In this sepia photograph, Boris had watchful serious eyes shaded by a cap with the lieutenant's insignia, his still boyish mouth holding back a smile, hands clasped on a rifle. A real soldier! At the back of the photograph, she kept a small glassine envelope with a pressed red poppy.

Boris fell in love with Zhenia when she was bandaging his shoulder. Apparently, he did not cry out once when she pulled the stray bullet out. It was the first love for both of them. They had a whole long month to get to know each other and plan for the future.

Then the unthinkable happened. He was sent on a routine reconnaissance mission when a bullet struck him. His companions carried him, lifeless, to the field hospital.

This tragedy changed my mother overnight. She decided that she would never love again. With renewed dedication, she plunged into her hospital work, feeling guilty to be alive, while Boris was dead.

One of the patients at the hospital frequently asked for her. Captain Cazimir Chengeri was seriously wounded in the spine and Dr. Fomin predicted that he would never be able to walk again. Cazimir claimed that only Dr. Zhenia's gentle touch on his brow could make him free of pain. She was glad to help. She let him hold her hand, oblivious of his loving looks fixed on her face. She felt she was giving of herself to someone who really needed her.

Cazimir was not handsome or particularly interesting. A small moustache did nothing to hide his receding chin and a weak mouth. But he was very much in love and persistent in his efforts to inspire pity, if not love.

There was a quiet period in Abbas Touman trenches as the front line changed direction. The field hospital became a convalescent center for the nearby regions. Cazimir was well enough to sit up in bed, but still could not walk.

Encouraged by Zhenia's kindness, he surprised her, one day, by declaring his love, asking her whether she would marry him. He said he knew she did not love him, but said that he would never make any demands on her. He would be content to have her kindness and friendship. Mother, believing that Cazimir would always be a paraplegic, agreed. Moreover, she also thought that it was a sign from above for her to make this sacrifice. She held his hand and agreed to marry him.

A month after the wedding, Cazimir made an amazing recovery and started walking. He and Zhenia rented a small house, and it eventually dawned on my mother that her new husband did not need her medical care any more. Cazimir, delighted to be well again, promptly demanded that my mother share his bed. Mother was aghast. All her good intentions flew out the window and she realized that her sacrifice was in vain. She was married to a man she did not love and who was repulsive to her. Their relations took on a nightmarish tint as Cazimir became extremely insistent of his rights and my mother continued to not be very accommodating, to say the least.

It was by pure chance at that time that Cazimir found out that a fellow officer he had previously met was recovering at the nearby clinic. This officer's name was Anatoli Markov.

Seven

In his memoir, Father recalled meeting Cazimir:

I was glad to see my fellow officer, Cazimir Chengeri. An attractive young lady, whom he introduced as his wife, Dr. Evgenia Constantinovna, accompanied him. Cazimir was obviously enchanted with his tiny new wife. However, it soon became apparent that something was wrong with their marriage because Dr. Evgenia's blue eyes seemed filled with unshed tears when Cazimir put his arms around her and said she was his "loving bride." To dispel her sadness, I asked her about herself, and she told me about volunteering to serve as doctor at the Eastern Front. I was astounded at her courage and patriotism. She talked with much enthusiasm and dedication about her work, while I admired the way she held herself, and the wealth of chestnut hair, piled in a crown on her head. Of course, I knew that I could not show my fascination with the wife of a fellow officer, but that said, I still thought that she was wasted on such a dullard.

* * *

Cazimir was excited to have found an old schoolmate. The three of them met nearly every day. In a short time, Zhenia and Anatoli became good friends, staying late into the night, talking about the war and how it affected their lives. Years later, my mother told me that she felt there was a special chemistry between them.

Obviously, Father's impression that something was not going well in the Chengeri household proved to be right. At times, Cazimir would bait his wife with some ironic remark, and she would fall silent, lips pressed together, or would leave the room.

Father noticed once or twice that her eyes were red. That tormented him. Although he tried to convince himself that it was wrong to have fallen in love with Cazimir's wife, he still felt that there was something akin to electricity between them. He had never been in love before. Life in military schools did not allow him any time or opportunity to court

21

the pretty girls he saw on summer vacation at Pokrovskoye. He did have a few passing adventures with peasant girls, but there were no promises on either side, and they were soon forgotten.

Father was a very reserved person in later life, and it surprised me to read in his diary the endearing expressions of his feelings for Mother. I was deeply touched when I read the following lines:

I reasoned that this was just infatuation and tried to suppress my feelings, but I could not conceal them entirely when I looked at her, unaware that she might have already guessed my secret. I was not prepared to deal with my new emotions. Although honor would not allow me to declare my love to a married woman, all my resolutions crumbled one fateful afternoon. Cazimir and Zhenia had invited me for dinner, but when I arrived, Zhenia was home alone. She said that Cazimir had been summoned to the Tiflis General Headquarters for a review of his medical condition. Before leaving, he raised the question of Zhenia's joining him should he be transferred to another military battalion. A heated discussion ensued and Cazimir became very angry when she told him that it was impossible for her to follow him, as she was still under orders to stay at the Abbas Touman military hospital.

Distraught at the idea of not being able to see Zhenia anymore, I begged her not to leave, took her hands and kissed them. She offered no resistance and that gave me hope. I wanted to take her in my arms and console her, but only managed to tell her that I would give my life to help her if I could. Then Zhenia confessed that she and Cazimir had quarreled constantly and that their married life was a sham. She then told me about the circumstances of their marriage and the mistake she had made in marrying him. She said that at the time, she wanted to sacrifice herself in taking care of him, but when Cazimir had miraculously recovered, she realized that she could no longer live with a man she did not love. Apparently Cazimir, his health restored, assumed that they should become lovers, but Zhenia told him that she could not go on with the marriage.

On hearing her story, my hopes soared. In spite of my good intentions, I was unable to suppress the love I felt for Zhenia. I finally blurted out that I was deeply in love with her, but that honor dictated that I could not yet seek her love, and was prepared to wait until she was free. I was rewarded by a wonderful warm look, which made my heart beat faster.

I must have sounded utterly stupid as I tried to calm her down with clichéd phrases like "everything will turn out well."

Although I still did not hear an encouraging word from her, in my heart I felt that although she returned my affection, she was not in a position to promise anything. She just put her hand on mine and said that when Cazimir returned, she would ask him for a divorce.

Back in my small room at the convalescent center, my doubts returned. I cursed myself for not being more eloquent; for not finding the right words to console the woman for whom my love was deepening. I feared that she would not find enough strength to break away from her disastrous marriage.

Eight

My mother's version of their first meeting was more romantic. I was in my early thirties and I suspected that Mother still had not told me everything about that time of her life. Mother and I always had a special friendship, which went beyond our mother-daughter relationship, and one afternoon when we were alone, I asked her.

"Mother, tell me again about your life with Cazimir Chengeri. You told me before that you did not love him, but was he such an unpleasant man? Was he cruel, demanding, and did you have any happiness with him at all?"

Mother sighed.

"No, he was not cruel or unpleasant. I was fond of him, but my heart was not involved and probably I was not fair to him. I should never have married him in the first place. He was infatuated with me and could never reconcile himself to the idea that I was not able to return his passion. He tried hard enough, but I felt I could not pretend to have any feelings toward him.

"When Cazimir recovered from his paralysis, he demanded that we sleep together. When I reminded him of his promise not to make any demands on me, he simply dismissed this with a laugh, saying that he was then too sick to know what he was promising. He said it was my duty as a wife to comply with my marriage vows. I felt caught in a snare. Under pressure from Cazimir, I decided to suppress my disgust and gave in to his pleadings, although I did not hide from him that I never loved him. I will not describe the hell I went through and how progressively angry and sarcastic he became as time went on. One day, I discovered I was pregnant. I welcomed this pregnancy, for I thought that at least I would have some joy out of our marriage by having a child to love."

Mother stopped talking. She sat very still, lost in her thoughts, and I held her close. Her revelation was a big surprise to me and I thought that maybe I had a sister somewhere. But the questions died on my lips as I looked at Mother. There was anguish in her face. She continued:

"My happiness was short-lived, for after five months, I lost my baby. I had wanted that child so much and I was completely devastated. Instead of supporting me in my grief, Cazimir blamed me for not taking better care of myself. Now we were quarreling constantly and I started to think about ending our marriage. When I broached the subject of divorce, Cazimir would beg me to give him another chance."

"But, Mother," I said, "why did you not leave him at once? What stopped you?"

"It was not that easy," said Mother. "I felt sorry for him. I was convinced that I could never be happy again. He begged me not to leave and I was too weak to oppose him."

"What happened next? How did you have the courage?"

"Well," said Mother, smiling, "I told you this story before, but you look like you want to hear it again."

"Yes, Mother, tell me again,"

"At that time," said Mother, "Cazimir asked me to accompany him to visit a fellow officer he had met a couple of years before, who was recuperating from his wounds at the convalescent center. When we arrived at the half-empty ward, we were met by Cazimir's friend. I found myself looking up at a tall young man, with startling dark eyes. He must have been sleeping when we arrived for his hair was all mussed up, with stray locks on his brow.

" 'This is Lieutenant Anatoli Lvovich Markov,' said Cazimir. 'Anatoli, I want you to meet my wife, Dr. Evgenia Constantinovna.'

"Anatoli Lvovich gazed speechlessly at me, then lifted my hand and kissed it reverently. He said, 'I salute you, Dr. Chengeri, as a representative of the courageous Russian women who are giving their life for Russia.'

"Although it was the recognized polite form for greeting a married woman, his words and the kiss moved me as though they conveyed more than respect.

"Cazimir was very pleased that Lieutenant Markov was so gallant to me. He embraced him and started telling him how lucky he was to have conquered me. He actually used the word 'conquered,' while I stood aside and tried not to compare Cazimir to this handsome man, who was still using a cane. His left arm was also bandaged and I could tell that he must have been seriously wounded.

25

"Anatoli served a bottle of native wine and we talked about the war and our previous lives. He did not talk about his war experiences, but asked me many questions. While we talked, I could feel his eyes on me. Cazimir became instantly jealous and on our return home, he subjected me to a scene of jealousy and rancor. He accused me of paying too much attention to Anatoli and that I did not behave like a decent married woman. This time, I did not mind. I was not listening to him."

"Tell me, Mother," I said, "is that when you fell in love with Father?"

"No, not then, but soon after. It is so strange how in a short time, my world changed. Anatoli, Cazimir and I met often when I was not on duty at the hospital. We talked about our families. Anatoli told us about his mother, who died tragically in a fire when he was still a boy. I wanted to put my arms around him when I heard the pain in his voice. But I looked away so that he would not read my eyes. It was Cazimir who always initiated our meetings. After the first outburst of jealousy, he never again mentioned Anatoli's interest in me, but his watchful gaze followed all our movements."

"A month later, Cazimir received orders to proceed to headquarters in Tiflis for possible transfer to active duty. Before he left, we had a violent quarrel. He said that a wife's place was with her husband and that if I refused to accompany him, he would be justified in his suspicions of my infidelity. Cazimir insisted that I apply for a transfer to wherever he would be posted, but I had already decided that I would not follow him. We had an ugly scene, after which he left, and I was still upset when Anatoli appeared at our door."

Knowing what was coming, I squeezed Mother's hand. "So how did you feel, without Cazimir's watchful eyes?" I asked. "Were you emotional?"

"Of course," said Mother. "Although I was very upset, I tried to compose myself. I told Anatoli that Cazimir was recalled to Tiflis, but before I knew it, I poured out all my misery to him, while he held my hands in his. I was embarrassed at having lost control of myself, but I felt so alone in the world that I opened my heart to the only friend I had.

" 'I shouldn't have told you all my problems,' I said. 'I feel ashamed at having to burden you with problems that do not concern you.'

"But Anatoli would not let go of me. 'Zhenia,' he said. 'Zhenia, please, do not go away. Do not leave me. I need you. I need to see you, to hear you, to speak with you. To me, you are the only tie to reality in this world of war and destruction.' He pressed his face to my hands while my heart overflowed with emotion. Although his words filled me with happiness, I felt I had no right to hear them. I was married to Cazimir and I was not free to love another man.

"As if reading my mind, Anatoli lifted his face and looked at me with deep love. He said, 'I have no right to express my feelings to you, for you are married to my friend. I can only put my life in your hands. Should you be free, I will be waiting for you, but this is a decision which has to be completely yours.' I could only hope that he would read my eyes as I looked up at him."

"Oh, Mother," I said. "This is so romantic! What happened next?"

"After he left," said Mother, "I was determined to ask Cazimir for a divorce, but as it turned out, fate took things into its own hands."

Nine

Indeed, at that time, providence was about to change not only the course of my parents' lives, but also that of every Russian family, without exception, from the Tsar to the most humble peasant. My parents' destiny was a microcosm of what happened to millions of people when the storm of a civil war swept over Russia.

Father's memoir eloquently describes the following events. He wrote:

Before Cazimir's return, I received my own orders to report to Headquarters to join my division. In Russia, there were already signs of growing unrest, especially in the big cities, but at the Eastern Front, it was relatively calm, although a feeling of uncertainty prevailed and people gathered in groups, whispering fearfully as to what might be the outcome if the Tsar were to abdicate. To me, growing up in a conservative monarchist milieu, it seemed unthinkable and I missed my father and uncles, who would be better informed as to the true political situation.

After arriving at headquarters I was billeted with some fifty other officers eagerly awaiting postings to their divisions spread along the front lines. We were all recovering from wounds received in the line of fire and, to tell the truth, we were not very patient with red tape procedures. Being in our early twenties and decorated for bravery, we thought that by virtue of having been wounded on the battlefield, we deserved respectful treatment from our particularly arrogant colonel. This unpleasant individual treated us like schoolboys. What irked us most was that he had spent his whole career in administrative jobs and had never set foot on the battleground.

One unfortunate afternoon, after a few weeks of inaction and boredom, I decided, once again, to ask the hated colonel whether he had received orders for my transfer. I felt I needed to know where my life was headed. Without any news of Zhenia, or from my family in Pokrovskoye, I was full of anger and impatience. I presented myself in front of the colonel and asked him formally, and very politely, as to the status of my return to active duty.

The colonel, without lifting his bald head from the papers on his desk, waved a dismissive hand at me and said, "Just leave me alone, Lieutenant, I am busy. Please go!"

At that, all the blood rushed to my head and I lost control of myself. In a blind rage I snatched out my sword and rushed at him with a cry of: "You peace-time bastard. Do you know that I am a decorated officer? How dare you treat me like a schoolboy?"

I was immediately disarmed and arrested. Brought in front of General Marchenko by two guards, I was repentant and humble, cursing my foolishness.

The general examined me with curiosity.

"Do you realize, Lieutenant," he said, "that you have committed an unpardonable action against a superior officer? I see you have an excellent war record, and I just want you to tell me why the hell did you behave like a stupid ass?"

"I am sorry, sir," I said, noticing a St. George's cross on the general's chest. This cross is one of our highest awards for bravery on the battlefield, and it suddenly gave me an idea to weasel out of the serious situation, which threatened me with a court martial.

"I could not contain myself, sir, when I was reprimanded like a child, by an officer who had never been in the line of fire."

"Well, well," said the general, trying to suppress his merriment. "So you are a young fighting rooster, eh?"

"Yes, sir," I said, praying to all the saints.

"I tell you what, Lieutenant," said the general. "Didn't you just complete treatment for injuries to your chest and had been recovering in one of our field hospitals? Wasn't there a psychiatric ward as well?"

"Yes, sir! But I was not in that ward."

"Too bad, too bad, but maybe we can improve on that. Now, I suggest that you return immediately to that hospital and ask them to do a better job of rehabilitating you. There will be no court martial, and I will appease the frustrated colonel myself. Understood?"

"Yes, sir. Thank you, sir."

"Dismissed. And Lieutenant?"

"Yes, sir?"

"When back on active duty, try to use some of this fiery temperament when fighting the enemy, not your own superior officers," said the now smiling general.

That same afternoon, I was put on a train back to Abbas Touman. Two guards who were visibly impressed with the "psychiatric patient" in their care accompanied me. I was handed over to the hospital staff for further rehabilitation and to the competent ministrations of—Dr. Evgenia Chengeri.

Cazimir had not yet returned and Zhenia and I saw each other every day. We put our mutual feelings on hold until his return and I spent two heavenly weeks at the hospital, after which I was summoned back to Tiflis. It turned out that I was to be posted to the newly formed Transport Battalion in the recently occupied Turkish territories. Zhenia had also received orders, to proceed to the town of Erezerum, so we parted with sad hearts, not able to predict what fate held in store for us.

Ten

At that time, the front line spread from the south of Trapezund to the frontier of Mesopotamia, towards Persia. The new battalion was in its initial stages of formation and our cadre of officers was increasing every day. I was surprised one day, when meeting new arrivals, to see none other than Cazimir, who was pleasantly surprised to see me. Once enrolled, we were offered a month's leave and I left for Pokrovskoye while Cazimir joined his parents in the Don region.

This was the last time I visited the cradle of my family. It was Maslennitza (Mardi Gras) and the old house hummed with happy voices of aunts, cousins and friends. That unforgettable month of joy: rides in the sleds, endless parties and fun remained as the best of my memories. In spite of the growing unrest in the country, our happy crowd was determined to have as much fun as possible. Our Uncle Bobrovski would lovingly shake his head, saying, "Make the most of it, children, for all this will end soon. The peasants and the factory workers are organizing themselves for something sinister and tragic." But we laughed, not believing a word he said. True, there was talk of uprisings in the city of Kursk, and we heard that crowds gathered around speakers who bore red flags, but somehow, this all seemed unreal to us. We also heard one evening that Rasputin, the evil monk who was said to be close to the Tsarina, was found assassinated in St. Petersburg, but nobody was sorry for him.

Although Mother was no longer there, Pokrovskoye was still our home. Maria Vassilivna was now Father's legal wife and, to give her credit, she never took advantage of her position and she showed Sonia, Evgeni and me her utter devotion and care. Of course, Nicholas no longer lived at Pokrovskoye, but only came as a visitor. During his time there, he ignored Maria Vassilivna as though she were invisible, and avoided speaking to Father. Fortunately for us children, Mother's sister, Elena Bobrovskaya, was always present on festive occasions, and we loved her. In her looks, she was remarkably like our mother and treated us as her own.

In the train going back to Tiflis, I noticed a change in the attitude of soldiers and the working people. The soldiers often appeared hostile and insolent, their uniforms in disarray. They were manifestly trying to create incidents in public places, while the workers muttered audibly about the bourgeois and democratic revolution, and that "times were changing." I started thinking about Uncle Bobrovski's warning.

In Tiflis, Cazimir met me and said that Zhenia was to join him soon. She would spend a few days in Abbas Touman before being posted to another hospital.

She arrived a few weeks later and we resumed our old life, spending much time together. She said that before her departure, she was going to speak to Cazimir about getting a divorce.

After she left, Cazimir asked me to visit him and as soon as I arrived he asked me point blank: "Will you marry Zhenia if I give her a divorce?"

I was taken aback and said, "That is for her to decide. However, I want you to know that at no time did your wife and I do anything that might bring dishonor to your marriage. We just fell in love and agreed that we would not make any plans until you granted her a divorce. I am very sorry. I respect you as a friend, but my love for Zhenia is stronger than anything I have ever experienced."

To give Cazimir credit, he behaved like a gentleman. When Zhenia arrived again, they had a final talk, and he agreed to a divorce.

Eleven

In February of 1917, we learned that there was a revolution in the capital. The Tsar had abdicated and a provisional government was established, which put an end to all speculations of where the country was going. Now meetings and uprisings sprouted all over Tiflis. They were limited to lengthy speeches while crowds of supporting workers and soldiers waved red flags. There was no violence yet, and all the military and civil officials continued in their designated posts. Our regimental flag was changed from yellow with the black eagle to St. George's flag of the Caucasus Army.

A spirit of rebirth surged everywhere and there was talk of a better life. The word "revolution" was on everybody's lips, and Zhenia and I believed that something good was going to happen. Cazimir, not as optimistic as we were, mistakenly attributed our good spirits to something else.

Soon enough, ominous news of violent incidents against officers of the army reached us. Russia had already withdrawn from participation in World War I and we no longer had orders from the central command. We were told unofficially that we were free to seek transfers to other branches of the army, and Cazimir and I decided to go to Baiburt, where we hoped to serve in the occupied territories. The divorce papers were signed and we were waiting for the final documents. In the meantime, Zhenia had to return to the hospital in the Tshvartshanaki region.

In spring of 1917, I was finally summoned to proceed immediately to Baiburt. Cazimir also received orders to travel to Trapezund, and we were both relieved not to be together in the same part of Caucasus.

Baiburt was formerly an important administrative center of Turkey, now in Russian hands. Traveling on horseback along perilous mountain roads took us more than a week. Another officer accompanied us, while the rest were recruits from Tiflis, riding in horse-drawn carts, loaded with everything from ammunition to personal belongings.

A pelting rain welcomed us to Baiburt. An ancient fortress dominated the town; its rusty cannons, overgrown with weeds, pointed at some invisible intruders. Below the fortress yawned a deep canyon where a rapid ribbon of foaming water warned the passer-by not to go too near the edge. Two years earlier, Baiburt was destroyed by artillery fire and abandoned by most of its inhabitants. Now in Russian hands, it was mainly an administrative rear center, but the sound of artillery was a constant reminder that for the Turks and Austrians, the war was not yet over.

My duties consisted of keeping order among the sparse population of Turks and Armenians. It was not an easy task. For many years, the Turks were determined to cut out all the Armenians and they had partially succeeded. Now, with the male Turkish population away at war, the Armenians systematically paid them back by killing the remaining few Turks. These were mostly women, children and old people, too weak to leave the town, but the avenging Armenians, who had suffered too long at the hands of their tormentors, had no pity. To my consternation, I was also appointed to be part of the judicial council and my duty was to question the prisoners as they were brought in front of the small tribunal. Although I knew the historical fact that the Turks had been massacring the Armenians for centuries, I still had to uphold the law and ignore the eye-for-an-eye philosophy of the offenders.

At that time, I was particularly worried about the fate of my father. I had learned from one of the newly arrived officers, who was from Kursk, that my father had been arrested and jailed for "sympathizing with the old regime." This officer informed me also that many soldiers in Central Russia were abandoning the army in droves and trekking back home.

All the officers were asked to pledge allegiance to the new government under Mr. Kerenski, and my first impulse was to refuse. Only the kind interference of our general saved my skin. He advised me, in a fatherly way, not to provoke the newly formed committee of soldiers, who openly waited for a pretext to arrest any officer. New revolutionary committees were sprouting everywhere and a Council of Soviet Deputies was formed in Baiburt. It was composed entirely of civilian clerks and soldiers from the disbanded army who proclaimed they were the legal representatives of the new Russian government.

When I thought that things would never get better, I had an unexpected joy. One day I was told that someone wanted to see me, and as I stepped outside I saw that it was my own Zhenia, who had arrived to join me.

Twelve

Apparently the revolution had reached the Tsvarhanski coal-mining town to the south of Baiburt where Zhenia's field hospital was located, next to the military barracks. To celebrate the good news, the soldiers and the civilian workers, in a drunken avenging spree, killed the director and the supervisors of the mine by throwing them into an open shaft. Seeking new victims, the crowd started to eliminate the officers of the small military detachment. By pure chance, Zhenia and three army officers escaped in the night, riding horseback until they reached a nearby native village, where they were able to hire a horse with a cart, which brought them to Baiburt.

Although Zhenia was exhausted after her perilous journey, her eyes were shining with happiness to be with me, and I marveled at her courage and resilience, which was, as I learned later, one of her wonderful qualities, which saved our lives many times during the terrible years ahead.

We were married by the Council of Soviet Deputies, which took no longer than five minutes. It did not matter to us that we were lodged in a tiny room with a narrow bed. We were at last together and from then on, shared whatever destiny had in store for us. Zhenia was now my wife.

After a week, we started receiving disturbing news of more incidents among the soldiers. In addition, a new element of civilian commissars started to flourish. They held much power in their hands and were typically former minor employees of the government who promoted themselves to top positions. Daily arrests of "traitors to the people" were made, and too often we heard shots in the night from nearby houses raided by orders of the new commissars.

A further plague on the unfortunate Armenians was the push of the Turkish mullahs who, emboldened by the disarray of the Russian military forces, mandated the Armenians to convert from the Russian orthodoxy religion to muslimism. Failure to comply was equivalent to a death sentence. The Russians, who traditionally protected the

35

Armenians, were powerless to do anything and a day did not go by without another Armenian family being massacred by the Turks.

Echoes reached us that a White Army was forming to fight the revolutionary Red Army, and Zhenia and I decided to leave the Army, or what was left of it, and proceed to Tiflis. From there, we knew we would find a way to join the White Army headquarters in the Don region.

Dressed in civilian clothes, we started our long journey across Caucasus. Our first stop was in Zakatali, where we spent three days, sheltered by the owner of a caravan-sarai (roadside inn). Zhenia immediately made friends with the pregnant wife of the innkeeper by attending to her medical problems, although her small bag of medicines was ridiculously insufficient, but this was a healthy young woman who soon became mother to a husky baby.

In Zakatali, we also found out that the Armenians had started a systematic killing of the Turks. The innkeeper confided that he feared his life could be in danger, since besides being a Turk, he was considered to be a wealthy man. The second night, while the other womenfolk and Zhenia went to the public bathhouse, heated by large timber logs, a crowd of drunken "comrades" forced their way into the roadside inn and demanded that the frightened innkeeper hand over the silver and gold coins which they said he had. By that time, everyone knew that paper money was not worth anything, and in this remote area, silver and gold coins were still in use.

The innkeeper, a shrewd man, did not keep his valuables in plain sight, but had on hand, just in case, a handful of silver coins and one or two small swords with silver hilts. He handed them over to the gun-toting commissar, who left muttering, "We'll be back, you blood-sucking profiteer!" As they left, they discharged their rifles in the air, laughing at the terrified neighbors scuttling down the street.

The sound of shooting reached the bathhouse where the women were bathing. A panic ensued and five minutes later, I saw, with amazement, my wife and the women of the innkeeper's household rush back to the inn. They were wrapped in towels only, and presented a laughable sight. Zhenia ran in front of the others and jumped on my neck with tears streaming on her face. She babbled, "Thank God you are alive! We heard the shooting coming from the inn and thought that they had killed both of you."

I was touched and embarrassed to see so many scantily dressed women, and did my best to calm down my dear wife, who was crying hysterically. This incident prompted us to take leave of our hospitable host and we left the next morning on two horses, which we had bought by selling a couple of guns.

It was slow going, mostly down along narrow mountain roads. There we joined several groups leaving town. These were Turkish families seeking to get away from the avenging Armenians, and they were friendly to us, letting us pass ahead of them. I rode in front and from time to time, turned to look at my little Zhenia, her slender figure swaying on her mountain horse as it carefully made its way over the stony narrow road. A wave of tenderness engulfed me as she gave me a loving smile and I thought I was the luckiest man alive. I thought fondly of how in spite of all her efforts to appear older and braver, she still could not conceal how feminine and vulnerable she was. Much to my road companion's surprise, I laughed aloud, remembering her pleasure as she tried on the colorful Circassian costume given to her by the innkeeper's wife.

This time, we stopped only overnight in small mountainside inns, until we finally reached, Kiev.

Thirteen

Our final destination was to continue by rail to Odessa, an important junction to our final destination – Novocherkassk. The trains were not running on schedule and we had to wait as long as twenty-four hours in Yalta, giving us time to visit this beautiful city again. What was once a charming holiday resort was now unrecognizable. The streets were empty of the vacationing crowds and only bands of former soldiers roamed the streets. Their dirty uniforms were in disarray and the civilians took cover at the sight of them strolling in the center of the wide boulevards, shouting political slogans, while brandishing bottles of vodka in their hands. Most of the street lamps were broken and many houses had shattered windows; only a few shops were open and food was not easy to find. We huddled at the train station, preferring to wait in a sheltered corner, rather than walk the dismal streets.

The Yalta/Odessa train arrived in the early morning, but we had no choice other than to share accommodations in the wagon transporting several cages of fowl. We were too tired and cold to care about the smell and the lack of ventilation, and we slept all through the night hours until we reached Odessa.

Zhenia remembered the address of a friend, and we finally located the house. We knocked a long time at the closed door. Then a cautious voice from inside asked us who we were. After a while, we were admitted and found to our surprise two families living there. These were also friends of Zhenia's sister Mania.

To our complete surprise, they told Zhenia that Mania and her husband were hiding in Odessa, quite nearby. Zneinia had told me that her sister and her husband belonged to the S.R. (Social Revolutionaries), and were condemned to ten years imprisonment by the Tsarist government just before World War I. What we did not know then was that during the Provisional Government of Kerensky, they were liberated from prison, but to their surprise, the newly-formed Bolshevik committee declared them "enemies of the people." To avoid being arrested again, they fled to Odessa., where their only hope was to merge with masses of people fleeing south.

We immediately rushed out to find Mania and it was heartbreaking to see the sisters clutch each other, laughing and crying. We met Mania's husband, Andrei, a tall bearded man with sad eyes.

We spent the night listening to their story. They had been completely devastated to find out that after having spent three years in prison for wanting a better government for Russia, they were now being hunted down as enemies by the very people they wanted to free from the Tsarist yoke.

My father was a staunch monarchist all his life and could not fathom how an educated scientist like Andrei Chicherin could plot against the Tsar, but he held his peace when he saw that both Mania and Andrei had by now lost all illusions about the cause for which they had suffered so much. Father told me later that they paid dearly for their mistake and he felt sorry for them. He described the scene.

Zhenia was appalled at the change in her sister. I had not met her before, but I had seen a sketch of Mania by a talented artist. In it, a charming blond beauty was gazing pensively at a book, her hair piled up on her head in a shining crown. I had difficulty reconciling this middle-aged woman with extinguished light in her eyes to that image of the beautiful young girl.

We found out at the railway station that the trains for Moscow were not running on schedule, and were often used to transport groups of newly organized government officials in torn uniforms with sewn-on red bands.

The grim stationmaster said, "If you're lucky and come early enough, you may squeeze in."

We left early the next day. We never saw Mania or Andrei again. They disappeared in the sweeping wave of revolution and carnage, and although we tried many times, we never found a trace of them.

Fourteen

When the noisy locomotive pulling the Odessa/Novocherkassk train entered the railway station, the crowd waiting on the platform rushed forward, pushing us from all sides. Clouds of steam rose into the frigid morning air as we were swept forward. The cars swam past us in seemingly never-ending processions. First came the sleepers and first-class green cars, all full of armed people. Some were in uniforms and some in civilian clothes; the new elite of the revolution, all sporting red ribbons, symbols of their power. By now we learned to recognize that the civilian officials were the most to be feared. These were the secret police who had wide powers over the lives of the citizens: the precursors of the ominous N.K.V.D. (political secret police).

Clutching our two cloth bags, containing whatever we could glean from our hospitable friends, we had no option but to scramble onto the nearest platform within our reach.

All compartments were occupied, but we found enough room in the drafty passage where we sat on our bags. We were lucky when, in the late afternoon, two passengers left from the nearest compartment, and finally Zhenia and I could sit and lean against each other, our bags safely tucked under our feet. The cars were not heated and it was bitterly cold. The other occupants of the compartment were an older couple and a mother with three small children. The youngest one was a tiny baby who cried all the time. Zhenia offered to help the woman and lent her a woolen scarf to wrap up the baby. The elderly couple shared some bread with us and Zhenia produced a piece of cheese given to us by her sister. We were all tired and I fell asleep in spite of the poor baby who did not stop crying.

The train did not stop at all stations. It was supposed to be an express train, but it moved slowly. Often at night it would stop for no reason known to us; sometimes we even heard gunshots. Everyone in our compartment was quiet, except for the baby crying. His mother prayed from time to time, murmuring soothing words of prayer, reminding me of my childhood when my nanny used to pray over us children after we were tucked safely in bed.

I thought sadly then that I had lost forever the security of my family home and that the foundations of Russia were shaking. This thought gave rise to the strong determination of enlisting as soon as possible in the White Army, where I would fight alongside brother officers to wrestle back our beloved Russia. The thought of my father imprisoned in Kursk set my blood boiling. How could they arrest him? He was a good man. For all his defects as a husband, he had been an excellent father. He was also a generous employer towards his peasants. He let them use his land for their own harvests, and the men and women of the two neighboring villages considered themselves lucky to be employed by Leo Markov. He paid them well, even though he demanded in return hard work and loyalty. Then my thoughts drifted to Nicholas, from whom I had heard nothing for a long time. I hoped that once in Novocherkassk, I would be able to find out more about everybody.

I woke up shivering from the cold. Although it was late spring, the windows outside had icicles framing the glass. It was unusually quiet in the compartment; there was no crying anymore. Then a thin keening cry broke the silence. The young mother was crying as she held the baby.

"He's dead," she cried, "he's dead."

Zhenia jumped from her seat and looked at the baby. The small features were white with bluish smudges under closed eyes. Zhenia touched the baby.

"He is with the angels now," she said, as tears flowed down her face.

She put her arms around the woman, who was too numb with grief to react.

* * *

As the train made its slow way towards the Don basin, our compartment gradually emptied. The weeping mother with her children and the elderly couple got off at the last station before we reached Don. There, several young men in students' uniforms boarded our train. Three of them settled down in our compartment.

They were going to Novocherkassk to enroll in the White Army and soon we were all talking enthusiastically about the possibility of joining the ranks of a newly-organized force against the Bolsheviks. Untying our cloth bags, we fished out whatever vestiges of military uniforms we had hoarded and donned them. Zhenia produced some thread and a needle and sewed to our sleeves makeshift white, blue and red rosettes, symbols of our beloved Russian flag.

Before we reached Novocherkassk, we passed a small station. The platform was nearly empty, but clean of the usual rubbish we encountered in the zone occupied by the Reds. I saw a Russian national flag gently waving in the breeze above the station, and the elderly figure of the stationmaster in his clean uniform. His bushy white whiskers and serene pink face was such a welcome sight, after the disorder we had left behind, that I wept with joy. To me, he was then the symbol of order and law of the Russia that I loved and respected.

Fifteen

At last, we reached Novocherkassk. This was the wealthy Don Cossack country. The people were fiercely chauvinistic, recognizing only their own laws. Traditionally they were free of obedience to Russian law and submitted only to their own authorities, which consisted of a democratic collection of Atamans or chiefs, who governed each region called *Stanitsi*. The Cossacks were allowed to have their own regulations for in times of war, they were the first to join the Tsarist forces to defend Russia.

As a rule, the Cossacks held a negative view towards the non-Cossacks, mainly the Russian peasants, whom they considered spineless because they did not resist the feudal system of dependence which held them in bondage before the liberation of the serfs. This general opinion extended also to the rest of the non-Cossack population, especially the Jews, towards whom they were openly hostile. As a result, most of the non-Cossacks joined the Bolshevist movement. However, the Cossacks were all determined to fight the Reds, and cooperated with leaders of the White Army to fight the common enemy.

As soon as we arrived in Novocherkassk, we rented a cheap room near the railway station. Leaving our meager possessions in our lodgings, we went in search of the White Army recruiting center.

Novocherkassk sat on steep hills, dotted with wealthy estates, the town sprawling on the foothills. We quickly found the Recruiting Center, occupying a large corner house with white columns, which was the former hall of the Noblemen's Association. When we arrived, it was teeming with young officers in uniform, students and nurses. These were volunteers ready to defend their country in time of need. With our service documents in hand, Zhenia and I were directed to a line in front of a closed door. When interviewed, I was told that there were three regiments in formation, and because of my experience in the south as a cavalry officer, I would be posted to Colonel Kutepov's regiment. The three volunteer regiments at that time consisted exclusively of officers who had taken part in World War I. This cadre of men had considerable experience, and it was not surprising that at the start of the civil war, the

Reds suffered defeat in the Don Basin. As long as there was that strong push of volunteers to defend Russia, we were winning, but soon after, the generals in charge created a hierarchy of red tape and declared a compulsory mobilization. This gave birth to an army of clerics and high-ranking officers who, unfortunately, sought to occupy administrative posts behind fighting lines. This was a different element of soldiers and officers, and in no time the White movement started to deteriorate. But that was still in the future, and in the summer of 1918, we were indestructible, pushing the Reds even further from their positions.

What was incredible is that although we were often not paid at all, we never complained. Zhenia and I were given nine rubles each pay day. We ate at the military dining rooms, and never had been happier as during that wonderful period of self-sacrifice, yearning to liberate our great country from terror and ignorance.

At that time, the territory of the White Army was spread as follows. In the north, Don Cossack regiment was headed by General Krasnov, and the east, where we were, was protected by the regiments of General Dennisov. To the west, the German army was still occupying the Ukraine frontier and was helping us, unofficially, against the Reds.

I was to be posted at once to General Kutepov's regiment in the region of Kuban, which was occupied by the Reds. We left by train early in the morning and I kept looking back, as the train gathered speed, where my dear Zhenia stood crying her heart out. She had to remain in Novocherkassk, where she was to work in the main hospital. Although I hated to be separated from her, I was still relieved that she would be out of immediate danger.

Sixteen

After a few hours, we entered Ekaterinodar. This Kuban Cossack territory was known for its wealthy agriculture, now run mostly by women, as anyone who could hold a rifle had joined the White Army.

Our long train stopped before the main station, where a large armored car, bristling with guns, was attached to the last car. After unloading us, the train was to proceed later to Ekaterinodar, but the armored car would stay with us as we advanced along the railroad into the occupied enemy territory. At last we reached our destination. The officers with rifles and machine guns spilled out, while I hurried to the car with the horses, where my black Arab welcomed me with a gentle neigh. Here, we were to chase the Reds from one stanitsa to another.

It was mid summer and fields of ripe corn stretched in front of us as far as the eye could see. Except for the buzz of insects and the call of small birds that did not know there was a war, it was quiet. As we advanced, I was lulled by the gait of my horse, and it seemed incredible that our enemies could be hiding beneath bushes and trees, ready to ambush us at any moment. Then, as if by magic, a staccato of machine guns broke the silence. The foot soldiers crouched in groups, firing back. Bullets whistled, mowing down the golden heads of corn. A loud whistling sound overhead was followed by a heavy thud of a large gun. However, it landed far behind us, and one of my companions even laughed, shouting, "They cannot even shoot straight." Our frightened horses were difficult to control as we raced forward, protecting our infantry. Dust was in the air, and screams of wounded soldiers and neighing of horses surrounded me.

"Down!" screamed our captain. "Dismount!" he ordered as we came upon another nest of machine guns. We obeyed, running, crouching low among the tall stalks of corn. As I ran, I held tight the reins of my horse, trying to calm the frightened animal. Then we heard cries as a group of enemy soldiers rushed out of a clump of bushes where they were hiding.

Suddenly, there was a deafening roar behind us. Two heavy guns from our motorized car were shooting back at the retreating enemy. A happy shout arose.

"They're retreating. They're running away. Let's go get them."

"Hold your fire," cried the captain. "Pick up the wounded and the dead." We were lucky not to have had many dead, but there were quite a few wounded soldiers, and those we carried to the railway line where they would be picked up.

This type of skirmish was repeated time and time again as we chased the enemy through fields and farms. To our surprise the Reds offered little resistance and our regiment was welcomed by the Cossacks, who fed us as well as they could, to show their gratitude for our having liberated them from the fighters of the "glorious revolution."

Our regiment moved steadily forward, pushing the enemy from their positions, one stanitsa after another. The Bolsheviks did not expect an organized force of professional soldiers, and after three weeks, we cleared the area, which was occupied since 1917.

Our next move was to take back the port of Novorossisk, which, curiously enough, was still occupied by the German Navy. The Bolsheviks were also encroached there from the beginning of the revolution. This curious situation arose because in 1917, the turmoil in Russia prevented a definite disposition of the terms of a separate peace agreement by which Russia had to withdraw from participation in World War I. Therefore, waiting for further instructions, the German Navy was anchored in Novorossisk, officially trying not to interfere in Russia's civil war.

Seventeen

While Father's regiment advanced in the Don and Kuban region, my mother's life followed a different path. Posted to a field hospital in Novocherkassk, she was working day and night shifts taking care of the wounded soldiers as they arrived by trainloads.

Occasionally she would receive a note from Father, hurriedly scribbled on a scrap of paper, and she would carry it with her all day, grateful that he was still alive.

Up to that time, the White Army was pushing the Reds out of their positions and the expected siege of Novorossisk was a hopeful sign that our side was gaining ground.

When Mother discovered that she was pregnant, her first impulse was to find a way to be as near to Father as she could, but her good sense prevailed and she decided to seek a transfer to Novorossisk, but only after that town was cleared of the enemy.

* * *

In the early morning of the summer of 1918, General Kutepov's regiment reached the city of Novorossisk. The city and the Communist officials were still asleep when all army offices and the city hall were quietly taken over. The commissars, cozily cocooned in their civilian jobs, did not expect any military intervention from the White Army and did not offer any resistance when they were relieved of their functions and placed under arrest. Their offices were packed with numerous crates of fine wines, plundered from the wealthy citizens of Novorossisk. There was no fight, only a parade down the main street where the liberated citizens celebrated their release by throwing flowers at the marching officers.

Anxious to have some news from Pokrovskoye, Father rushed to Gelindjik, a suburb of Novorossisk, where the Markov family had a large estate attached to a vineyard. He wrote in his diary about that event:

I had spent many summers in Gelindjik and my heart jumped as I saw the gates of our property leading to the house overlooking the "Tonki Mis" Bay.

The windows were shuttered, but I knocked on the front door, not really expecting anyone to be there. When, after a time, the door cautiously opened, I did not believe my eyes when I saw the familiar face of my father. Maria Vassilivna was peering over his shoulder and was also staring at me in amazement. We hugged each other and sat down in the half-empty house, asking questions, and laughing with joy.

I was shocked to see in the half-light of the closed shutters that Maria Vassilivna had an artificial leg, which she tried to hide in the folds of her skirt.

A sharp pang of pity replaced my familiar feeling of dislike towards the woman who was the cause of my dear mother's unhappiness.

"What happened to you?" I gasped in disbelief.

Father answered, as Maria Vassilivna vainly tried to control the tears streaming down her face.

"It's a long story, son," he said. "Let's have a glass of wine and I will tell you what happened to us since your visit two years ago.

"When the revolution reached Kursk," he said, "all our county officials were arrested and replaced by commissars from the ranks of junior clerks. Many of them were from the two villages near Pokrovskoye. They requisitioned everything from our estate and I was also arrested as an 'enemy of the people' because I was the elected marshal of nobility of the Kursk region. I was held in the local jail, awaiting transfer to a bigger facility, to be judged and dispatched in the same way as many of our neighbors. Maria Vassilivna was allowed to visit me, because she was considered to be one of the exploited citizens, as she was governess to my children.

"These were still the early days of the revolution and there were many changes in the prison administration. Maria Vassilivna was able to bribe two of the guards to arrange my escape. We made our way to Moscow, where I was hiding in her sister's house. After a few days, I left Moscow, alone, trying to make my way south in order to reach Novorossisk, while Maria Vassilivna was to follow me in a few days. Later that week, she was trying to board a trolley when a crowd of hooligans pushed her off. Her leg below the knee was mangled and had to be amputated. I knew nothing about that and only learned of her accident when she arrived here two months ago, with an artificial leg. She is doing very well, and I am proud of her. She saved my life."

He stopped talking, and put his arm around her. She was crying quietly, her hands crossed on her knees.

I just stared at them, as I was struck with the full realization of the irrevocable tragic destiny that befell our family. My father, the invincible proud head of our clan, arrested, humiliated, and obliged to flee like a criminal, for the simple reason that he was part of the old order which was crumbling around us. The courage and loyalty of Maria Vassilivna impressed me, beyond words.

I found out that day that my brother Nicholas had died from typhoid fever when he was discharged from his regiment two years before. His widow, a pretty peasant girl from a nearby village in Kursk, did not mourn him for long, and married a peasant lad from the same district. Sister Sonia remained in Moscow to be near her husband, who was arrested as a "wealthy capitalist." It was much later that I learned that he was executed, together with many others, without any trial.

I told Father about Zhenia, and about our plans to meet eventually in Novorossisk.

I left them with a heavy feeling of loss, and felt even more acutely how much I needed Zhenia to be by my side.

Eighteen

According to my father's diary, he did not remain long in Novorossisk, as he was ordered to the shifting front where the Red and White armies fought for every inch of their motherland. By that time, it was obvious that the White Army was losing on all fronts. It was difficult for me to read of the terrible carnage that took place in those bloody encounters. Even to a seasoned warrior like my father, the sight of dead bodies along the streets of towns and villages gave him nightmares. He wrote:

There were bodies lying along the roads, their young faces frozen in expressions of surprise, agony and pain. No one took any notice of them anymore as they lay there, anonymous, all alone, and only some family somewhere would always miss their father, son or brother.

One of my father's worst experiences was the battle for Kiev, which changed hands twice, when the civilian population evacuated from the beautiful city, fleeing along the roads with whatever they could carry. Some were lucky to have a cart, but these were few, and many, too tired to walk, just collapsed by the wayside. No one stopped. They all just walked on, driven to indifference by exhaustion, not noticing their fallen brothers. Life had no value any more and the civil war, which fed the thirst for revenge and destruction, transformed the kind Russian men into vengeful robots.

At last, disillusioned and already sick with the first symptoms of typhoid fever, Father was making his weary way from Kiev to Novorossisk. At one of the train stops, he witnessed a crowd of Communist soldiers literally tear apart a young Cossack officer, who still wore his military epaulettes. This incident was the last drop in the overflowing cup of horrors that he had seen in his young life. His mind, already clouded by fever, refused to accept the awful reality of what Father had seen, and he collapsed, unconscious, in the crowded compartment where he was traveling.

His diary, written much later after this incident, did not detail his return to Novorossisk, as he did not remember much of what happened, except for the elderly colonel who was his companion. It was that same kind man, Colonel Dimidov, who took care of my father and was able to finally transport him to Novorossisk.

But Novorossisk was again under siege, now losing its battle against the Reds, and most of the White Army forces were outside the city, trying to staunch the approaching forces of the Bolsheviks. Many citizens were leaving town and a new wave of terror was sweeping over that seaport. A large group of deserters from both the Red Army and the Kuban Cossacks Division, together with opportunistic civilians, organized a band calling themselves the "Green Army." This was because they were hiding in the green woods surrounding the city, and under pretext of "catching spies," they plundered and assassinated whenever there was an opportunity of stealing and robbing, especially unprotected women and old people who did not want to leave their homes.

* * *

My mother was already five months pregnant when she decided to join my father, who, she knew, was also returning from Kiev. Tired from her long journey, she reached the Markov vineyard, only to find that both Leo and Maria Vassilivna no longer lived there. Uncertain and frightened, she knocked at the neighbors' house and was lucky to find out that Katia, the young daughter of the family, still lived there alone. She had lost her parents in a raid of the Greens, and she only survived by hiding in the bushes outside the house. Katia also needed a friend, and the two women decided to stay together in Katia's house, hoping that it would be of no interest, since it was already thoroughly ransacked.

They made makeshift beds on the floor in one of the rooms and Katia scrounged some eggs and bread from neighbors. After a week, when they were seriously running out of food, Mother decided she would go to the local hospital to apply for a job.

The two women set out one morning, happy to have each other's company, when the driver of a cart stopped them, and an elderly gentleman leaned out and asked for directions to the Markov vineyard.

When my mother told me about that incident, there was always a catch in her throat.

" 'Who are you?' asked the military-looking stranger.

" 'I am Eugenia Markov. Maybe you bring me news of my husband? He was with the White Army, and he is Captain Anatoli Markov, a cavalry officer?'

"The stranger got out of the cart and came towards me.

" 'Madam,' he said, 'my name is Colonel Dimidov. I am so glad to have found you. We have in our cart your husband, Captain Anatoli Lvovich. He is very sick and needs immediate attention. At this moment, he is unconscious, but he has moments of clarity. He has probably typhoid fever and I pray that he will survive. Let's get him quickly into the house.'

"I rushed to the cart and lifted the blanket under which Anatoli was lying. I did not need to diagnose him, as I was only too familiar with the deadly scourge of typhoid. It took only one look at him to realize how desperately sick he was. With the help of the cart driver and the colonel, Anatoli was carried into the house. I put wet sheets over him to subdue the fever, and sent Katia to the city hospital for medical supplies.

"I sat on the floor next to him, keeping the bed sheets moist as he tossed in delirium. He did not recognize his surroundings, or me, and in his fevered mind he was still seeing piles of dead bodies and bloodied limbs. At times, he would become violent. We had to tie him up with strips of bed-sheets as we were afraid that he could hurt himsel or attack us."

Nineteen

"How terrible," I said. "Did this last a long time?"

"No," said Mother. "After a few days, the fever subsided, the medicine and his strong young constitution eventually pulled him through. I was already making plans to offer my services at the military hospital, when something happened that left a mark on me for the rest of my life.

"One afternoon, while it was still light, we heard gunshots nearby. These shots were followed by screams and more shots.

"'It's the Greens,' whispered Katia, trembling with fear. 'That is the Sapozhnikovs' house. There is only the old grandmother and her young servant. Oh God, please save them.' She crossed herself and clung to me, crying.

" 'Evgenia Constantinovna,' she asked, 'what if they attack us next? What shall we do? I am so scared!' She was trembling with fear.

"I glanced at your father. He was still tied down but sleeping through all the noise. I prayed briefly. My mind went blank. I just had to do something to save us. I had a revolver, but I never had to use it, though I ldid learn to shoot. At that moment, I knew there was only one way out. I took the small revolver and decided that the Greens would not take us alive.

"After a while, we thought that the danger was over when, through a crack in the shutters, we saw a man with a Mauser in his hands and another handgun tucked in his belt. He was creeping towards the front door, trying to open it, and then knelt down to peer through the keyhole.

"At that moment, I did not hesitate. I knew exactly what I had to do. I held my revolver steady with both hands and put it against the keyhole of the door. Then I pulled the trigger. There was no cry. Only the thud of a heavy body as he fell backwards.

"We carefully opened the door, listening for sounds. All was silent as we looked down at the dead man. There was no blood flowing, only a small hole in his forehead. He reeked of vodka and he was dead.

" 'Quickly, Katia,' I said. 'Let's hide him in the vineyard.'

"We got hold of his legs and dragged him as far as we could, out of sight. We threw a heap of dry leaves on top and returned quickly to the house, trembling with fear.

"I had been terrified that I would miss and that he would come in and kill us all. As to killing a human being, I know that I will answer someday before God, and I will let him judge me. When I became a doctor, I took the vow to save lives, and here I was obliged to kill a man in order to save my husband, Katia, my baby and myself. Morally I had no choice and this was war."

Fortunately nobody came to look for the dead man, and the following week, my mother and Katia enlisted the help of Colonel Dimidov, who dug a hole big enough to bury the unlucky comrade of the Greens. He also congratulated and hugged Mother for getting rid of one more vermin.

Today, as I write this, I am amazed at the strength and courage of that extraordinary woman, my wonderful and unique mother.

Twenty

On May 1, 1919, Mother gave birth to a baby girl, my sister Evgenia (Jenny), at the military hospital in Novorossisk.

Father was still too sick to be of any help, but Katia proved to be invaluable. It was a difficult birth, and in addition to that, Mother developed a high fever, which was due to an infection from the poor sanitary conditions at the hospital. Rather than remain at the hospital, Mother asked to be transferred back to Katia's house, where she was taken care of by Katia and by friends from the medical staff at the hospital.

At last, weak but alive, she was able to take care of little Jenny, who was a healthy child, in spite of the fact that mother was not able to breastfeed her. However, later on in life, little Jenny suffered the consequences of the lack of healthy food during her early childhood. She developed rickets some time later and nearly died.

While Father was recuperating, Mother started working at the military hospital and Katia took care of him. Father was much stronger and, in spite of Mother's objections, was making plans to offer his services at the local military command center. He had no memory of how he had arrived in Gelindjik.

He still was not fit for active duty but was readily accepted in the law enforcement section, which needed experienced officers. He was put in charge of a small detachment that policed the city. Too often, it was a losing battle against the bands of Greens who became bolder with each day. There was no denying that the gallant forces of the White Army were losing and the ominous news of defeat could no longer be just rumors.

Money had lost its value and yesterday's new paper currency was not worth the paper it was printed on. People stood in the streets under the pelting rain waiting for Cossack carts loaded with frozen potatoes and pumpkins. The Cossack women, mostly from Kuban areas, stood on the carts with mocking smiles as crowds of city women, with their high heels sinking in deep mud, pushed their way to get nearer to the provisions. They pocketed the money offered by outstretched white hands, obviously enjoying the plight of the White Russians, who, they believed, deserved their destiny.

Unfortunately for them, that same destiny awaited them when the Communists organized themselves as rulers of Russia. All Cossacks were pursued and eliminated as enemies of the people. Both the Don and Kuban Cossacks had ceased to exist with the advent of the Soviet Union. Some were able to escape abroad, but those who lived became Soviet citizens, but were always looked upon with suspicion, with all the disadvantages which that entailed.

Another element of horror was the hospital for infectious diseases. In that long low building, the sick, the dying and the dead were all bedded side by side. A sickening stench emanated from the broken windows, and there was no one to bury the dead.

To avoid the sickness and the cold, my parents were able to secure two bunks in a car on an unused train, off the main line. There they huddled at night, warmed by a small coal heater emanating poisonous fumes.

Father was now helping to register the refugees for departure on whatever ships accepted them for destinations in Turkey or Europe.

In January 1920, the Red Army finally pushed the remnants of the White Army as far South as the Black Sea, to the port of Novorossisk. Masses of civilians and military personnel invaded this last bastion of safety, in the hopes of escaping certain death at the hands of the pursuing enemy. The former Allies, British and French authorities, sent ships to rescue them. The British Navy ships stood in the port, with daily departures. And the huge dreadnaught *Queen Mary* lay at anchor, awaiting her next load. Even the Germans sent a couple of their Navy ships, but in spite of all the efforts, it still was not enough to cope with the growing number of arrivals.

Leo and Maria Vassilivna left on one of the British steamers headed for Yugoslavia. In February, there was no longer any military or civilian authority, and with the fall of Rostov, Ekaterinodar, and Novocherkassk, it was only a matter of days before the Reds entered Novorossisk.

Father' s diary describes their departure from Russia on March 21, 1920:

Early in the morning we loaded a cart with our meager belongings. Zhenia was suffering the first symptoms of typhoid fever, and could scarcely walk. I held our little Jenny while supporting my wife with the other hand. We were afraid that the ship's officers would discover that Zhenia was infected with typhoid fever, and refuse to accept her on board. We knew that many exiles were also sick, but it was unthinkable to remain any longer in Novorossisk.

"Just a couple of hours more, Zhenichka," I said. "Smile and pretend that you are well, or they won't let us on board."

We got out of the cart and stood in line to board the *Saratov* looming above us. Zhenia gave a big smile, but I could feel her hot trembling hand. The officer examined our papers and little Jenny gave him a smile with her two front teeth as we passed at last to safety. We descended carefully down into the hold of the ship on wet slippery iron steps.

The enormous hold was already full of people with their bags, blankets and boxes. There were officers on crutches, old women leaning on the arms of others, crying children and nannies, and even an elderly lady with two dogs.

"Madam," an officer was shouting, "we cannot have dogs here. Please get them out."

"Go to hell," shouted the lady. "Who do you think you are? My husband is a colonel!"

"Madam, I am General Potapenko, and I am in charge of this hold. The dogs must go."

And so it went, but I was not listening anymore. I found a place near the wall, where Zhenia was lying on our belongings, and sat down on the floor, holding our sleeping little girl on my lap.

A painful feeling of uncertainty continued its hold on me. What if something went wrong and we couldn't leave? Our future was shrouded in darkness. No one on board, including the captain, knew where the *Saratov* was headed with its human cargo of refugees, as this information would only be received in Istanbul from the British military authorities. But I concluded that whatever was awaiting us could not be worse than what we had already experienced or what could certainly be our fate had we remained in Novorossisk. Unable to overcome the feeling of anxiety,

I made sure that my little Jenny was sleeping, wrapped in a blanket, and made my way to the upper deck.

It was a gray and windy evening. Rain clouds raced across the sky where blue searchlights crisscrossed the horizon, skimming across the restless waters and gliding across the foothills. From the distant shore of Tonki Mis came sporadic sounds of heavy artillery, while the rising northwest wind intensified its winter song.

I stood a long time watching my homeland for the last time. At dawn the *Saratov* lifted the anchors and slowly glided along the quay. A deep urgent vibration of motors arose from the depth of the boat as she gathered speed and turned away from shore.

My last glimpse of Russia was a lonely silhouette of a soldier in a tall fur hat, clutching a rifle as he stood on guard at the edge of the pier. Next to me someone was weeping loudly while the *Saratov* headed east into the foggy cloud of an uncertain future.

PART II

One

When the refugee ship *Saratov* gently bumped the wharf of the ancient Alexandria Harbor, my father, Anatoli Markov, watching from the upper deck, could hardly believe his eyes. Huge bearded Sikh soldiers in turbans and khaki shorts formed a receiving line to welcome the motley crowd of Russian émigrés as they tottered unsteadily, going down the planks. Only in books had he seen such exotic-looking dark-skinned people, where they were portrayed in scant African clothes, while here they were dressed in British Army uniforms. An English officer, in a cork helmet, stood impassively on the side, supervising the operation, as the soldiers helped the wounded and the weak onto a military truck.

Father had heard earlier that the King of Egypt, Fouad I, had kindly agreed to give shelter to Russian refugees who, pursued by destructive forces of the Bolsheviks, had abandoned their homeland. By this time, everyone on the ship knew that Turkey and Greece had refused to let them disembark because of the typhoid fever that had been raging on board the *Saratov* during the three-week odyssey at sea.

Both my mother and father had just recovered from cruel bouts with typhoid fever, and Father, still weak, felt as if his knees would not support him. The refugee ship was not sufficiently equipped with medical supplies and they were lucky to survive at all. A heavy military overcoat thrown over his shoulders was now too heavy and he shrugged it off. He inhaled the unfamiliar fragrance of oranges and some kind of spice drifting in the morning air. A small boat filled with fruit approached the steamer, and a smiling Arab was waving a peeled banana in his outstretched hand.

Father felt dizzy, but thought he was lucky just to be alive. *How strange*, he mused. *Here we are, after all our terrible experiences, about to start a new life. I wish I could do something memorable at this moment—something symbolic.* Suddenly, he laughed. His innate sense of humor found an immediate solution to his solemn thoughts. He felt like doing something silly. He snatched the fur hat from his head. That warm hat had served him well from 1914 to 1920, during the war against the Germans and in the White Army. He decided that this hat, with its population of lice, would be the symbol of the unwanted in his life. He twirled it several times and sent it sailing into the shimmering Mediterranean.

Meanwhile, the passengers were headed for the quarantine, their dirty green uniforms still proudly displaying the gallant insignias of some of the most heroic and legendary regiments of their beloved country. Waiting for them to disembark, a small detachment of Russian officers was still on board, standing at attention over a dozen body bags. These were bodies of people who had died the day before and were not yet buried at sea. A priest with a white beard stood at their side. This sight sobered Father, and the serious mood returned him to reality.

We lost the fight, he thought, *but we are not losers. Yes, we have lost the battle against dark forces, but we are not beaten. We are withdrawing from our land occupied by a clique of Bolsheviks, who tried to destroy all that was sacred and noble. They desecrated our Church and killed their own brothers, all for a foreign philosophy.* A surge of determination swept through his mind. He lifted his head. "I swear on my love for Russia," he whispered, "that I will never give up the struggle against Communism. I don't know how, but as God is my witness, I will fight in my own way so that one day Russia will return to its true destiny, with God guiding all our steps."

A familiar form materialized near Anatoli and a small hand clasped his arm. "Here you are, Zhenia," he acknowledged, embracing my mother. "You are always there for me, in all the important moments of our lives. Look at that sunshine, feel that warm air. We have arrived at last at a peaceful haven. Who knows what the future will hold for us here?"

"Well, Tolia," she said, "our new life is to begin. I have been asked to help with the seriously wounded and I will drive in the ambulance with them while they process everybody. I found out that once we arrive at the quarantine camp, we will be housed together, so I will leave you now. I have already packed our belongings. Little Jenny is with the Platonov family, and she is well taken care of." Watching the hat float away, she laughed. "I'm glad you got rid of that fur hat with its village of lice. You won't need it here, that's for sure."

My mother was then only twenty-nine, but she was already a certified doctor with invaluable experience on the Eastern Front and in the White Army. Of small stature, she seemed younger than her years, especially when accompanied by her giant of a husband. She quickly kissed him and joined the group of nurses and doctors accompanying the wounded as they went down the gangway.

She drove in a military ambulance. It was filled with seriously wounded officers, some of them unconscious. She was cradling the head of a young man who was moaning with pain. His face was flushed with fever and she knew he was suffering from a hip wound. "Help them, Father," she prayed silently. "We have done what we could with the few medical supplies we had, and I am glad that there will be doctors and nurses at the British hospital who will care for them."

* * *

Descending to the darkness of the hold, Father grabbed his battered suitcase and gave a last look around the smelly, airless area that had sheltered them. He smiled bitterly, thinking that whatever lay in the future could only be better than those three last weeks. He did not remember much of that time, except that he was constantly thirsty. There were no beds, and the sick and dying were lying together on blankets. The filthy hold was empty now and a sickening stench rose from the floor. Anxious to get out, he joined the rest of the passengers and went down the swaying gangplank, relishing the feeling that he would at last stand on firm land. Reaching the last step, he was unceremoniously snatched off his feet by a grinning Sikh soldier, who hoisted him onto a high truck, where he was handled by another bearded monster who gently sat him down. Too stunned to speak or protest, Father found that he was jammed between a general and a young cadet.

"Surprised, Captain?" laughed the general. "I was also treated with the same consideration by our colorful saviors, but I had the privilege of being informed earlier that we would be driven as soon as possible to a quarantine camp. There is no time to lose as we are all carriers of typhoid fever, and should not be in contact with anyone until we are pronounced safe to join the rest of our group."

"How exciting, sir," squeaked the young cadet. "These soldiers are Egyptians, aren't they? We studied about Egypt, but I never thought I would meet some, because we lived in Petrograd. I learned that they write in pictures and I wonder how it sounds."

"Well, Kostia," replied the general, noticing the boy's nametag pinned to his chest, "actually, these soldiers are from India, and they are called Sikhs, recognizable by their beards and turbans. They are wearing British military uniforms because India is a British colony. To answer your other question, the majority of Egyptians today are not the descendants of the old Egyptians. Today their people are Arabs, who conquered Egypt after Alexander the Great, and the Romans after him occupied Egypt."

Kostia looked disappointed. "You mean, sir, that they don't walk around in loincloths with funny striped headwear?"

"I don't think so, son," smiled the general, who was probably an experienced traveler. "But today's Arabs wear quite colorful kaftans, while the women wrap themselves in heavy black material. If they are married, they wear a veil, but the unmarried girls do not need to hide their faces."

"How exciting this is going to be," cried the boy. "I will have so many things to tell my parents when I see them."

The general looked with compassion at the young boy. "So you have come very far away from your family?" he asked.

"Yes, sir," said the cadet. His eyes reddened, but he tried not to cry. "Mamochka and Father joined the White Army and my school was evacuated south. I hope that I can find them soon. Before we were evacuated from Novorossisk, I was waiting to hear from them, but the Bolsheviks cut us off. I saw some fighting while we waited for the

Saratov to arrive. Then I was sick on board and do not remember how long we sailed."

Father's heart contracted with pity. He knew that many cadet schools were evacuated with the retreating forces. These boys were aged ten to sixteen, and many of them perished from wounds and neglect, although the officers accompanying them tended them with love and care.

The general sighed. He put his arms around Kostia, too moved to speak. He turned his face away, watching more trucks arrive, and to hide his emotions, he joined in the banter of his fellow passengers.

After an hour on dusty roads, they reached a military compound surrounded by barbed wire. Upon entering the camp they were taken to the bathhouses, where their hair was shaved off by a number of barbers. Once despoiled of their locks, they were given smelly disinfectant bars of soap and told to take showers.

After the welcome luxury of hot water, Father wrapped himself in one of the gray cotton robes laid out for them and joined his laughing companions as they examined each other in their new attire. There were no mirrors, but he knew that he looked as ridiculous as any of them, with shaved heads and short robes. He realized with pleasure that he heard laughter for the first time in a long while. He felt he was young again. He closed his eyes for an instant to savor the moment of exhilaration, and then joined the group of new Russian émigrés about to start a new life.

* * *

In 1920, Egypt had just been placed under the protectorate of the British Empire. After the end of World War I, Turkey, with the support of influential Turkish princes living in Egypt, was trying to extend its influence into Egyptian politics. Egypt was a choice morsel because of its rich cotton crops and the unique advantage of the Suez Canal.

Following its policy of colonization, the British, in a brilliant political move, set up a new king in Egypt to replace the ruling Khedives, who were mostly Turkish appointees, and offered to give its protection to the new kingdom, establishing British military camps in the larger cities. This arrangement not only protected Egypt from Turkey, but also facilitated British aspirations to the neighboring Sudan, on which they cast their greedy eyes.

Egypt now had a new king. Fouad I was educated in Europe and his wife, Queen Nazli, was of French descent. Attracted by economic possibilities, English businessmen flocked to the new protectorate with their families, acquiring vast agricultural lands for growing cotton and rice. The French also came and prospered. The Greeks and Italians, who always lived in Egypt, were generally lower-middle-class merchants and restaurant owners. Quite a large population of wealthy merchants of European origin, including Armenians and Lebanese, formed a multilingual society

With hardly any taxes, they prospered and grew rich. They employed *fellahins*, Egyptian peasants, to work the fields, but the wages were low and the villages remained poor. The British did not sponsor village schools and neither did the Egyptian government. The British, by virtue of being English, did not have to be wealthy to be part of an exclusive class. When the Russian émigrés were invited by King Fouad to make Egypt their home, the High Society unanimously followed suit and adopted the homeless Russians as their own. Due to the fact that the small émigré community included several titled members of Russian aristocracy, an enthusiastic welcome was extended to the entire group. Most of them were well-educated, spoke French, English and German, and in no time, White Russians blended seamlessly into the multilingual society.

The pages of the Sunday newspaper, *La Reforme Illustree*, regularly supplied its readers with the important events of high ociety, reporting such select happenings as engagements, marriages, baptisms, receptions and balls. These articles listed every "well-born" person who attended those functions, and woe to the reporter who forgot to insert the name of such-and-such personality. An erratum of such an omission would be found in the following week's edition. The Egyptians, unless they were princes of Turkish origin or p*ashas* (an Egyptian title given to important wealthy people), were not invited to such functions.

The Egyptians quickly learned that they were second-class citizens, and meekly accepted that fact. Even after the protectorate agreement came to an end in 1954, nothing changed in Egypt.

But a new generation of Egyptians, mainly from the educated middle class, was growing up. The young men and women learned in schools and universities that they were heirs to a wonderful country, which, owing to a rich fertile soil, could produce, every year, two crops of the best cotton in the world, and where the wheat and rice crops were in abundance.

Such was the political climate in Egypt when the small Russian group landed in Alexandria in February of 1920, for whom a different life was just about to begin.

Two

Life at the refugee camp was challenging, to say the least. Each family was allotted a small tent while the bachelors and single women lived in segregated large tents.

At the beginning, there were more than 2,000 people in the camps, but soon, many refugees who were not in quarantine were allowed to travel to Yugoslavia and France. These countries readily accepted them, while the rest decided to stay on and seek employment in Alexandria and Cairo.

A makeshift Russian church was established at once in a big tent and life revolved around church and communal dining rooms. Food was supplied by the British Army. It was plain but plentiful, with emphasis on canned food. Many lifelong friendships were established and groups of mutual interests sprung up. Choir singing and amateur acting were popular in an effort to survive the inevitable boredom and lighten up the feeling of uncertainty that plagued everyone.

My parents remained in the camp at Tel El Kebir for six months, until Father was able to obtain a job as a taxi driver.

Since all business transactions in Egypt at that time were conducted exclusively in French, several émigrés soon found suitable jobs. Teachers, doctors, nurses and engineers were in great demand, but the rest were military career officers, such as my father, with no professional skills

Circumstances decreed that my parents would remain in Alexandria, the main reason being that my mother was expecting a child, yours truly.

I was born on December 2, 1921, without much fanfare, in a British military hospital at the Mustafa Pasha barracks. Two other Russian babies were born on the same day, one of whom, Leonid Sisoyev, was to play an important role in my later life. A large tent, grandly called the "maternity ward," was reserved for wives of military personnel, and for Russian refugees.

Mother told me I was a quiet baby who slept most of the time, waking up only for feeding. She was relieved because my older sister,

Jenny, was born during the revolutionary years, when my parents were constantly on the march with the White Army, and as a result, she was sickly and high-strung. Jenny did not welcome the idea of another child competing for the affection of her parents, and declared war on me from the moment my mother brought me home. Even in later years, she would remember the event with a disgusted curl of her lip

"You were such an ugly baby, lots of dark hair and a red shriveled face," she would say, relishing a howl of protest from me. When Mother protested that I had indeed improved after a few days, Jenny would toss her head and say, "But, of course, I was born a beautiful baby with golden hair and blue eyes. Just look at my picture and tell me who is prettier."

Alas, years did nothing to improve my sister's attitude. The spirit of competition never left her, and in her mind, she remained a victim of circumstances throughout her life.

* * *

Father, a career officer in Russia, had no practical skills for earning his living. In Russia, it was not unusual for young men of his class to attend cadet schools and military academies, from where they would be absorbed in the many select regiments. It was understood that to become a member of these regiments, one had to be independently wealthy and a member of the gentry, for these were honorary appointments for which no salaries were paid. To be a member of a select regiment involved considerable expenses. The officers were responsible for maintaining stables of several horses, male servants, and several changes of expensive colorful dress uniforms. After serving their monarch for a few years, they were expected to retire and devote their time to their estates. When a young man of landed gentry, not inclined for military service, would elect to continue his studies, he would seek occupations to serve the motherland, as it was considerably more honorable. Lawyers, doctors, teachers and engineers who worked for salaries were considered to be of the professional class, quite distinct from the gentry.

* * *

Father tried several unsuccessful ways to earn money. When he enrolled in a taxi-driving school, he soon lost his job. Natives, who dominated that line of work, were not about to welcome a bunch of foreign competitors who could not even speak Arabic, and were hostile to newcomers. To tell the truth, Father would often fall asleep at his taxi station waiting for a fare, but fate had other plans for him.

One day, he learned that there were several openings for applicants with military backgrounds at the Anglo-Egyptian Police, for duties as Constables. The brigade of European Constables was a unique organization attached to the Anglo-Egyptian Governorate. The brigade of Constables was then recently introduced into the police organization due to the unusual circumstances existing at that time in Egypt.

The Constables were recruited from qualified members of the international community. Their functions consisted of keeping order among the foreign nationals, who were not subject to Egyptian law, but rather, to the laws of their own respective countries. These were Italian, Greek, French, Spanish, etc., nationals who worked closely with their consulates. In legal cases involving foreign individuals, a special Mixed Tribunal of foreign judges was appointed to process cases according to the laws of their respective countries. Most cases were of a criminal nature and did not present any complicated diplomatic problems. The Egyptians had their own courts and did not interfere with the Mixed Tribunals. Father applied and was accepted immediately into the Constable brigade.

This was interesting work, which afforded him some free time to do his writing. My earliest memories are of Father's typewriter clicking away far into the night. He wrote about his childhood, about Russia, about his experiences during World War I, and his service in the White Army. One of his bigger works was a detailed history of the White Army, which was acquired by the California branch of the Hoover Library in 1961.

But already in the early 1920s his articles in the Russian newspapers in France attracted the attention of the Russian communities. He then expanded his writing activities to other European countries, and later to the American newspapers in New York and San Francisco. His weekly reports in the Alexandria French newspapers, such as *La Bourse Egyptienne* and *La Reforme*, often dealt with the political climate in Russia, shedding light on the events in the newly-formed Soviet Union.

The source of Father's information came from the many escapees from Soviet merchant ships, who frequently jumped ship in Alexandria, seeking political refuge, and invariably, Father helped them. Although the Soviet citizens were not allowed to leave Russia, there was still a steady trickle of refugees, who were immediately integrated into the Russian community. They had many stories to tell, and brought with them Soviet newspapers, where the "great achievements" were printed for the benefit of the Russian population. These articles were the start of my father's long writing career.

* * *

It was at that time that Father received an unexpected summons from His Egyptian Majesty, King Fouad.

At first, Father was astonished and curious, as he could not think of any reason for the summons, but he donned his Constable uniform of the Anglo-Egyptian police and presented himself at the Montazah Palace, the summer residence of the king.

Years later I read the details of that visit in Father's diary.

I arrived an hour early and my taxi left me at the gates of the palace, where I showed the invitation to the guard on duty. I was asked to follow a tall Nubian dressed in a white robe with a wide red sash. He wore a white turban.

We entered a large vestibule with blue marble columns. The floor was covered with a green and gold mosaic design. We went through several doors guarded by attendants, and I was invited to sit on a chair in the vast antechamber.

After what seemed a long time, I was finally ushered to a large balcony overlooking the Bay of Montazah.

King Fouad was sitting in a recliner with a coffee cup in his hand.

The Nubian approached the king and said in Arabic, "This is Constable Markov, your Majesty."

The king looked up. He smiled as I saluted.

"Ah, he said in French, "Constable Markov. Please have a seat."

I sat in the chair across from the king, a small glass table separating us. The Nubian brought a cup of black coffee, placed it in front of me and withdrew.

"Constable Markov," said the king, "you look like you had military training. Tell me about yourself. I know, already, that you arrived in Egypt with the remnants of the White Army, seeking political asylum, and I was glad to welcome them. The assassination of your emperor and his lovely family was such a cruel and unnecessary act."

He wistfully shook his head. His face was familiar to me from his photographs in the Alexandria periodicals and also on postage stamps: a round face with a receding hairline, and a mustache with upturned ends. Trying not to stare, I watched his kind face. There was no pretense about him. Here was an aging king, I thought. Another absolute monarch who could also be toppled by a crowd of ignorant rabble, seduced by lying promises of "equality."

Our eyes met for a moment, and maybe my face showed my unguarded thoughts, for the king smiled at me.

"It has been reported to me," he said, "that your political articles in our European press deal mostly with the spread of international Communism. I am becoming more and more aware that Communism is no longer a Russian commodity, and that Moscow is discreetly operating in European universities, seeking talented agents for the spread of what they call 'international' Communism."

He paused, watching my expression. "Any comments, so far?" he asked.

"Yes," I replied. "Only they don't tell those young idealists that the so-called 'international' side of it begins and ends in the Kremlin."

"Of course," said the king. "While the newly-recruited members of the Communist party will be convinced that they are real patriots who are liberating their own country from unfair government, they will, in fact, be working for the Soviet Union's ambition of world domination."

He put down his cup and the Nubian attendant appeared immediately from nowhere and placed another steaming cup of Turkish coffee on the table in front of the king. Since I seldom drank strong coffee, I took only a sip from my cup, but apparently, his majesty loved the bitter stuff.

He continued: "Our universities, both European and our own, are breeding grounds for revolutionary ideas. Young people always search for new forms of government, and are easily influenced by their teachers. Since you have had ample opportunity to observe first hand the initial birth of Communist ideas among the military and civilian population in your country, I would like to pick your brain from time to time."

I said, "Your Majesty, all my life, I served my emperor and my country faithfully. I had lost both, but due to your Majesty's hospitality, I now have a country and a monarch to serve in every way I can."

"Thank you," said the king. "I want to ask you a few questions. I will ask my secretary to take notes. I hope you don't mind. This is quite unofficial and I want you to keep this session, and the ones that may follow, quite confidential."

He rang a bell and spoke briefly to the servant. As if by magic, the door opened and a middle-aged man entered the room. He sat nearby and prepared to take notes.

This took about two hours. After the secretary left the room, the king talked at length with me about some of his concerns. He told me that he would let me know when he wanted to see me again. He said that he trusted me to keep these meetings confidential, and I gave him my word.

When Father told me about that momentous meeting with King Fouad, I remember that I was very excited, and urged him to tell me more. To my disappointment he told me, quite firmly, that this was confidential information, and that was that.

I believe, however, that Father shared this secret side of his life with Mother, but she never said anything about it to me, although I tried very hard to worm it out of her. What I found out, by observation, was that Father visited the king once a month in summer at his Montazah Palace, and every two months when the king was in his winter residence in Cairo.

King Fouad died in 1936, succeeded by his son Farouk, who was sixteen at that time. Whatever anti-Communist activity Father was involved with, I never found out, but as the political climate of Egypt changed through the years, his secret service had probably triggered a series of unfortunate and tragic events for him in 1958.

* * *

After I was born, my mother had no doubts that she could return to medicine, at least part time, but soon encountered a roadblock. Although she was already planning to set up a clinic, she was soon told that foreign doctors had to pass a board examination in Arabic before being granted the right to practice medicine in Egypt. That created dismay among the newly-arrived Russian doctors, but soon the authorities relented and announced that it was acceptable to pass the examination in French. Hopeful again, she and the other doctors applied for certification. Because she was the only woman doctor among them, another disappointment awaited her. After she passed the required examination successfully, the Egyptian administrator minced no words as he told her in bad French that a woman's place was at home, and refused her the necessary permit.

I was still a toddler when my parents rented an apartment in a native neighborhood on the margin of the desert, east of Alexandria. Our landlord was Hag Abd el Aziz, a chieftain of the tiny village called Siuf. The villagers lived mostly in large tents among groves of palm trees, and Hag Abd el Aziz was considered rich, since he had built himself a two-story house made of local bricks. My parents occupied the ground floor, while Abd el Aziz, with his two wives, Fatma and Ratiba, occupied the upper level. Abd el Aziz was a quiet man who lived in peace with his two wives. He told my parents that he had married his second wife, Ratiba, only when it was obvious that Fatma could not have any children. The two women lived happily together, bringing up Ratiba's three children.

At that time, Siuf had no medical clinic or doctors, and the natives had to travel far, often on foot, to get medical help. My mother, determined to put to use her medical knowledge, thought of a plan which would achieve her purpose. She put up a sign on the door advertising a free clinic. Soon, female patients flocked to her door. They had no problem being doctored by a woman. Mother did not accept any fees, and the grateful natives brought her fresh eggs, vegetables and dates. Since this was a free clinic, the Egyptian authorities did not object and left her alone. There were several Russian doctors in Alexandria, and through them, Mother took every opportunity to read about the latest achievements in the medical field.

Every morning, before Mother would open the front door, a collection of women wrapped up in black *abayas* (floor-length wraps) congregated around the small apartment house. They waited for Mother to see them as they sat on the beaten ground with their children, chattering like magpies among themselves.

Of course, I was too young to remember anything, but later, when my parents spoke about that time, it seemed to me that I could remember those days. When, six years later, we came to Siuf again, I believed that I could remember living there. By that time, modern civilization had changed that remote area. Gone were the low Bedouin tents. They were replaced with small yellow-colored brick dwellings.

When we returned to Siuf, we found out that Abd el Aziz had built a villa for rent, and was glad to lease it to us. He did not want to rent it to locals, as the Europeans paid a higher rent, and that got him in trouble with his sister. She had built an apartment house, too, but was unable to find good renters, as it was sub-standard and only natives wanted to live in a house with toilets which were nothing more than a hole in the ground. This competition with her brother led to an unfortunate incident, which I will explain later.

After we moved in, my mother started to accept private nursing jobs among the small European community nearby. It was not much, but it was enough money to supplement Father's starting salary with the Governorate.

The villa had three bedrooms, a small kitchen, and a bathroom with just a shower. A large central room served as dining room and sitting room. The floor was gray tile, while the bedrooms had polished wooden floors. Every window, as in all houses in Alexandria, had wooden slat shutters. This was a comfortable house where Jenny and I had the freedom of a big garden filled with jasmine bushes.

I was eight years old at the time, and Jenny was ten-and-a-half. A high wall surrounded our villa and the garden where we played. We had firm instructions not to go outside the gates, but one day, they were left ajar, so I slipped through. As I stood outside, I saw that a new tent had just been erected a few yards from our house.

I had never been inside a Bedouin tent and I was very curious. By then, I was quite familiar with the sight of their women who came to my mother for medical help. These women were quite different from the native *fellahin* (peasant) women, who were always wrapped from head to toe in heavy black wraps. The Bedouin were nomads and their women did not cover their faces. They wore long robes of light black fabric, with two or three vests of different lengths. Their eyes were heavily underlined with kohl—a charcoal powder mixed with water—and their hair was braided like numerous snakes, adorned with bright coins. Even the poorest Bedouin girl wore gold-colored bracelets jingling on her arms.

I approached the entrance to the tent, a canvas flap, and peered inside.

A voice came from inside, *"Ahlemwasahlem"* (Greetings), and a plump Bedouin woman lifted the flap and invited me to come in.

A heavy odor of spices, incense and garlic assailed my nostrils while my eyes adjusted to the low light created by the sunlight forcing its way through the holes in the tent.

Leila (her name, as I found out later) sat me on one of the several cotton pads loosely arranged around a primus stove. Something appetizing bubbled in the kettle, and she filled a plate and set it in front of me. She brought a pitcher of water and a bucket and told me to wash my hands. Then she handed me the plate with a large piece of flat bread, still warm from the stone on which she had baked it. I used the flat bread to scoop the sauce into my mouth. Leila smiled at me. *"Maashallah!"* she said, something approximating *bon appetit.*

Many decades have passed since, but I can still taste the spicy okra I ate that day, and feel the warm welcome from a nomad Bedouin woman. This was my first independent excursion into the world away from my family, but it taught me the Bedouin tradition of hospitality and kindness to strangers, practiced even by the poorest of the poor. Then my mother appeared at the flap, relieved to have found me. I lost interest in Leila during the friendly exchange between her and my mother and examined the interior of the *Koshk*—the tent. The sides of the tent sloped from the center, supported by four posts, about seven feet high, creating a square ceiling over the eating area. A curtain of undetermined color separated the eating area from the sleeping quarters, concealing the bed pads. Several ropes were strung, hung with pieces of clothing, and at a lower level, I could see bunches of dried dates and clusters of plump garlic.

Leila became a frequent visitor to our house. She would come to the kitchen door bringing such sweet treats as a handful of fresh juicy red dates, or a piece of sugar cane. Mother treated her elderly husband, who suffered from arthritis, and applied soothing ointment to his painful joints. When he passed away after a couple of years, Leila packed up her tent and moved away to live with a married daughter. We missed her, for she had become a friend.

Three

I was five years old when my parents rented a small apartment near the beach known as the Sporting Club Station. The apartment was on the terrace of a two-story house. In a previous incarnation, it was a two-room laundry, before being transformed into a rental apartment by the addition of a small counter with a Primus burner and a tiny bathroom with a shower.

My sister, Jenny, had already started school at the Franciscan convent nearby. In addition, Jenny also attended Sunday school classes, where the Russian kids were taught reading and writing by a former lawyer. Father Alexei, our Russian priest, taught New Testament to the children and the basic prayers of the Russian Orthodox Church.

I was very impressed with my sister's school activities. Jenny always tried to show off her newly-acquired skills. She was already a fluent reader in Russian. When we were not fighting, she taught me the Russian alphabet, and before long, I could read our few children's books, over and over. I had no difficulty speaking our native language, but it would be many years before I mastered the mysteries of Russian grammar. The reason was simple. When I became old enough to attend Russian Sunday school, the Russian teacher became a taxi driver, and to fill the void, Father Alexei decided, instead, to introduce the children to the interesting stories of the Old Testament. That was a lot of fun. We all giggled when he went on and on about who begat whom. I particularly enjoyed the story of Abraham, who was about to kill his son. All the boys were disappointed that he did not kill him. The practical side of the Sunday school was that although I did not learn the Russian grammar, I never forgot who begat whom, and could rattle my knowledge of Hebraic names to the hilarious amusement of my parents.

It was fun living on the roof of an apartment. Mother was a doctor, but she was not allowed to practice medicine. She packed away her reference books and the few medical instruments she possessed and stayed home, learning how to be a housewife. Father said that it wasn't necessary for her to learn how to cook because he would eat whatever she served. One day, he even ate my mother's burnt meatballs while she cried. Jenny fed her meatball to the cat, but I believed my father when he said they were tasty, and even today, I like my meatballs on the crusty side.

I did not know that we were poor because all our Russian friends were living in the same condition. We had a large table in the main room and four chairs. Our visitors usually sat on two cots, which served as beds for Jenny and me. They were covered with military-issue, dark-green woolen blankets with just a few holes. Our parents' cots were in the other room, with a desk wedged between them.

Father's old typewriter was strictly out of bounds to us, and we learned early, the hard way, not to mess with it or Father's papers.

We did not have conventional toys, but I always found some way to entertain myself. On Sundays, when Father did not go to work, I would snuggle up to him on his cot and ask him to tell me the story of the little boy. This was the only story that Father knew, and he always told it with a lot of feeling, his eyes lost in the distance as he spoke about the young boy who lived in a big house by a river. (As a child, I never suspected that he was really telling me about his own life in Russia; only later did I make the connection.) That boy had two brothers, a sister, and a beautiful mother. They had many cousins and playmates and they ran in the fields and swam in the creek. Sometimes, Father would stop in the middle of the story and I could see that inside his head, he was still telling me the story, but no sound came from him. I thought that he was tired from working all the week and I did not speak to him, but played my own game on the wall next to his bed.

There was a crack the size of a big pencil in the wall, and I could see little round insects busy going in and out. I tried to help them get out and scratched with my finger to loosen the peeling whitewash paint off the wall. The round little creatures were happy to come out and some even managed to land on the bed. I picked one up and probably pressed it too hard. It stopped moving and released a bad smell. Father came out of his dream and asked me, "What are you doing, Vicka?" I held my hand to his nose and let him smell my fingers. He was not very happy. He yelled, "Zhenia, did you know we have bedbugs?" Mother came running and stood gazing speechlessly at the small crack, which had just become bigger.

"Do something!" said Father. "I still remember their stench when they attacked us at night in the Baiburt hotel during the revolution."

"My God!" said Mother. "I have some alcohol, but that probably won't help."

"They will probably enjoy the alcohol, like vodka," said Father. "But maybe these are not like Russian bedbugs. They are Egyptian and therefore they do not touch any spirits."

"Mamochka," I asked, "what are bedbugs?"

"Get away from that wall, child, and let me wash your hands. These are vermin and we have to destroy them before they destroy us. Anatoli, get off that cot and go down and ask Maria Ivanovna if she knows how to get rid of bedbugs!"

Maria Ivanovna was the supreme authority on everything that Mother did not know about practical living. She lived on the floor below us, and was a fountain of information on everybody and everything. Whether or not she knew what she was talking about, her imposing stature and ruddy complexion inspired confidence, and Mother relied on her for valuable advice on household matters. Maria guided Mother through the rough apprenticeship of adapting herself to new rules and conditions of life in a new, exotic country. Mother had little experience whatsoever with how to prepare food, handle money, and deal with everyday emergencies. On graduating from medical school, she volunteered as a doctor on the Eastern Front, and later on, with my father, joined the White Army. At thirty, mother of two children, she had to learn fast how to survive in a foreign and strange land. My father was just as unprepared as she was to face a life of responsibilities, even to a lesser degree, having spent his school years in military academies and officers' schools. Although his father was wealthy, Father never had the opportunity to handle money, as during his school years, and the war experience, he had little need to do so. In Egypt, whatever my father was able to earn, he would bring home, expecting Mother to handle such mundane details. Much later, when I realized what challenges she faced, I could appreciate her courage and flexibility.

This was my first, and luckily last, experience with bedbugs, as Maria Ivanovna advised us to call in "the mattress man." I learned later that the bedbug scourge was known to all living in old houses in Alexandria. The only way to get rid of them was to call in the bedbug man, who would whitewash the walls to cover every tiny hole and crack. He would then lock himself in the empty room with the mattresses. These mattresses, about ten inches thick, were filled with raw Egyptian cotton. The bedbug expert would undo the cotton cover, pull out the filling and then fluff it up on a harp-like tool with two or three strings. Taking handfuls of cotton balls, he would twang them on the strings, releasing thick clouds of dust. The cotton fibers would thus become airy, silky and voluminous.

After washing the covers, he would dry them, creating new and clean mattresses, expertly sewn with rounded corners, to serve for another year.

The beds were metal mesh, covering coils of springs. The bedbugs thrived in the damp heat of Alexandria's summers, and made their nests wherever they could, in the mattresses or in the tight metal coils of the *shustas*, as the metal beds were called. The procedure to destroy the bedbugs in the metal coils was simple and effective. A Primus stove would be lit, and the mattress man would pass the Primus stove like a blowtorch under the surface of the metal mesh and the coiled springs. A sickening sound of popping roasted bedbugs would fill the air, while the mattress man would urge them on their way to oblivion with suitable jokes and encouragement.

I often think with sadness of these humble workers, who risked their lungs to make a few *piastres* (in Egyptian currency, 1 piastre = 10 cents) to support their families. They were performing a wonderful social service, as anyone who has ever experienced the close proximity of bedbugs will agree.

Four

Mohamed Ali was our friend for thirty years. He was a professional Holy Beggar, who entered our life when I was seven years old.

At that time, we lived at Siuf, where such beggars were a familiar sight. Though most of our neighbors were poor themselves, they always gave them something, be it a few ounces of sugar, rice or beans. In exchange, the beggars would bless them, calling upon the Lord to grant his benefactors health and protection from evil.

Mother was not surprised when the beggar appeared at our door. When he stretched out his hand, Mother said, "*Stana shwaya*" (Wait, please) and was turning away to bring him something to eat when she noticed a bloody rag wrapped around his hand. She realized that he was recently hurt, and invited him to come in. He came in willingly and, ignoring the proffered chair, sat down on the floor.

Mother unwrapped the dirty bandage, exposing a festering wound.

"*Mush kwaiess*" (Not good), she said, while he gave her a toothy grin and nodded his head several times, obviously happy to have his hand attended to by a serious-looking doctor, even though a woman. She disinfected his wound and wrapped his hand in a gauze bandage, all the while examining her new patient.

He was dressed in the usual Bedouin garb, ample pants and a *ghalabieh*, a tunic with long, wide sleeves. He wore a white turban with a green top, which Mother knew meant he had been to Mecca at least once.

She also noticed that his alms cloth bag was almost empty, and asked him to wait.

I was in the kitchen at that time, usually banished from the consulting room, but that did not prevent me from peeking through the half-open door.

"Mama, is the beggar sick?" I asked. "Is he going to die?"

"No, silly," said Mother. "He's just got an infected cut, but I think he must be hungry. Hand me that bottle of milk while I make him a sandwich. Then go speak to him while I cut the bread."

Full of my new importance, I sidled through the door and sat on the floor across from the funny-looking man.

He was studying me as well, with kind, intelligent eyes that were surrounded by a network of fine wrinkles. He was the first to break the ice.

"*Esmak ey? Enta bint oula waled?*" (What's your name? Are you a girl or a boy?)

At that age I desperately wished I were a boy, and had talked my mother into giving me a drastic haircut, so I was very pleased by his question.

"*Ana bint,*" I said regretfully. "*Bint Factoria.*" (I am a girl, my name is Victoria).

"*U enta, esmak ey?*" (And what is your name?) I asked, very proud to be conversing like a grown-up, and hoping he would ask how old I was.

"Hag Mohamed Ali," he said, proudly lifting his chin. Young as I was, I could not but be impressed by the aura of dignity about him. Suddenly shy, I was about to beat a hasty retreat when to my delight, he asked me my age. It was on the tip of my tongue to lie that I was already eight years old, but then my mother entered with a tray of food and I decided to tell the truth.

"I am seven, but soon, very soon, in about nine months, I will be eight." I said.

Then, all excited with my new acquaintance, I cried, "Mother, Mother, his name is Mohamed Ali, and he is Hag. Does that mean that he is a holy man? Ask him if he is holy like our priest. Has he got any children? How did he hurt himself?"

"No, dear," Mother said. "Hag is just a title of honor because he visited Mecca, where the Prophet Mohamed is said to have died, and the pious Muslims revere that place like we do Bethlehem. Now, stop asking questions. I want to talk to him, and you can stay, only if you are quiet."

Mother talked to him in Arabic, in what I knew later was as much as she could learn of that complicated language, which she had to learn

81

in just a few years. The Arabic language belongs to a group of languages that have no roots in either the Cyrillic grammar or in the Roman.

It seemed that Mohamed Ali cut himself while peeling a sugar cane the previous day. Sugar cane was a cheap and tasty treat that all the natives enjoyed. After peeling the hard skin, they cut it into pieces and chewed the soft fibrous strands that yielded lots of juice.

Then Mohamed Ali told Mother that he could read and write Arabic, and that he listened regularly to the news every day, when he stopped at one of the numerous cafés during his daily peregrinations along the streets.

The cafés in Egypt were the preferred meeting place of men only. There, over tiny cups of strong coffee or sweet ink-black tea, political events of the day were discussed, with much waving of hands. The radio was always on full blast, broadcasting news of the day or transmitting some endless moaning and cooing song.

Mother was pleasantly surprised that Mohamed Ali could speak of politics, when he voiced his opinion on the topics of the day. Moreover, he had no trouble understanding when Mother told him we were White Russians.

Now, when I look back, I can understand why Mother warmed up to him, since he discussed and commented on the situation in which White Russians tried to survive in a friendly, but very different exotic environment.

The following month, Mohamed Ali returned and was greeted warmly by my mother. Thus a pattern was established which was to last for thirty years.

Sitting comfortably on the floor, he would unwrap some little gift that he brought us. Sometimes it would be a few grains of incense that he would place on a flat stone and light it until it glowed. Holding the stone on his open palm, he would move his hand in a slow circular motion, sending clouds of fragrant incense into the air, thus blessing our home and us.

On other occasions, he would bring some native herb medicine and discuss its merits with Mother, or fish some gooey candy out of his cloth bag, which I always gobbled up with relish, despite my mother's admonitions. Father was seldom home when Mohamed Ali visited us, but whenever they met, Father liked to chat with him, and later, he even wrote a short story about him.

After the ritual gifts and blessings, he would start on the latest news, sipping cups of strong Turkish coffee and enjoying Mother's cigarettes, which she always carried with her. She became addicted to smoking while in medical school, because, as she told me, the smoke helped her to overcome the stench of decomposing bodies, when practicing on cadavers brought from the city morgue.

Politics were the main subject of conversations with Mohamed Ali.

"What's new in this crazy world of ours? What more do the *Inglisi* [English] want from us? They have our frontiers, our cotton, and they are masters of our Suez Canal. They want to own Sudan, but if our government is not stupid, they will not allow this to happen. But do you know why? Far, far in the Sudan, there is much wealth under the ground, but only the British have the money to get it out." Thus, for months, followed by years, the dialogue continued between a Russian doctor and an unusual Egyptian beggar.

As a child, it seemed to me that Mohamed Ali was there forever. He seemed to appear whenever we had some crisis at home, and once was even able to resolve a threatening problem which was very frightening, to say the least. I was then ten years old, when a horrible incident happened which shook my little world. Mohamed Ali was to play an important role in that tragedy.

It all started when our landlord, Sheikh Hag Abdullah, quarreled with his sister, Zeinab. She lived next door to the villa we were renting from him. A recent widow, with many children, she offered for rent the second floor of her house, but there were no takers, and she blamed her brother, who had no problems renting his villa to us.

Her children, encouraged by the mother, were always throwing garbage and stones at our pets. On advice from the Sheikh, we decided to ignore her, but that only fueled her resentment and hate, and in desperation, she devised a diabolical plan.

One morning, I opened the green shutters of my bedroom, which looked out at the small kitchen porch, to find, to my terrible dismay, our small black puppy dead by the door. Crying loudly, I called my mother, who rushed to see what happened, but there was nothing she could do, so she just held me in her arms, trying to console me.

At that moment, our garden gate opened and Mohamed Ali walked in with a big smile, blessing us in the name of Allah.

Upon seeing the dead puppy, he looked around and stopped short.

"Don't move, Doctora. Don't touch anything, and get *bint Factoria* out of the way," he cried. Then he bent down and withdrew a piece of paper stuck in the wooden shutter. Relegated to my bedroom, I watched from the window.

Mohamed Ali held the paper close to his face, reading something in Arabic that was written in dark red ink. When he looked up at us, stern-faced, I could see that something was really wrong.

"This is a terrible curse," he said. "Some evil person wrote this in blood. This curse has the power to kill the smallest living thing in your home, and it is only by sheer luck that your little puppy saw it first, and paid with his life, as he sniffed it."

He sat down and searched in his cloth bag, withdrawing the flat stone and the incense. "Get me a piece of paper," he commanded, "and a pen and ink. I do not know who wrote this, but I will turn the curse back upon the author of this evil."

Although my mother was skeptical, she still brought him the paper and the ink and Mohamed Ali wrote laboriously and slowly, filling almost half a page. He then lit the incense on the flat stone, held the paper to the flame and slowly burned it. The fragrance filled the air and Mohamed Ali waved his hands and mumbled a prayer.

I was very impressed and felt important, while my mother watched, smiling indulgently at her friend. She was glad about the intervention of Mohamed Ali, for I seemed to have forgotten about the puppy.

In the evening, when Father came home, Mother told him about the incident and they both laughed a little, remembering our beggar's worry.

At that moment, a loud shriek came from Zeinab's house. We ran to the window and saw her out on the balcony. She stood screaming and crying, then to my surprise, with a strong jerking motion, she tore her dress in half and started to pull out her hair.

"What happened?" Father asked Sheik Hag Abdullah, who ran out of his house with his sons. "Has anybody died?"

"Something terrible did happen," he answered. "Her youngest child has just died suddenly and she is crazy with grief. She is out of her mind, for she is saying that she is to blame for his death."

My parents looked at each other, Mother pale, her blue eyes dark with worry; Father frowning, a puzzled look on his kind face.

"I think it is best that we look for another house," he said. "There are too many unexplainable events happening here. I'll start looking tomorrow, and you better start packing."

"Yes," Mother said. "I want to get away from here as quickly as possible." She clasped me close to her. "Vicka, when you see Mohamed Ali next time, thank him, for I believe he may have saved your life."

As we moved from one house to another, Mohamed Ali always found us. It was not difficult, as we usually had friendly neighbors who would direct him to our new address.

In the meantime, I started school, but was soon moved from the Holy Mothers of the Apostles to the Scottish School for Girls. This change was not because of my particular preference, but due to an incident, for which I was, alas, partly to blame. One of the Holy Mothers, namely Mother Cecilia, chastised me one day because of my extremely lively nature by repeatedly banging me against the wall. Such uncivilized treatment resulted in my being yanked immediately out of their tendercare. I was then submitted to endless questions as to the reason for my punishment. When under unmerciful parental pressure, I finally revealed what had triggered such extreme measures, and I mumbled, "I just rang the bell, that's all."

Mother could not believe that I was so severely punished, until quite reluctantly, I added that when I was placed on the dais near the Holy Mother to keep me from mischief, I crawled under her ample skirts, grabbed the bell and rang for recess.

My parents said they were quite upset with me, but I could tell that my father could hardly contain himself from laughing. Mother kept a straight face, but she could not fool me, either, although I tried to look suitably contrite.

Mother told her friends that the change of schools was a good move and that in a relatively short time, I would be over my unruly phase of behavior. In fact she was right and in the course of the first year, I grew accustomed to the Anglo-Saxon manner of education. I was reasonably well behaved (in my opinion, of course), although there was that unfortunate incident involving a broken water faucet, which was a complete misunderstanding.

During afternoon recess, I noticed water running from a garden faucet and tried to shut it off. Since it would not budge, I helped myself to a flat piece of rock and banged it shut, but the stupid thing shattered the metal connection and a fountain of water erupted sky-high, to the delight of all my classmates. The only person who was not delighted was the math teacher, Miss Rosy, who happened to pass by. Drenched and unrepentant, I was dragged by the rather wet Miss Rosy to the office of Miss Williams, our feared Headmistress. The latter reprimanded me in front of the whole school. "Victoria," she said in her clipped British accent, "keep in mind that the Russian Benevolent Society is paying for your tuition." This tactless statement made her my archenemy, but from then on, I was on my best behavior, and much more careful not to get caught.

During my early teen years, we moved periodically from one house to another, as Father was promoted rapidly to captain through the ranks of the Anglo-Egyptian Governorate. We were now able to live comfortably. Jenny and I had our own rooms. This was a relief since we never got along well, and we both welcomed the change. My parents realized that they were not returning to Russia in the near future, so Mother started acquiring better furniture, and soon our house started looking like a home.

When I later became interested in boys, I learned that Mohamed Ali could predict, without fail, how my innocent infatuations would turn out, just by looking in the dregs of my coffee cup.

"Yes," he would say. "Yes, I can see in your cup that you are thinking of a young man. A fair-haired young man, but I can also see that there is a woman behind him. Yes, an older woman, maybe his mother, who wants him to stay at home and study." He would point his thin finger at some blob in my cup and his expressive face would take on a worried expression. "Aha, look there on the other side—there is a tall man behind you. It could be your father, who is not very pleased with you." Shaking his head in warning, he would say, "*Y bint Factoria*, I advise you not to think about that young man, not now. Wait a few more years and I will tell your fortune again, and then maybe I will see a wedding."

Thus my friend Mohamed Ali would coax me in his own way to stop dreaming about the sixteen-year-old neighbor who went to St. Andrew's School.

In my teen years, I am sorry to say, I took Mohamed Ali for granted. He was always there, visiting us wherever we lived. Once a month, he would show up, settle comfortably on the kitchen floor and have long talks with Mother. It was not until later, when, from the tomboy I had been, I became a young lady of seventeen, that my own friendship with Mohamed Ali began in earnest, and I shared my little sorrows and successes with him.

During the war years, Mohamed Ali was there as usual, commenting on the losses and gains of the Allies. He had aged somewhat and probably did not eat too well, but he never complained, and he joked about the severe rationing of cooking oil, potatoes and wheat. We knew that many stray bombs destroyed the humble hovels of the poor native quarters of Hadra, where he lived, but these casualties never made the daily papers.

Throughout the good times and the difficult last days of our life in Egypt, he was always there for us. We never knew how old he was, but at the end, he looked quite frail, although he still carried himself with his usual dignity. My remembrance of our life in Egypt would not be complete without honoring this special friend in the pages of my memoir.

Five

From the day the White Russians moved from the refugee camps into rented homes, they immediately formed numerous clubs and associations, such as the Patriotic Club, Former Officers Fraternity, and the Monarchist Association, whose members were mainly former officers like my father. Russian social clubs and dining rooms became popular centers where everybody came to discuss their lives, politics, and their attempts to find jobs.

We all lived along the narrow suburban area of Alexandria, conveniently serviced by the excellent public transportation of the Belgian Tram Company. In those days, when automobiles were still a great luxury, members of our community traveled by trams along the relatively short distances between stations. This mode of transportation facilitated frequent visits between families sharing common interests. This was very important in those times when not everyone had radios and telephones (costly commodities enjoyed only by wealthier households) and they relied for news on daily papers that reported local and European political events.

Our community adhered to all religious observances of the Russian Orthodox faith at our small apartment chapel. Every service ended by the priest intoning, "And now let us pray for our suffering Mother Russia and the suffering Russian people living there." A solemn moment followed, with a few furtive tears shed by a group of people who had lost their country.

In addition to Saturday evening and Sunday services, important church events such as Easter, Christmas and Lent were opportunities to enjoy special traditional dishes and desserts served on these occasions. Thus, just before Lent, each housewife served "blinis" at the Mardi Gras. These plump yeast pancakes, doused with melted butter, were eaten with pickled herring, caviar and smoked fish served with dollops of sour cream. Cold vodka would be served with these dishes. Vodka was not sold in Egypt and families had to make their own brew. In my early teens, since I hated the taste of alcohol, I was elected to prepare vodka in our small bathroom sink. It was not difficult. Mother bought pure alcohol at the pharmacy, where it was sold freely, and I had to mix it with the same amount of water and filter it at least three times. As a finishing touch, the vodka was flavored with grated lemon or orange peel. Although our Russian guests greatly appreciated my masterpiece, my father never drank any kind of spirits. On these occasions, Mother would sometimes have a shot of vodka, but neither Jenny nor I developed a liking for our national drink.

At Easter, every family went to midnight Mass. This was an all-important celebration in our community. It was followed by a late supper upon returning home from church. Most adult churchgoers had been fasting during Lent, especially the last week before Easter, and were therefore looking forward ravenously to the traditional dishes prepared for that night. After Mass, we would return home holding, according to ageless tradition, our lit candles protected by paper shields, and it was important not to let the candle go out. I can still remember the care with which I sheltered my light to get it safely home, where it would be placed in front of the holy icons.

Once at home, Mother would bring out various delicacies to the table. It would have been already set for the holiday feast. Dish after dish of sliced cold veal and pork, cabbage and salmon pies; bowls of Russian salad, looking like a colored mosaic of tiny pieces of beets, carrots, green peas and potatoes tempted the eye; and, of course, traditional colored eggs side by side with narrow dishes of pickled fish, cucumbers in brine, and fish in aspic.

But the centerpiece was, of course, the rich sweet *kulichi*, baked tall in large coffee cans. These were glazed and decorated with silver and gold candies. The crowning glory was the *paskha*. *Paskha* means Easter in Russian, and is a traditional elaborate pyramid-shaped confection, similar to cheesecake, with candied fruit and slivers of almonds. In the Egypt of my childhood, it was difficult to find anything resembling farmer's cheese that was the primary ingredient in the *paskha*, and Russian housewives were forever trying to find a milkman who could obtain some fresh cheese for that yearly treat.

Of course, in my early childhood, the festivities were very modest, but no matter how small, the holiday table was the best that our family could afford.

Although I grew up in Egypt, for all intents and purposes, it was as if my parents never left Russia. The members of the Russian community who settled in Alexandria organized themselves into a closely-knit colony, which gathered around the Russian Orthodox Church. As White Russians we were represented by our own Consul General, Alexander Petrov, who was empowered to issue identity documents and register marriages, births and deaths. However, when traveling, we carried special *"Laissez Passer"* (Allow to Pass) issued by the Egyptian government. This served as a passport for non-Egyptian citizens.

My sister and I attended a bilingual English and French school, but at home, we only spoke Russian. In addition, we were tutored at a Russian Sunday school run by our priest and several teachers.

We spoke colloquial Arabic in native shops and with servants. Colloquial Arabic differs considerably from literary, and, to my regret today, I never learned to read and write in that language, because in my time, it was taught only in native schools.

To supplement our education, Father made it a point to teach us geography and history. After dinner, he played games with us, questioning us as to who was the reigning monarch of such-and-such a country or who the president was of a given republic.

Jenny and I competed avidly with each other, making sure of our answers by looking up correct information in the fat *Larousse Encyclopedia*.

The geography lessons consisted of us naming countries of a given continent, and much emphasis was put on Europe. Both North and South American countries were difficult for us, as well as the countries of the East, because at that time, little was written about them in the local newspapers, and to us, they seemed like places on a different planet, while Australia and New Zealand were a real challenge.

We were also taught who the Allies were during World War I, then called the "Great War." Also, we had to know who the enemies of the Allies were, like Germany, Italy, Austria and Turkey. We learned the hated names of all the top Bolsheviks, and above all, to disapprove of Communism. Father left the rest of our education to schools, which unfortunately, at that time, had weak programs in science and mathematics.

My teachers in primary school paid more attention to calligraphy and sewing than to my arithmetic skills. After a particularly bad report card, Mother hired a math tutor for me, much to my disgust, and I spent one miserable summer catching up. Unfortunately, my calligraphy never reached the desired perfection and I still cannot decipher my own shopping list. But it was Father's love of history and politics that fostered in me a taste for political arguments and debates, and a definite distrust of Soviet Russia and Communists.

My high school years were as unremarkable as those that preceded them, with the difference being that I gradually settled down to the unavoidable fact that I was never going to be a boy with the privileges and perks granted to the "better half" of our human race.

I refused to be part of a clique led by forceful bullies, and remained convinced that I, indeed, was different. I resisted all attempts to enroll me in the sheep mentality of our class. I graduated in the tumultuous year when World War II began. I never made any real friends in school and surprised my teachers with my graduation essay on "Are We Our Brothers' Keepers?" in which I went to great lengths discussing the British attitude toward Egyptians. My other skills were fair-to-middling, and in the summer of 1939, I graduated with nothing to show for the ten years I spent at Scottish School for Girls but a leather-bound volume of John Galsworthy plays.

When I was sixteen, my best friend and companion was Mike Tsoukaris. He was only a year older than I, but even at that early age, he showed much promise as a pototenial businessman.

He came from a very modest Greek family and his father was always out of work, but Mike, quite early in life, decided that his own life was going to be different. A natural storyteller, he was also absolutely charming, in addition to being an incorrigible liar. An example of his early achievement was his hilarious association with an English lady, wife of a wealthy businessman. Mrs. Cornish wanted to help the bright twelve-year-old boy get a good education and offered to pay for his education at the select Victoria College. However, there was a string attached. As a condition, she asked Mike to become a Baptist, if he wanted to, of course.

Mike did not think twice. He said there was nothing that he wanted more than to become a Baptist and was speedily converted to "the right faith." From then on, he never missed accompanying the good lady to the Baptist church, learning to sing all the hymns by heart. This, of course, did not stop him from attending the Greek Orthodox Church with his mother for late services, especially since he was the lead tenor in the St. Nicholas Greek Church choir.

He graduated with honors from Victoria College, acquired a British accent, and made lifelong friends with a number of princes in his class from Saudi Arabia.

But to me, Mike was my only brother and a loyal friend. He chaperoned me to our teenage parties, where he was always the life of the party. He was also my encyclopedia on all secret subjects never mentioned by Mother, and any information about sex I gleaned was from the creative liar, who probably had great fun telling me outrageous stories.

But we bonded for life as brother and sister. During the war, Mike fought in the Greek Army. On his rare furloughs, he would appear with gifts from the British NAAFI (Food Supply Division of the British Army), such as a ham or boxes of chocolates, and would smile mysteriously when asked how he obtained those goodies.

After the war, Mike left for Australia, but we never lost touch, and visited occasionally in ur later years.

Six

Looking back upon my life, I find an intricate pattern of influences, which shaped me over the years. I owe my choice for independent thinking to my dear mother, who, in spite of her own conservative upbringing, fostered in me a free spirit and guided me gently to think for myself. As for Father, he believed that his two daughters should follow his own beliefs in all areas, and my sister, Jenny, had no trouble adjusting to his expectations. Unlike me, she never questioned the suitability of applying his ideas to her own life.

As I was growing up, I sensed progressively that, although my parents agreed on most important points, there was a vast difference between them. Whereas Father was completely immersed in politics and his writings, Mother was an intellectual whose interests ran the gamut from literature and philosophy to fine arts and mysticism. She was quick to explore new ideas and her gift to me was her constant sharing of her multiple interests. I listened without tiring about her early years in Vladivostok, Siberia, when, at the age of nine, she accompanied her father on horseback on long journeys, and how, later on, she overcame her mother's resistance to enroll in St. Petersburg Medical School.

When I was ten, all the dramatic events of my mother's life seemed to have happened eons of years ago, although, in fact, her participation in World War I and the White Army had been no more than a dozen years earlier.

Father also shared with us his memories of Russia, but in his busy schedule, he never had much time to spend with us, and only much later, after he left us forever in 1961, did I learn about his fascinating life. Mother was not able to survive without the man she loved and joined him three months later. They were both in their mid-sixties.

My relationship with sister, Jenny, was, at the best of times, more like a short truce than a friendship, and only in our mature years were we able to establish a closeness which was lacking when we were young.

At the age of twelve, I was pleasantly surprised and excited to receive an unexpected invitation to go to Cairo. The circumstances that led to my invitation were amusing, more to an outside observer than to the people involved in that tragic comedy.

As Disneyland is to American kids, so Cairo was to those living in Alexandria. It was only three hours from Alexandria by train. The Pyramids, the Nile, the Egyptian Museum, the Cairo Citadel, and the famous Khan Khalil markets were the magic spots that simply had to be visited, and I, of course, had never been anywhere, outside my native Alexandria.

I was invited to stay with the Babanins, a Russian family from Cairo, with two daughters, Marousia and Lydia. These two girls were, at that time, our frequent houseguests because Mother was very kind and welcomed the two sisters after hearing their sad story.

Apparently, Lydia, seventeen years of age, had a real problem. Besides being very plain, she had an oversized nose. To her, it was a big sorrow, particularly because her sister, Marousia, was extremely pretty. She was in her early twenties and endowed with big brown eyes and a cute upturned nose.

Their loving parents could not bear to see poor Lydia become more and more depressed and they decided to send her to Alexandria to see Dr. Nicholas Solovtsoff, a famous Russian plastic surgeon, who, reportedly, performed successful "nose jobs." As far as Mother knew, the good doctor was an eye, nose and throat specialist, and she was surprised to hear that he had suddenly become a plastic surgeon. But since the two girls turned up on our doorstep only *after* the operation, there was nothing that Mother could do, except pray for a miracle. Dr. Solovtsoff assured the girls that the operation was a success and even gave Lydia a discount by virtue of her being Russian.

The operation panned out to be one of those unfortunate mishaps. When reshaping the offending protuberance into a smaller version, the doctor somehow cut off too much of the cartilage and replaced it with an artificial joint of waxy paraffin. He gave strict instructions to keep the nose out of the sun, and to return in a week. Delighted with the promise of a shapely nose, Lydia celebrated by going to the beach. As instructed, she sat in the shade, out of the sun. However, shade or not, the artificial joint started to melt in the hot Alexandria afternoon and when, a week later, the doctor removed the bandages, he gave an amazed whistle. The artificial bridge had melted down and only a small crooked trumpet reminded him that once a nose had been there.

Undaunted by his failure, the inventive doctor tried to correct the mishap but in spite of several attempts, the result was an ugly potato-like hump, with a decidedly purple hue. He said brightly that the color would improve with time, bade them good-bye, and advised Lydia to return home.

There was no question of a lawsuit, for the family had no money, and they wanted to believe the doctor.

Devastated, the two girls had to return to Cairo. This coincided with my summer vacation and the two sisters asked my parents to allow me to go back with them for three weeks. They were hoping that my presence would somehow soften the parents' ire. They still hoped that Lydia would look better one day. Unfortunately, this was not to be, but on a lighter note, we learned several years later that Lydia had married an English corporal during World War II, and went to live in England. Whether her nose was reborn remained a mystery.

I was very excited and begged my parents to let me go, and after some arguments between Father and Mother, they finally relented on the condition that I would write them every week.

The Babanins lived in Choubrah, a suburb of Cairo. This was my first experience with a real apartment building. The Babanins lived in an apartment on the ground floor of a large three-story building that occupied a whole block, separated by wide circular iron staircases. Hanging from them were endless rows of laundry stretched from every window, ballooning gaily in the breeze like multicolored poppies.

During the day, the staircases were buzzing at all times with voices of housewives calling to each other and to the ambulant merchants below, in Italian, Greek and Arabic. Ringing voices of children laughing and playing created a symphony of sounds. Occasionally, snatches of a song reached me as I stood in the Babanins' kitchen, bemused by this overwhelming kaleidoscope of life. This was so different from my life in Alexandria, and I felt I was entering a new world, exciting and free. I drank it all in, hoarding all the impressions to share with my family upon my return.

Although I loved going to parks, I hated going to the zoo. When, at the age of six, I was first taken to the Alexandria Zoological Garden "Nouzha," I was given a bag of peanuts and invited to throw them to the monkeys, who picked them up with lightning speed and lost interest in me when my bag was empty. They were scuttling around in a large cage or sitting in groups on palm tree trunks. I thought they were cute, but soon wanted to go home, so Mother took me to see the bears.

These were enormous shaggy creatures sitting listlessly in cages too small for them. Mother said, "Look, Vicka, these are Siberian bears. When I was a little girl growing up in Vladivostok, these bears lived in our dense forests." I looked at them and something tore at my young heart. There was such sadness and misery in the eyes of those big, unkempt animals that I started crying.

"Why are they in prison, Mama?" I asked. "Are they bad animals?"

Mother tried to calm me down. "No, sweetheart," she said. "They are not bad, but if they are not kept in cages, they will run away."

This made me cry all the more and I was begging Mother to ask the keepers to let them go free again to roam in their green forests. This incident left a deep mark on me and even in later years, when I visited modern zoos, my heart remembered the pity and outrage I felt at seeing wild beasts deprived of their freedom.

But now that I was in my teens, I had learned not to be rude when the Babanins offered an outing to the Cairo Zoo, and I accepted the invitation with appropriate grace. I decided that once there, I would find a way of avoiding the idiots who gaped at lords of the animal kingdom, baiting them with sticks and laughing at their reaction.

When we arrived at the zoo, under the pretext of finding the bathrooms, I detached myself from my friends and sought refuge on a bench near the picnic grounds. I watched idly as a family of four arrived, laden with a picnic basket and lawn chairs. Two boys about my age threw themselves on the green lawn, obviously enjoying the cool feel of damp grass. The two women, heavily overweight, chatted amiably while unloading the picnic basket. One of the boys cried, "Mama, did you pack our ball?"

"Of course I did," said the mother, and threw the ball, which fell short, near my feet. I jumped up and, seizing the ball, feigned to throw it to the boys, a teasing maneuver I borrowed from watching neighboring boys at play. The two boys laughed good-naturedly, and when I finally handed them the ball, they asked, "Would you like to play?" I readily agreed and the three of us started a lively game.

When the women sang out, *"Bambini, a mangiare"* (Children, let's eat), the two boys dropped the ball and rushed to the spot where a checkered red-and-white tablecloth was spread under the trees. I hung back, minding my manners, suddenly shy, not wanting to intrude on the family meal. I finally remembered that I was supposed to be back with the Babanins. I waved good-bye and turned to go, but one of the oversized ladies got up with unsuspected agility and put her plump arms around me.

"Where are you going, little girl?" she asked. "This is lunch time and you are invited to share our picnic. Aren't you hungry? We have enough food for a crowd. Even Ernesto and Mimi won't be able to eat it all." She nudged me to a spot near her. "Sit down near me. There."

I was too surprised to protest when she spoke again.

"First of all, let's observe the etiquette. What is your name, child? Vicka? What a pretty name. Now I am Louise Stefanos, and this lady here is my sister in-law, Nara." She pointed to the two boys, who were already nibbling on something.

"This curly rascal is my eldest son, Ernesto." Ernesto raised his hand in acknowledgement, while chewing on a piece of chicken. She then pointed to the second boy, who rose and clicked his heels. "And this gallant young gentleman is Dimitri, my youngest. We call him Mimi. Now that we know each other formally, let's eat."

She handed a plate to the other woman. "Nara, fill this child's plate, and give her a large piece of that delicious cake you baked this morning."

The unexpected warm welcome of my new friends made me forget completely that I was expected somewhere else, and I joined my pleasant companions in devouring everything that was piled on my plate.

While we ate, Madame Louise asked me about my family and told me about herself. The boys chimed in, and I learned that they both were students at St. Joseph's Academy, and that though Mimi was a good student, Ernesto hated schoolwork and would probably not make the passing grade in the fall. Madame Louise gave her firstborn a loving look. "Ernesto, what am I going to do with you?" she said. "You really have to try harder at school. One day, you will grow up and what will you do then?"

"Mama, Mama," cried Ernesto, jumping up and embracing his mother. "I won't have to work, for you will always have enough money for us all." He addressed me. "Do you know that mother is one of the best dress designers in Cairo? Have you ever heard about the establishment of 'Madame Louise'?"

I mutely shook my head, amazed at the way he spoke to his mother.

"Well," insisted Ernesto, "she is even the favorite dressmaker of the queen. You don't believe me? Ask Aunt Nara. Ask her. She'll tell you!"

Aunt Nara only shook her head in disapproval, and Mimi nudged his brother. "She lets you get away with anything,: he said.

So it went, the animated ribbing and laughter between mother and son, which became so very familiar to me in the long years of my friendship with this unconventional family.

Before I left to join the worried Babanins, who by then were looking for me, I learned that indeed Madame Louise was a well-known designer, and the family lived in the center of Cairo in an old apartment house, dating back to the Khedives—the Ottoman rulers of Egypt before the reign of King Fuad. The boys told me that Aunt Nara had been married to Uncle George, Louise's brother, who had long ago chosen greener pastures, leaving Nara as a permanent fixture with his sister. This arrangement was perfect, for Louise was working long hours at her business, and Nara took care of the household and the boys.

There was never any mention of the boys' father and I thought it was better not to ask. Before we said good-bye, we exchanged addresses, and thus began our lifelong bond.

This was the time of my life when I discovered that I could make friends outside my family circle. It was an exhilarating experience to be just *me*, treated as a person, not just my parents' daughter, but also someone different whom I did not quite recognize, myself. When Madame Louise and her family came into my life, I found I could speak freely about myself, and not just answering questions, such as "How old are you?" or "Do you like going to school? that were usually asked me by my parents' friends.

I hoarded jealously my chance encounter with new friends, and did not speak of them to the Babanins, but waited until I got home to tell Mother about them.

As always, Mother understood me when I told her about that new feeling of freedom I experienced. She embraced me and said, "Yes, you are maturing and starting to think. You are noticing how other families behave, and learning to value kindness and candor. I am sure that one day, I will also meet Madame Louise, and will have the opportunity to thank her for her kindness towards you."

A few months later, Mother did meet Madame Louise, when the whole family came to spend Christmas holidays in Alexandria. Mother had that rare quality of being able to strike the right note when meeting strangers, and when the two did meet, there was no doubt in my mind that they liked each other. Mother admired Madame Louise for her courage in overcoming the odds of bringing up two boys alone, and praised her business acumen in building up a thriving haute couture business. At that time of my life, she did not allow me to spend my vacations so far away from home, but she trusted Madame Louise and let me visit her from time to time.

To Madame Louise, I always remained her little girl. When in 1958 we left Egypt forever, I spent a few days with her, thinking sadly that I would never see her again. She passed away in Athens in 1961, having lost her battle against diabetes.

From our first encounter at the zoo, her two sons, Ernesto and Mimi, adopted me as their baby sister, and with the passing of years, a strong bond of tolerance and understanding was forged. Their two lives followed different and unconventional paths, but, learning not to judge, I became the trusted recipient of secrets they dared not share with their mother. I spoke French with Mimi, Ernesto and their mother. In Egypt, everybody spoke French when communicating with other Europeans; the exception were the British, who only sometimes spoke French.

Mimi, kind, sensitive and loyal, was a loving soul. One day, he revealed to me that he was homosexual. These were times when this was only spoken about in whispers, especially in Egypt, and Mimi suffered constantly, trying vainly to hide his life from his family.

Madame Louise never let on what she knew about Mimi and hid her unhappiness under a mask of serenity and loving composure. To me, it was sad that she went to her grave without being able to understand her unhappy son.

Mimi was always looking for a perfect partner, but never seemed to find one. He was constantly disappointed in love, and would suffer through throes of jealous despair. This state of mind alternated with periods of euphoria that would last, alas, only until the next betrayal.

As for Ernesto, he never changed. After his lusterless graduation, he left for Europe. There, he quickly gravitated towards a group of international happy-go-lucky adventurers who were always available to escort wealthy aging beauties to gaming casinos.

Although I never condoned his way of life, Ernesto found in me a sister he never had. In spite of his cockiness, he frequently had the need to talk about fears and doubts, which plagued him from time to time. On his return to Egypt, several times a year, he invariably came to see me, unloading the varied baggage of his unruly life.

On rare occasions, when I thought I had to speak up and berate his untidy way of living, he would just embrace me and say, "Don't scold me, little sister. Life is meant to be enjoyed. I am young now and I want to live it up. When I will be old, I will settle down. I promise."

It was useless to moralize to Ernesto, and I just hoped that one day, he would grow up. Unfortunately, he never did, but one day, something happened to him that changed him overnight. Ernesto fell in love, head-over-heels for the first time in his carefree life.

Her name was Lucrece, Lu for short, and she was from Switzerland. She was of medium height with ash-blond hair and incredibly beautiful gray eyes, shaded by dark eyelashes. She looked delicate and fragile, but underneath, she was all steel. After a month of passionate love, Lu told him she was going back to Geneva, but Ernesto was not going to let her go. He asked her to marry him and promised he would do anything for her.

So Lu sat him down and told him in a blunt Swiss manner that she would love to marry him, provided he abandon completely his gigolo friends, and start earning enough money to give her the comforts of life she was accustomed to. She also stipulated that unless he complied right then, she would be out of his life, pronto. To his own surprise, Ernesto promised at once and they were promptly married.

When the newlyweds arrived in Cairo, we were already in the process of liquidating our life in Egypt, and I was going through the most difficult period of my life. To my regret, I was able to spend only a short time with Ernesto and Lu, and before leaving, I asked Ernesto what I could give him as a wedding present. I said I wanted to give him something really meaningful, and to my surprise, he said at once that, indeed, there was something that he wanted.

He said, "Do you remember when you showed me the ancient leather-bound volume from your father's library, with colored plates of the coats of arms of the Russian nobility?"

"Yes, of course," I said. "What of it?"

"Well," said Ernesto, "you did say that some of those coats of arms belonged to families now extinct, as there were no more descendents."

"Yes," I said, still not understanding.

"Could you let me have a colored reproduction of one of those crests?" he asked. "I want it for a joke. Of course, if this is too much to ask," he pouted, "then forget it."

"Oh, Ernesto," I said. "This is not difficult, and I will do it for you with pleasure. Let me get the book and you can pick the one you like, provided it's an extinct family."

I got the book and we went through it, and soon Ernesto chose a colorful plate of a family whose last descendant perished in the war with Napoleon. He left happy as a lark.

I contacted a friend of ours, a talented graphic artist, and after ten days, Ernesto got his wedding present. It was a magnificent color reproduction on parchment paper, and I mailed it to Ernesto with my best wishes.

* * *

Ernesto never changed. He and Lucrece seemed to lead a charmed fantastic life. They established themselves in the south of France, and although Ernesto never worked, they never seemed to run out of money. They occasionally stoped in California on their way to some famous vacation resorts and visited me.

One day, dying with curiosity, I asked Ernesto, "Tell me, you rascal, what do you do for a living?"

He laughed, happy that I asked.

"I am an in-vest-or, little sister," he drawled. "Business is good and I recently gave Lu a new yellow car. A Rolls. You should see her drive it along the Corniche in Nice."

Still incredulous, I pressed on, "And what kind of investments, Ernesto?"

"Well, I invest in various commodities, you know—diamonds and things, a little of this, a little of that... We travel a lot and I have, how you say, good connections with useful people like that ugly Greek shipping guy, what's his name, Lucrece?"

"If you mean Aristide," said Lu, "he is not ugly. He is too rich to be ugly."

I could hardly believe my ears, wanting to believe it was a joke. "Go away, Ernesto. You must be joking. I don't believe you."

"I don't know, Vicka, you still think that I am that little nobody you knew in Egypt. Well, that was long ago, and I want to show you something. Hey, Lu, let me have my pocket book," said Ernesto. "Thank you, love."

He pulled a card from the wallet and handed it to me. "This is my business card. You can keep it."

I looked at Lu, who was smiling as if relishing the moment. "Read it," she said. "Please read it."

I read aloud:

> *Count Ernesto de Stefanos*
> *Investments.*
> *Paris – London – Hong Kong*

Seeing that I was speechless, Lucrece laughed and said, "As you can see, Vicka, Ernesto kept his word when he promised to be a good provider."

Although that was the last time I laid eyes on the "Count and Countess de Stefanos," I received several phone calls from the Count himself, who always assured me that he was doing well. "No," he would insist. "No, I have never been arrested. You don't have to worry, little sister, because I am an honest investor, and a very respectable member of the high society."

I understand that at present, Count Ernesto and Countess de Stefanos are still living in Nice, and are still respected members of the "high society."

Seven

Early in 1940, many German male citizens either fled to their fatherland or were interned in concentration camps near Ismailiah, north of Cairo. My parents became very concerned about my plans to attend the Egyptology Institute in Cairo, since most of the faculty members were German. Their fears were well founded, and we soon learned that the Institute had closed its doors.

I was devastated by the finality of that blow, as my application to the Institute had already been approved prior to the beginning of the hostilities.

Until then, I was cocooned in our friendly international community and felt safe from menacing events in Europe. I thought, naively enough, that Egypt could not be involved in a mere border incident between Germany and Poland. In my ignorance, I reasoned that since our German friends were all nice, decent people, as were the Italians, it would have been ridiculous to think of them as enemies. *It is not our war*, I thought. *We are too far removed from any military action, and probably Germany is bluffing in a strategic show of force, over some territorial dispute.*

I secretly criticized my parents for being too concerned with events happening somewhere in Danzig, and convinced myself that soon everything would be resolved satisfactorily.

But my youthful optimism was shaken to the core when many of my Italian friends, wearing brown shirts and waving the Italian flag, left on the last boat headed for Italy. Their young voices singing *"Giovenezia, giovenezia, primavera di Venezia,"* Mussolini's national anthem, made me cry as the sound lingered in the wake of the boat leaving Alexandria, never to return. But that was just the beginning. All the Italian men who did not leave were soon interned, and at last, the realization that Egypt, too, was at war dawned on me.

Soon, downtown Alexandria become a tower of Babel. Army, Air Force and Navy uniforms filled the wide Boulevard Zaghloul, representing British, Australian, New Zealand, French, Greek and

South African Allies. Shortly after, the Polish Army of General Anders arrived in Alexandria, and everybody became familiar with the sight of their officers' caps, square in shape, called *confideratkas*, worn at a rakish angle.

I started working as a volunteer at the Sidi Gaber railway station, handing out mugs of tea with milk to hundreds of soldiers arriving from Cairo, where there was, at that time, the only airport. Streams of soldiers erupted from the cars, to be loaded on military trucks—lorries, as they were called—and I became expert at handing out tin mugs of hot tea to eager hands of smiling young men.

* * *

We did not know then that this influx of military men was a prelude to the fierce battles of the Western Front under the command of General Montgomery. These battles of Tobruk, Benghazi and El Alamein marked some of the saddest pages in the history of World War II, which left behind heartbreaking fields of white crosses in Tobruk. When I visited Tobruk some years after the war, I was struck by the irony of those yesterday's enemies, sleeping together side by side, linked forever by the final dates of their young lives.

* * *

Huge camps were hurriedly erected on the outskirts of Alexandria, to accommodate and supply the human sacrifice in the name of freedom. On the main arteries, convoys stretched for miles, and often, military police directed the traffic downtown.

Restaurants and nightclubs prospered, filled to capacity with soldiers on leave or awaiting postings. My circle of friends diminished even more when my buddy Mike joined the Greek Army, and was immediately sent to some unknown destination. I started taking lessons in typing and shorthand, as there was an urgent demand for civilian personnel in military camps. I was eager to help, and although I was already twenty, my parents, very protective of me, still considered me a child. When we went out with friends to many of Alexandria's nightclubs, I gazed with envy at the dancing couples, and when occasionally invited to dance by young men in uniform, I was inevitably warned by Father, in no uncertain terms, not to date any military man unless I was chaperoned.

In spite of my age, I was, no doubt, very naïve. French and English novels fed my romantic imagination. When reading John Galsworthy, I imagined falling in love with a member of the British Parliament, who would carry me off to a big country house in England, and Colette's novels thrust me into the world of sophistication and nostalgic drama. I fancied myself a woman of the world, blasé and aloof. To that end, I borrowed a silver cigarette holder from my mother and practiced smoking in front of a mirror. I imitated a French singer I admired by throwing my head back, with eyes half closed, sending streams of smoke in the air. Fortunately for me, cigarettes made me cough, and I never became a smoker, while sister Jenny, wanting to imitate Mother, became an incurable addict.

I wanted to appear sophisticated, but my problem was that I still looked sixteen. I imagined I knew all about sex, gleaning all I could from my world-wise girlfriends, while Mike pretended to teach me and made fun of me, shocking me with stories, real or imaginary, about his erotic adventures. Some of my knowledge came from a tattered magazine with "dirty" pictures that we passed under our desks in class. My dear mother was useless in that respect. She could never speak to me about sex, and knowing that, I never brought up the subject.

My experiences with boys my age were limited to furtive kisses outside our front door and dancing at our teenage parties, allowing sweaty cheek-to-cheek contact to the scratchy sound of the phonograph. Secretly, I was always dreaming of meeting a tall and, most importantly, a blond hero, with whom I would have a romantic involvement, and who would carry me off to live happily ever after. The blond part was, of course, due to the fact that most of the boys I knew were from the Mediterranean basin, dark-eyed and dark-haired. Although some boys in our Russian community were blond, I turned my nose up at them; knowing them all my life failed the requirements of "romantic" or "mysterious."

* * *

We learned that now we were on "military alert," which required all windows to be shrouded in dark fabric, but we still were surprised when the bombing started. We knew that reconnaissance planes flew over Alexandria, for then the sirens would sound long wailing alarms to announce the beginning of a raid, when we were supposed to go down to shelters, and short ones when the raid was over. However, everybody went up on the flat roofs to enjoy the sight of searchlights in the sky, illuminating tiny planes to the sound of anti-aircraft guns. We all laughed and said that these were the Italian bombers, harmless since they did not drop any bombs. Although our villa had no bomb shelter, there was one nearby, but nobody ever went there. That is, until the Luftwaffe planes started bombing.

That night, sirens did not warn us. We just heard the heavy drone of planes, followed by distant thumps from the direction of the Alexandria port. Only then the sirens went off, while the sound of explosions became louder. Up on the roof, we watched, horror-stricken, as the searchlights illuminated parachutes with bombs attached, slowly descending over the harbor and the environments. The western sky was alive with long fingers of light, trapping dozens of fighter planes like fireflies caught in crosshairs. The next day, the radio reported serious damage to native houses near the port, but, of course, no mention was ever made of any military targets.

After that, we were bombed at frequent intervals and the nearby air-raid shelter became a social center. Father and sister Jenny went willingly when the alarms went off. Father would meet his friend Ivan Psiachis to talk about the war, while Jenny flirted with our next-door neighbor. As for Mother and me, we could not stand the suffocating atmosphere of the shelter and we would sneak up on the roof to watch the action. My mother was fearless, and she and I shared the thrill of danger, arms entwined around each other. It was one of our many wonderful quality times together, when I found the closeness and understanding that bound her to me. We were more friends than mother and daughter and I would confide all my dreams and little secrets to her, with the exception of some incidents later, which would have hurt her, had I dared tell her. But more about that later.

Eight

One night Father insisted we follow him to the shelter. The bombing of the civilian neighborhoods was now increasing, and two blocks away from our house, a three-story apartment building was leveled to the ground by a torpedo attached to a parachute.

At the shelter, we met our Yugoslav friend Orsolina, whose husband was a prisoner of war. Orsolina was not alone. Two young officers in blue Air Force uniforms accompanied her. The markings on their shoulders were unfamiliar to me, and when she introduced us, I learned that they were Yugoslav war pilots recently arrived.

"Meet Vuko Shiakovich and Toma Zhivanovich," said Orsolina. "Vuko is from Sarajevo and Toma is from Belgrade." I was about to say something in French, but Orsolina laughed and said, "You can speak Russian to both boys, Vicka, for they speak Serbian, and this is so much like Russian."

Both officers were very good-looking. Tall and fair, they were decidedly unlike any of the young men I knew. Vuko's bright-blue eyes and ready smile set my heart racing. Toma zeroed in on Jenny, and soon they were deep in conversation while Vuko and I went through the initial stages of two young people who had just met. I was not quite twenty years old, and Vuko was twenty-three. I was probably the first civilian girl Vuko met after his arrival. Encouraged by my sympathetic reaction to his plight, he poured out his tragic story. Apparently, his parents had perished in an air raid while he was enlisting in Belgrade. I could see tears in his eyes when he spoke about his loss. He said that a few weeks later, his squadron was obliged to flee the Germans, who had by then occupied Belgrade. They landed in a sheltered bay near Abuquir, the historical town made famous during the Napoleonic wars.

As I listened to Vuko's unhappy tale, my heart went out to him. My romantic juices started flowing and my imagination supplied the rest. I wanted to be in love and I desperately needed a Prince Charming. Looking back, I now realize that this was the moment when I first started endowing unsuspected suitors with qualities that were most important to me. It was an unconscious process and one that caused me, later on, a lot of unhappiness and pain.

So, I created Vuko in the most desirable and romantic version. In my mind, he fulfilled the necessary attributes, the first one being coming from a country where I would not be stateless. Since he was unquestionably good-looking and unhappy, I supplied the rest of the requirements: an intellectual capacity to converse with a fine sense of humor, knowledge of politics, music, art and literature. Falling in love with him was then a cinch and during the following days, I listened with a thrill to his declarations of love in Serbian, which was the only language he knew, having spent all his life on his father's farm near Sarajevo.

Vuko fell in love with me, while I thought that at last, I had met my hero. At first, I was flattered to have someone tell me how wonderful I was, and he was indeed very eloquent, and had such blue eyes. But as days went by and the newness paled, I had to admit to myself that he bored me.

I was brought up to explore as many interests as I could handle. I was an avid reader and loved opera, never missing the winter season when the Milan Opera came to the Alhambra Theater. I often attended the symphony series by famous orchestras visiting Alexandria, and at home, politics were the frequent subject at our dinner table, so I expected Vuko to share my interests. When I asked him what books he had read, he enthusiastically admitted that his favorite book was *The Three Musketeers*, in Serbian translation, that he had read several times. As to music, his only interest was the Bosnian folk songs, which he sang with much gusto, in the appropriate manner: closing his eyes and propping his head with his palm, while wailing Turkish inherited melodies—the joy of every true Bosniak.

I became disappointed and impatient with him. Was I snobbish? I probably was, but there was one other factor. He was extremely jealous and subjected me to long scenes of interrogation about anyone who cast appreciative eyes upon me, intentionally or not. I was accustomed to being on friendly terms with many boys, and when I introduced Vuko to my friends, he began to suspect that I was flirting with them. This, of course, stemmed from the fact that Vuko could speak only Serbian, and the friendly banter in English and French drove him up the wall, since he could not understand a word of what was said. As a result, I started avoiding my friends so as not to provoke a predictable fit of jealousy.

When Vuko proposed to me, I said I would think about it. After four months of puppy love, we were quarreling constantly, and I felt increasingly disappointed and frustrated with our relationship. The magic of having someone love me had gradually faded away, and I felt I was not ready to tie my life to anyone, in general, and Vuko, in particular. I thought I wanted to study, to travel, but the truth was that I was definitely no longer in love with him. Vuko's idea of a fun date was to accompany me downtown to Yougoslavenski Dom (Yugoslav club), where I watched the dancing couples while Vuko fraternized noisily with his compatriots, downing liters of Slivovitz. Sometimes, they would all launch spontaneously into some interminable ballad, featuring Vuko as soloist with a dissonant background chorus. No one ever asked me to dance, as Vuko would, from time to time, put his proprietary arm around my shoulders, making it clear to anyone who wanted to know that I was spoken for. When, in despair, I asked Mother for advice, she suggested I tell him I was not ready to commit myself until the end of the war. I decided that on Vuko's next visit, I would tell him exactly that. Both my parents were delighted with my change of heart, although Mother had a soft spot for him.

I had prepared what I thought was a clever little speech about the wisdom of waiting until the war would be over and things would be normal again before committing ourselves. My little plan did not work out as well as I had hoped. Vuko had his own little surprise for me. On his next visit, he arrived with a solemn look on his handsome face, and announced to Mother and me that he had something important to tell us. He produced a small red box and asked me to open it. Surprised and intrigued, I opened it and my heart fell as I gazed upon an engagement ring. Vuko tenderly slipped the engagement ring on my third left-hand finger.

I was about to protest, but Vuko silenced me with a tender look. He said, "I know that maybe this is too early to speak of a long commitment, but today is my good-bye visit. Our squadron is leaving tomorrow at dawn. I don't know where we are going and I don't know if I will ever come back. But if I do, I want you to know that at the end of the war,

I will come for you, and while I am away, I will know that there is someone who will be waiting for me."

He turned to Mother. "Dear Mamochka," he said, "you have been my second mother and I will never forget your kindness towards me. Please keep Vicka safe for me, and remind her while I am away, that I love her and count on her to be my wife one day."

Mother was crying as he embraced her and I sat unable to remember my prepared speech. Vuko did not wait for me to say anything, for he was crying, also. He embraced me, whispered, "Good-bye" and rushed out.

* * *

In the months that followed Vuko's departure for unknown destinations, I received only two postcards from him, with no address, just a brief message of affection. When, a year later, Vuko's memory was reduced to a few snapshots, Mother received an ominous buff envelope from the military authorities informing her, as the next of kin, that Lieutenant Vuko Shiakovich was reported lost in action.

I stared at the telegram, my mind refusing to accept the reality behind the brief message, while Mother just closed her eyes and was lost in her own grief. I could not imagine that Vuko was probably killed months before and I knew nothing about it. I remembered his buoyant vitality, his hopes for a future after the war, and the cruel memory of my indifference toward him and his dreams. I felt guilty and needed someone who would listen to me and absolve me from the feeling of culpability that troubled me so much.

Mother took my hand and said quietly, "My little girl, don't go blaming yourself for what happened to Vuko. I think I know what thoughts are tormenting you. In my own life, I, too, had suffered a great loss, and because of that, I chose a wrong turn, which nearly destroyed me."

"Each person has their own destiny, and our feelings of love or indifference cannot change that reality. I want you to mourn Vuko, and this will take some time. I, myself, will never forget him. He had lost his mother and I was happy to show him my love and affection while he was still with us."

But Vuko's loss left a deep scar on my young life. I blamed myself for not being more tolerant and loving towards him, and although I knew that this pain was irrational, I still grieved for many years. This was the end of my childish innocence and the devastating awareness of my own mortality.

* * *

As the war progressed, with every empty space at the family tables, we now knew that nothing would ever be the same again. There was no longer danger of an immediate attack, but the rest of the world was still involved in a war that seemed endless.

American Army uniforms started appearing on the streets of Alexandria, and were easily recognized by their darker green khaki color and better cut than their British counterparts. In 1942, we learned from radio and newspapers that the United States and Japan were at war, but Egypt did not declare war on Japan.

The attack on Pearl Harbor was, of course, reported, but with the bloody battles in Italy and later in Russia, this was just another war incident, which resulted in the United States joining the Allies against the Axis forces. So far and remote as it seemed to most of us, it wasn't until 1958, when I moved to the United States, that I learned of the horrors of the war in the Pacific.

But, of course, the end of the war for us was when the Russian forces finally entered Berlin, and Germany capitulated on May 7, 1945.

The Europeans in Egypt actively followed the developments on the front, and the White Russian community vainly hoped that something might change in Russia. The Yalta conference, which betrayed the hopes of many East European countries, was a cruel blow, especially to White Russians as they saw the Soviet Union appropriating the lion's share of the spoils of war, in which Czechoslovakia, Rumania, Hungary, Poland, Bulgaria, Yugoslavia, Finland, Estonia and Lithuania lost their freedom. My parents were devastated, especially Father, whose brother Evgeni, an active anti-Communist living in Yugoslavia, was sent to a prison camp in Siberia for twenty-five years, according to the terms of the Yalta conference.

Nine

As soon as I thought I was proficient enough, I applied for a secretarial position and was immediately hired by a British shipping company, which was in the initial stages of the Lease Lend project between the United States and England. The office was housed in a large storage building attached to Gate Six of the Alexandria harbor, and I had to catch a rickety bus to get to work.

I was interviewed by a pleasant-looking civilian, Mr. Boardman, who, after ascertaining that I was not German or Italian, hired me on the spot and rushed away on some urgent business. Returning home, I was floating on air with happiness. I was now part of the war effort, and very pleased that I was not tested on my less-than-perfect shorthand and typing skills.

When I reported for work the next day, I found out that apart from myself, there was only one other employee. An elderly Greek accountant, Mr. Grammatikidis, who at once took me under his wing. He assumed a fatherly attitude towards me and after half an hour, he knew everything about me, but never said anything about himself.

Gram, as he was nicknamed, was busy all the time, while I had nothing to do, because Mr. Boardman was always away somewhere. He would appear sporadically, look through the mail, make long-distance calls and rush away. When I asked him what my duties were, he said, "Oh, you will have plenty to do once we start working in earnest, and for the moment, familiarize yourself with the office, and help Gram." On rare occasions, he would dictate a few letters, which I had to retype many times, because I could not decipher my own shorthand, and often had to resort to longhand. Mr. Boardman would shake his head and promised that soon we should have a long talk.

I was not anxious to have that talk, for I felt only too well that the long talk would also be our last one.

Jenny, my older sister, preferred not to work. She stayed at home and was good company for Mother. Her decision was embraced by Father, who believed that his daughters did not have to work and frowned on my insistence on seeking employment.

My sister and I were separated by only three years, but at that time of our lives, this was an enormous difference, and we each had our own circle of friends. Jenny readily espoused Father's idea of what a proper young lady should be, while I, even as a child, resisted all attempts to influence my choice of friends. Thus, much to Father's consternation, I chose my friends myself—not always wisely, it is true, but at least they were all interesting individuals and that was very important to me. I was also stubbornly resistant to any attempts to lure me into Jenny's group of "proper" friends.

It was customary that in the evenings, friends dropped in and stayed for the inevitable high tea. I usually managed to escape to my room after a few minutes of diplomatic pleasantries. Mother and Jenny entertained them, and Father would sometimes appear later. He kept late office hours, or was busy at his typewriter, writing articles for the numerous Russian newspapers abroad or the local French press.

At that time, I was attending evening art sessions at the Atelier des Artistes, where they had live models. I started drawing in my early teens and took every opportunity to draw from nature, so when the Atelier advertised classes, I enrolled at once. The Atelier was located in the center of the city and my parents were reluctant to allow me to be out after dark. We had strictly enforced blackouts, and it meant that I had to walk in complete darkness, about five city blocks from the Ramleh tram station to the Atelier. Father decided to drive me there, and then pick me up after the sessions at eight o'clock.

I was the youngest member of the group. Everyone seemed to be an established artist, who greeted each other by first names, and whose stained and battered easels were proof of their status as ""artists." I felt out of place in that rarefied atmosphere, until I learned that several of our members were attempting to draw from live models for the first time.

The president of the Atelier, Joseph Sebasti, also worked at his easel, but during the break, walked around looking at some of the lucky artists' work, praising or correcting sketches. He stopped briefly at my masterpiece, on which I made a mess of the model's generous hip.

"*Tres bien, tres bien, Mademoiselle*," he said. "Try not to put in any details at first. Just deal with general lines. Like so." He rubbed out some lines and with the tip of the charcoal, created a couple of curves, which suddenly became alive.

I mumbled my thanks, feeling my cheeks go red-hot, because I noticed an amused smile on the face of the young man next to me. He was smoking a pipe and looked sophisticated and aloof. I hated him on the spot, until I heard him say something to Sebasti. Being born in Egypt, I spoke French since childhood, but as everyone knows, no degree of perfection could ever equal the accent and intonation of a Paris-born speaker.

And this pipe-smoking idiot spoke such beautiful French through the pipe clenched in his teeth that it took my breath away. Of course, all my friends were fluent in French, but we all spoke with the sing-song Mediterranean inflection, and only in French films did we hear this pure French accent, which was to me the epitome of culture and sophistication.

That evening, I learned that this young man's name was Pierrot Catzeflis and that he was a student at the Sorbonne University. While visiting his parents in Egypt, he was stuck in Alexandria due to the German occupation of Paris.

What a wonderful opportunity to have a real French friend who would tell me all about life in France, I thought. But how could I get to know him, since he didn't even realize that I was standing next to him? Except, of course, when he saw that I was a beginner in the art class. That amused curl of his lips when Sebasti made that loud remark made me feel inadequate. *But,* I thought to myself, *he doesn't know that I can be very eloquent on many subjects, and that although I am not very pretty, I can be funny. He will also learn that I am not just anybody. I come from a very good Russian family, although now we are not very wealthy or very well known.*

But in spite of my reasoning, when Wednesday evening came, I just stood before my easel, not able to overcome my shyness to get myself noticed by the pipe-smoking arrogant guy, who was completely engrossed in his work and did not pay any attention to me. His work was not very good, but that did not diminish my interest in him.

Back at work the next day, I wracked my brain for an opening gambit that would make him notice me. I was unable to come up with any face-saving approaches, and out of sheer boredom, was going through the telephone directory, idly looking for familiar names, when I spotted the name Emil Catzeflis.

At lunchtime, when Gram went off to the nearest coffee shop, I decided to dial the number that I just found. I really had no plan in mind as I dialed the six-digit number. I held my breath when I realized that someone answered at once. *"Allo,"* said a lazy voice with that unmistakable accent. *"Allo, allo. Qui parle?"* (Hello, who is speaking?)

I said, *"Allo,"* and then quickly hung up. *What am I doing?* I thought, my face afire and my heart beating wildly. *What can I say? That I am looking for a friend, or maybe he will think that I am one of those girls looking for an adventure? What if he recognized my voice? Nah, how could he? He hasn't even heard me speak. He probably thinks that it's a wrong number.*

Ten

The next time at the art class, the model failed to appear and Sebasti had an inspiration. He asked the Arab youth who had been painting the cabinets in Sebasti's workshop to pose as a live model. The man agreed and was placed on a bench, nude, with his shirt modestly draping his intimate parts.

The model was ugly, skinny and altogether uninspiring. Pierrot was sketching diligently, completely unaware of me, when the tall figure of my father appeared in the doorway. Father gazed speechlessly at the nude guy and then walked across the floor to me.

"Get your things together," he said. "Now!"

His face was stern. "Had I known," he said, "that you would be sketching naked men, I would never have permitted you to come to this class."

He grabbed me by the arm and led me out. I could hardly contain my tears at this humiliation, especially because I heard some tittering, which ensued in the quiet. I feared I had lost forever the opportunity of becoming friends with Pierrot.

In the car going home, Father went on and on about my becoming more and more like some of my girlfriends, whose parents were too liberal. I knew that once he was in that foul mood, it was useless to argue with him. I was hoping that once we got home I could rely on Mother to iron things out, and let me continue my art classes at the Atelier.

The next day, as soon as Gram went out for his Turkish coffee, I decided that I would take fate in my own hands.

When I dialed the number, Pierrot answered at once. *"Allo, j'écoute."* (Hello, I'm listening.)

"Bonjour," I said, "it's me, Solveig." (Why did I use the name Solveig? At the start, I just wanted to hear his voice, without him ever finding out. Solveig, to me, sounded romantic, as the love of Peer Gynt in Grieg's opera, and it was natural to me to think that he would know who Solveig was.)

"Solveig?" Pierrot said "Like in *Peer Gynt*? C'est marrant!" (That's neat! in French slang).

"Well," I said, "at least you seem to know a little about music, so maybe you are hopefully not completely dull."

A peal of laughter dissipated all my preconceived ideas that Pierrot was aloof and stuck-up.

"Dull?" he managed to gasp. "Do you know what dull is? I'll tell you. Dull is the description of the silly Alexandria youths who probably surround you. The ones whose opinions are drawn from the Sunday edition of your hopeless daily newspaper. That's what's dull. I have been here for five months already and I am bored, bored, bored. Isn't there anyone who thinks, who has an opinion of what is happening in the world outside their own small interests?"

I was stunned, and delighted. Here was someone who was echoing my own thoughts and in an instant I decided that I really wanted to know him better, even if it meant exposing myself to his ironic scrutiny.

"Well, I said, "you are right, if you are thinking about that crowd at the Sporting Club, who have no more brains in their heads than the horses they watch at the Sunday races. However, I can assure you that I don't belong to that idle group. As a matter of fact, I am working for an important shipping company."

"I am very impressed," said Pierrot. "As for me, I am a student of literature at the Sorbonne University, and I study painting whenever I can. I love music and I love pretty girls."

That last remark felt like a cold shower as I took stock of my insignificant physiognomy with Kalmuk high cheekbones and small brown eyes.

"Well," I said, "I like tall blond guys, but they are not always interesting or smart, so maybe the physical attributes should take second place to wit, charm and intelligence." I bit my tongue as I thought of Pierrot's small stature, although he did have interesting eyes, a woman's eyes, dark-blue with long lashes. At that time of my life, my hero had to be tall to comply with my preset romantic notions and alas, Pierrot did not qualify, for he was shorter than I.

"Now that we have determined that I am not stupid, but not very tall, and you are intelligent, but maybe not a beauty, let's meet somewhere and have some ice cream," said Pierrot.

"*Ça va*" (Okay), I said. "I'll meet you tomorrow at six o'clock at the Ramleh station."

I quickly hung up. My mind was in a turmoil. *What have I done?* I thought. What would he think of me? This definitely was not done. I was a young lady, and as such, was not supposed to initiate any social contacts. My sister would never do a thing like that. It was the men who were supposed to propose a meeting. But a stubborn little voice inside me wanted to assert her right to choose beyond the social rules, and to hell with proprieties!

Eleven

I boarded the city tram at exactly five-thirty, and tried to compose myself. My mind was whirling. I kept touching my hair because that morning, I got caught in a rain shower when I ran out for a bite to eat at the small falafel stand near our office. Since Gram was still out on his lunch break, I had quickly fixed a hair roller on my fringe, in hopes of improving my looks. That morning, I chose to wear my best outfit, a mustard-colored tailored suit, sewed by Toula, our dressmaker, who had assured me that it was "pure Chanel."

Of course, I did not say at home that I was meeting a young man. To ease my guilty conscience, I told Mother that I might be somewhat late as I was going for some ice cream with friends after work. I conveniently reasoned that I would tell her all about my little escapade—later on.

It was raining when I arrived in front of the Ramleh station. The yellow square building was the favorite rendezvous for meeting friends to catch a movie or go out on the town. That evening, it was packed with people standing shoulder-to-shoulder, seeking shelter from the rain. "*Pardon, pardon,*" I muttered, as I courageously squeezed myself into the damp warm crowd. My heart beating fast, I scanned the chattering faces around me. I thought desperately that Pierrot did not even know what I looked like and it was up to me to find him. I steeled myself, anticipating a look of disappointed surprise on his face. Then I saw him. He was standing with his back to me, wearing a gray sweater, holding his eyeglasses in his hand as he peered nearsightedly around him.

Here goes, I said to myself, and with a confidence I did not feel, tapped him on the shoulder and said brightly, "Bonsoir!" He turned around quickly and burst out laughing.

"But it's that little girl from the Atelier," he said. "*C'est charmant. Bonsoir,* Solveig!" (Charming! Good evening, Solveig!)

He shook my hand. "I am delighted that you turned out to be that cute little girl, who was so genuinely trying to sketch that ugly naked guy. Let's walk out of this crowd. My Theresine is waiting and is probably soaking wet."

Before I could ask who Theresine was, Pierrot rushed me out of the crowd. Outside, we ran hand-in-hand to the nearby corner, where a very wet old Renault was parked, its convertible top missing.

"This is Theresine," he said with pride. "She is still working very well, although the doors are permanently welded, so I hope you don't mind if we hop in from the top." We scrambled into the old soggy wreck and, sure enough, it fired on the first attempt, and off we shot onto the wide Boulevard de la Corniche.

Darkness had already fallen and a brilliant necklace of lights formed a half-circle on the beautiful Bay of Alexandria.

"So, Solveig, is this your real name?" asked Pierrot, while he noisily changed the speed on the car.

"No, I wish," I said. "I assumed that you were familiar with Grieg. My name is Victoria, but everyone calls me Vicka."

"*Ça va*," he said. "I will call you Vikette." He laughed. "And what else are you not, Vikette?"

"Well," I said, "to start with, I am not Scandinavian, but Russian. White Russian."

"Oh, probably a countess or a princess. That tall father of yours looked imposing enough to be either, when he glared at everyone around the room when he came to get you."

"No," I laughed. "We are not titled, although most of the men in my father's family served in the Duma, the Russian Tsarist parliament. You probably know about the Russian Revolution."

"Yes, what a tragedy it all happened," he said. "In France we have many White Russians, especially in Paris, and it is common to see former officers of famous regiments work as taxi drivers."

"What about your family, Pierrot? Do they live here or in France?"

"Well, my father owned a publishing house in Alexandria, but both he and Mother traveled often to France. I was born in Alexandria, but was studying at the Sorbonne. By a curious coincidence, when I came home for vacation, my parents got stuck in Paris. It was occupied by the Germans, so here I am, alone and abandoned, and glad to have found a friend, even if she is pseudo Scandinavian."

"That makes two of us, Pierrot. I think you, too, are a liar. To me, you don't look at all abandoned."

"Well, maybe I exaggerated a little. But seriously, I am bored with the Alexandria girls, parading on Sundays at the fashionable teashops and morning concerts where they listen with delight to Von Suppe! Do you ever attend those events yourself?"

"God forbid!" I said. "But my sister, Jenny, goes every time with her crowd of friends. I hate that kind of circus music."

So we chatted away while I got wetter and wetter, wondering when we were going to stop at a pastry shop. By that time, my hair was hanging in wet snakes and the charm of my new adventure was dampening rapidly.

Pierrot must have read my mind. "Vikette," he said, "what do you think if we have something to eat instead of the ice cream. We are both drenched and since we are not far from where I live, our housekeeper, Hussein, will prepare for us something tasty."

Seeing the look of panic on my face, he went on, "In case you don't trust me, he will be there to watch over you to guarantee your safety from my possible ardors."

The disarming simplicity of my new friend made me trust him. I agreed, quaking inwardly, surprised by my own temerity.

The Catzeflis house was not far from downtown, on a shady street. Typical of our suburban houses, it was surrounded by stone walls topped with broken glass shards to discourage intruders.

Pierrot honked his horn, and after a short while, the tall iron gates opened wide and we drove into a graceful arcade, which led to the house. An elderly Sudanese man, in a white robe with a red belt, stood aside to welcome us.

"*Itfadl, Boutros bey*" (Welcome, Mr. Peter), he said. "*Ahlem u wasahlem ya Mazmazelle*" (a polite salutation). He helped me out of Theresine and handed us dry towels as he listened to Pierrot with a smile on his ancient face.

"This is Hussein," said Pierrot. "He has been with our family since he was a young boy, and now he is an important part of our household. He is a widower and takes care of our family."

He proceeded to give Hussein instructions for preparing some hot food, while I looked with curiosity around the large drawing room. All chairs and couches were covered with dustsheets and it was obvious that the room had not been used for quite a while. In my heart, I was still apprehensive that I had been invited into a den of seduction, but I was somewhat reassured by the dreary atmosphere of the room, until Pierrot's next remark awakened my worst fears.

"Let's go to my room," he said. "I want to show you my collection of classical records, and it will be certainly warmer there. Hussein, please bring the food to my room. We will eat there."

Here it comes, I thought. *The first stage of seduction.* He had gotten me into his house and I would have to use my brains to get out of this predicament. *He will probably offer me something alcoholic to drink.*

Pierrot, completely unaware of my inner fears, led me without much ado to a well-lit room.

"This is where I sleep, work, and listen to my records," he said.

I gazed with surprise and astonishment at what I had thought to be the scene of my unspeakable doom. A large table stood in the center of the room on which piles of books were stacked among sheets of drawing paper, with sketches and half-finished paintings vying for space with tubes of oil paints and brushes. A tall chest of drawers stood near a large record player. A narrow bed was wedged between the window and a couple of straight-backed chairs. This was certainly not the typical set-up, staged for a predatory attack on a potential victim, and I finally relaxed. Pierrot opened the tall cabinet and showed me an impressive collection of records, carefully labeled and organized in alphabetical order of composers.

"I want you to listen to my favorite concerto," he said, tenderly wiping the record and setting it carefully on the turntable. "This is the *Sonata in A Major* by Cesar Frank, for violin and piano, played by Cortot and Thibaud. As you listen to it, you will understand why its beauty influenced Marcel Proust to include it in his first book, *A la Recherche du Temps Perdu, Remembrance of Things Past.*"

Of course, I had heard of Marcel Proust as a writer, but had never attempted to read any of his works. At my high school, our French literature studies were mostly devoted to classics like Victor Hugo, Balzac, and Georges Sand. I suspected later that our teacher, the elderly Mademoiselle Gizelle, did not see fit to teach us the liberal trends of more modern literature. That did not stop me later from reading avidly all that was available from the large lending library run by two Armenian sisters. I thought that here was an opportunity to read this controversial writer, and perhaps my new friend could help me understand Proust's philosophy.

Seeing my uncertain smile, Pierrot must have guessed that I did not read Proust, and as I listened, enthralled, to the dramatic opening of the dialogue between the violin and piano, Pierrot fetched a volume from a shelf and without a word, put it next to me. Thus we sat listening to music, forgetting the bowls of soup, which Hussein quietly set before us.

As I listened, I felt a surge of wonder wash over me. I sensed that there was a possibility that I had found a friend such as I always yearned for, from whom I would learn to appreciate so much of what was important to me. That feeling made me realize I was changing from an immature girl to an adult with different values from my teen years. This time, contrary to my previous behavior and dreams, there was no search for romance, but a definite wish for something real and serious, which was lacking in my life.

The rest of that evening followed the same friendly pattern that had begun. Pierrot, who was five years older than I, adopted a protective brotherly attitude towards me, which never wavered over the long years of our friendship. He was always eager to share with me all the things that he cherished, such as literature, art and music. He loved poetry and often read to me from Baudelaire, Verlaine and Rimbaud, while I listened to his voice full of emotion reciting the immortal lines that I can still remember now.

We always found time to pore over art books, as I learned to love the Impressionists and understand modern art, and we visited ancient and modern museums together in Alexandria and Cairo.

As a painter, Pierrot was not very talented, but he worked with an enthusiasm and persistence which, alas, never paid off. As I write, I often look at the painting he had made for me of the Alexandria skyline, seen from the Boulevard de la Corniche. It was painted on a rainy day, and the subdued colors of the Mediterranean seem to melt into the fog surrounding the Fort Kaid Bey, which was built on the foundations of the famous Alexandria lighthouse, one of the seven wonders of the world. But as I fondly look at it again, I am reminded of our first drive on the rainy evening of long ago.

After our first rendezvous, we started to meet weekly. When later I told my mother all about Pierrot, she scolded me, and insisted that he come to our house to meet her. When he came, he charmed her with his good manners and respectful, friendly attitude, and both she and Father liked him very much.

On weekends, we went for long walks along the Corniche, and attended concerts, but that winter, we generally stayed at Pierrot's house, where I now felt completely at home, always welcomed by Hussein, who developed a soft spot for me.

Twelve

Pierrot's personal life was quite tumultuous. He usually fell in love with the wrong girl, but shrugged off his unhappiness, saying that it didn't matter. But the time caught up with him when it did matter, because his latest girlfriend, from a wealthy family from Cairo, told him one day that she was pregnant. Surprised, but being the ethical man he was, he married her. But judging from his infrequent letters, the marriage was not a happy one.

* * *

While Pierrot was trying to be a husband and father, the Americans had entered Paris and travel to France was resumed.

The war was ending. I was uncertain as to which direction my life would take, since all the military offices were liquidating their personnel.

My employment with Mr. Boardman did not last long. He fired me when he discovered that my secretarial skills were below acceptable standards and advised me, in a fatherly manner, to return to my typing and shorthand studies. Mortified and humbled, I followed his advice, and as a result I was hired as Secretary to management of Ottoman Bank.

The excitement generated during the first years of the war gradually subsided, to be replaced with a general feeling of sadness and mourning as many of our close friends from the Polish Army were killed in the battles on the Western desert. Many Greek families were in mourning for their sons, and for more than a year, we heard nothing from my dear Greek childhood friend, Mike.

Now, evening gatherings at our house were subdued and quiet, often just listening to radio reports from Europe.

* * *

Pierrot returned to Alexandria from Cairo with his new family. Now, there was no question of resuming our usual friendly talks and outings. I visited him to meet Albertine, his new wife, and was met by an unhappy young woman with tear-stained eyes, a stone-faced Pierrot, and the house littered with baby bottles and opened packages of diapers. This was the wrong time for a visit, and I retreated after a stay of five minutes, hoping that it was only a passing phase in a young marriage.

Alas, it was not. A hasty departure for Paris was in the works and, this time, there was no chance of even passing a couple of hours with my dear friend.

He wrote from Paris three months later, telling of his painful separation from his wife and of the bitterness between them. He was now living alone in Paris, and had gone back to school. His parents returned to Alexandria, and I only saw Pierrot again two years later, although we corresponded regularly.

* * *

Years later, when my husband and I were living in the United States, already happily married, we finally planned a long vacation in Europe. I was excited and happy to meet Pierrot after so many years.

Unfortunately, it was not to be. Upon our arrival in Paris, we found out from the concierge of his apartment building that Pierrot and his daughter were killed in a car accident a week before our arrival. I tried, in vain, calling some of his relatives, but could not find anybody who knew of the circumstances of how this tragedy happened.

I visited the shady cemetery where a simple engraved stone read *Pierre Catzeflis 1916-1975.*

I never found out the details of what happened to my dear friend.

Thirteen

When the war ended, the world heaved a sigh of relief, and there was great joy in most countries. When survivors and prisoners of war from both sides began their trek home, some of them found that the nightmare of Communist rule over their country had just begun. This was the price of peace decided at the Yalta conference of 1945.

Egypt was the provisional haven of numerous international military personnel, as well as of many now homeless European kings. The crowned rulers were willingly accepted by France and the United States. The mere mortals refused to go back to their countries, and arrangements had to be made with Allied countries to accept them. The Free Polish Army, under General Anders, was nearly all absorbed by Great Britain, where the former soldiers found work mostly in the mining industry.

To us, the civilian population of Alexandria, this was a time of joy mixed with sadness. As our young friends came back from war, we were grateful to have them back, but the war had left its bitter imprint on their former carefree lives. I realized also that those who had stayed at home, including myself, were also changed forever. Many of our Italian and Greek friends who returned had trouble finding work, and some of them discovered that their wives and girlfriends had not waited for them. But after several months, all wounds started to heal and life became normal again.

My workday started at a quarter to eight when I left my house on rue Heliopolis and walked the short distance to the tram station. Apart from fortunate individuals who enjoyed the luxury of a family car, everyone who worked in downtown Alexandria traveled in those wide Belgian tram cars. They serviced the long strip of suburbia from downtown Ramleh to the terminal of Victoria station to the west. Victoria was also the site of the exclusive Victoria College for Young Men, attended by wealthy Alexandrites and more than a smattering of Arab princes from the Arab emirates.

When I left for work a little earlier, I would stop at the small Greek *loukoumades* shop, where crowds of customers waited in line for airy deep-fried balls of dough, redolent of cinnamon and dripping with honey.

Waiting at the station was fun, since it was the same familiar crowd. I would invariably meet someone with whom to indulge in friendly banter. By the time the tram arrived at our Ibrahimieh station, all the seats were already taken and I had to squeeze in between warm bodies standing on platforms at both ends of cars. Since there were no straps to hold on to, one would be thrown from side-to-side as the tram gathered speed, so I usually tried to find a place where I could lean against a partition, instead of having some sex pervert take advantage of the crowd by pressing too close to me. In those cases, a time-tested maneuver always worked. Bending my elbow, I would give a sharp blow backwards, taking the wind out of the jerk's sails. It was very effective, especially when I accompanied the punishment with a brilliant smile, and "Oh pardon, Monsieur, did I hurt you?"

At the Ottoman Bank, we had midmorning breaks for fifteen minutes, and we usually sent the numerous uniformed *suffraghis* (attendants) to buy us something to eat, like a falafel or a *foul* (lima bean) wrap. These were warm pita rounds, filled with wonderful falafel patties. The *foul* wraps were also very tasty, with steamed beans slathered in *tahini* (spiced sesame paste). Although this sounds like we ate a lot of food, most of us were slender, probably due to year-round swimming and outdoor sports, which we all enjoyed. Between the hours of 12:00 and 3:00 p.m., Alexandria enjoyed lunch and siesta time. After that, the same crowd of office workers trekked back to work, in a steady stream along the main street, Boulevard Zaghloul.

However, after work at five o'clock, it was a different matter. This was the time for social gatherings of friends. Our numerous pastry shops overflowed with happy crowds consuming gargantuan quantities of fine pastries and ice cream before going on to movies. We had excellent movie theaters, and in summer some of them converted to open-air seating.

Supper was after nine o'clock, when Alexandria society liked to dress up and celebrate life late, past midnight. Usually, parties ended up in one of the many cabarets, where there were attractions of beautiful girls from all over Europe. A dance band would play in the intervals and it was time for cheek-to-cheek tangos, with dimmed orange lights. I enjoyed dancing, but avoided cheek-to-cheek, finding it too familiar.

Jenny had been taking nursing lessons at the local Red Cross, and sometimes took part-time jobs at the Jewish Hospital near our house. As we grew older, we learned to settle our differences without undue hostilities. We each had our own circle of friends and often attended the same "potluck" parties held in private homes.

* * *

Recovering after the deprivations of war, the pleasure-starved society of Alexandria took every opportunity to make up for lost time. Every excuse was good for organizing charity events such as balls, bazaars, amateur plays and picnics. Each European colony attempted to outdo one another in originality and no expense was spared. It was an honor to serve on the committees, organizing festivities. The balls were very popular and the patrons gave lavishly to the charity organizations.

My sister, Jenny, and I were often invited to participate, as we belonged to various groups of these charitable institutions. The charity events were usually held in one of the casinos or even sometimes in one of the larger establishments like the Mohamed Ali Theater.

Although that meant spending part of the evening at different money-making games, or serving at champagne bars, located in four corners of the ballroom, we still managed to dance later on and have a wonderful time. This way, we had our fill of dancing to live orchestras and were, at the close of the events, chaperoned safely home by friendly matrons.

I will always remember one particular evening. I was watching the dance floor while I worked behind the champagne bar. A large orchestra was playing a Strauss waltz as colorfully-dressed couples whirled around like flowers bending in the wind. This was the year when the evening dresses were particularly beautiful, with tiny waists, bare shoulders and crinoline skirts. It felt to me like a nostalgic glimpse back to the last century.

My sister and I enjoyed dancing at the balls. Before the winter season, every self-respecting young lady consulted the latest fashion magazines from France. In Alexandria, everybody had their own dressmakers. Whether these were famous fashion houses, such as "Madame Olga" or "Annette," or not so famous ones such as Rosa, Toula or Zeinab, who turned out unique creations for their clients. Our own dressmaker was Madame Salama, who had her small but busy shop on Attarine Street, a native neighborhood, but who was very talented and ambitious. She turned out beautiful ball gowns for both Jenny and me at very reasonable prices, because she never forgot that I recommended her to my manager at the bank.

This happened when I was assigned to find a dressmaker to sew uniforms for girls working at the bank. At that time, there were no women tellers and the feminine staff, mostly typists, worked out of sight in the cubicles and lofts. My boss, Mr. Kenny, the bank manager, thought that it did not look good for the bank to have the girls wear street clothes, and decided that they should all wear uniforms at work. As to the details of the uniforms, he said he relied on my good taste and judgment, and left me to figure out the pattern and the color of the uniforms.

That little problem was resolved by hiring Madame Salama to sew the uniforms. We decided on dark blue, and Mr. Kenny was pleased with the results. Unfortunately, this earned me some enemies in the typing pool, since Mr. Kenny decided that I would not wear a uniform, because I had to be attractively dressed when I ushered important clients of the bank into his office.

I worked ten happy years at the bank. By my first year, I had already honed my shorthand and typing skills and had a very good relationship with my boss. All our managers were English, posted from London. I had a good salary which I could keep, since Father's position at the Governorate provided the family with an excellent income. Besides being secretary to the top manager, I was soon promoted to supervise the girls' typing pool.

Over the years, I became close to many of the girls. They were mostly from Greek and Lebanese families. The Greek girls were avid basketball players and we even had, at one time, a bank basketball team, playing against the Barclays Bank team. We won, owing to Maroula, our star center.

Although I was successful in my working life, my private life left much to be desired. At thirty, I still was not married. Several times, as with Vuko, I thought I was in love, but disillusion would follow, leaving me with a sense of relief. Deep inside, I cherished a dream of love, but it was too vague to verbalize and it certainly did not apply to anyone I had ever met.

* * *

In 1952, the political climate in Egypt was changing. Encouraged by their teachers in universities, young Egyptians began a courageous fight to redeem their country from King Farouk, who had inherited his father's throne at the age of sixteen, and was completely unprepared to govern. Spoiled and self-indulgent, he rapidly lost the support of his people, and his orgies and debauches made him a laughingstock of all Europe.

Events came to a head when, in the summer of that year, an obscure army officer, General Neguib, decided that Egypt did not have to put up with foreigners and a bad king. In a daring bloodless coup, he deposed the king, sending him packing to France on one of his luxurious yachts. Nobody was sorry for the playboy Farouk, whose appetite for women and food proved to be his undoing. Soon after, he died from overeating at a European spa.

General Neguib was in power for only a few years. His first action was to exile the wealthy Turkish princes, by appropriating their lands and bank accounts. He was succeeded by Colonel Nasser, who, during the Egyptian/Israeli War, expelled from Egypt British, French and Jewish people, and confiscated all their assets. In 1956, he also nationalized the Suez Canal Company, a multimillion-dollar European corporation, causing havoc among its shareholders.

But before that final debacle, several important events changed my life.

Fourteen

To me, friendship has been, and remains today, the most important facet of my life. In my adult life in Egypt, I was fortunate to meet many unusual people, with some of whom I have formed lifelong ties. At the top of the list is Father Josaphat. He was a Franciscan monk whose genuine friendship and subtle guidance gave a positive direction to the tumultuous years of my life after World War II.

In the spring of 1947, the war years were now a memory of kaleidoscopic events. The loss of many loved friends had changed me from an insouciant fun-loving girl to a rather skeptical individual. No longer did I enjoy the weekly parties—too many of our happy crowd were missing; some killed in action on the Western Front, some in Italy or Greece. What was left of General Anders' Polish Army had left for England. The military cemetery at Tobruk in the desert, west of Alexandria, was now home for many of our friends, where they slept companionably next to their German enemies killed in the same battle. Dear Vuko and all his comrades had perished in air battles over Monte Cassino, and Mike, my dear adopted brother, had left for Australia. To me, Alexandria now felt like an empty town. To make things worse, Pierrot had gone to France, and I felt isolated and despondent. Never having been particularly religious, I now had completely lost my faith in God, and stopped going to the Russian church, much to Mother's chagrin, but she was too wise to press me.

My hopes to continue my studies at a university were dashed since the German Archaeology Institute in Cairo never reopened, and my choice would have been to study in France or England, but I was now working at the Ottoman Bank in Alexandria, as staff secretary. I liked the people for whom I worked: British bankers and young trainees from England. These were carefree men, happy to escape the misery of post war reconstruction, and who found Egypt to be exotic and certainly warmer.

When home from work, I would withdraw to my room to read. Life resumed its routine. In the early evenings, family friends often dropped by, and usually Mother and sister Jenny enjoyed their company. As for me, I was expected to greet them, but then I would discreetly disappear under some polite pretext, rather than participate in the social chatter that bored me. Father sometimes came home late, as his versatile work at the Governorate was subject to erratic hours.

Even when at home, people often came to see him, asking for help in handling minor problems with the Egyptian authorities. Always willing to assist, he was well known for his generosity in volunteering to iron out the tricky formalities of permits and fines, so when I answered the doorbell one late afternoon, I was not surprised to see a stranger asking for him. A tall, portly Franciscan monk gazed at me with a friendly smile.

"I am Father Josaphat from St. Mary's Cathedral in Cairo," he said. "May I speak to Captain Markov? Is he home?"

He spoke in Serbian, which I understood well, as it was much akin to Russian.

"Please come in," I said. "My father will be home soon. May I offer you some refreshment? A cup of tea? A cold beer or some wine?"

He looked at me with twinkling brown eyes. "Of course," he said. "I would love to have something to sustain me in this heat. What is your name, young lady? How come you speak Serbian?"

"That is a long story," I said. "Why don't you go onto the balcony in the shade, and I will get some beer."

I returned with some refreshment and soon found myself telling Father Josaphat all about Vuko: how we met and fell in love and our stormy and unhappy engagement. I did not dwell long on Vuko's death, and really, there was not much to tell. How could I describe what I felt when I got the telegram from the war office?

After I ended my story, Father Josaphat was silent for a while. We watched the waters of the distant bay change from blue to gold in the setting sun. We sat drinking our beer, not feeling the need to fill the void with words, and I felt very comfortable to be with him. I was grateful to him for not preaching to me about the solace of faith.

Father Josaphat sat very quietly, lost in thought, as I looked at him from the corner of my eyes. A small grayish beard framed his round face, but his eyes were those of a young man. I thought I liked him, but my bitter mood engendered negative thoughts, dampening my first good impression. *What does he know?* I thought. *How can he possibly understand the feeling of pain, of anguish, of emptiness in my life?* How could he understand my guilt at being alive when Vuko, so happy and full of life, had suddenly been snuffed out, without even a grave to mark what was left of him? This monk was probably thinking of how to start a monologue to tell me I should not despair and not lose hope of happiness: that I was young and my whole life was before me. In my mind, I decided that if he would start talking about the merits of patience and hope for the future, I would clam up and not continue to make a fool of myself.

Then he said: "Victoria, I know that you are not expecting me to give you a prescription of how to pick up the threads of your life. Unfortunately, there are no words of hope or consolation. Every person is special and irreplaceable, and every loss marks us forever. It also teaches us to value more those who are still with us. Every friend is a gift and you can rest in the knowledge that this is the right time for you to be sad and mourn those who have disappeared from your life." He took a sip of his beer, and continued.

"When the war began, I was attached to our fighting forces, and even had to wear a uniform to be useful to the young soldiers going to war. My faith has been challenged all too often in the face of death and carnage of so many young men and women of my country. But in spite of that, I kept going, and one day, I understood that my function was to bring some small measure of comfort to soldiers going to their death. I could not change the world and I still don't know why some are spared and some are killed. But on the battlefield, I was the only familiar figure of peace to those young boys, and sometimes the last compassionate face they saw before they died.

"For some reason, God wanted me to be there and I accepted that. Today, the war is over, and my heart still mourns them, but life is continuing and so is my pledge to serve God and men." He sighed and covered my hand with his. "You fear the unknown," he said, "because you no longer see the familiar loving faces of your friends around you, but any day now, you'll discover those who will become your new friends, for you have much to give and also to receive. You haven't said so, but I feel that you do not believe much in God. The problem is that no words or speeches will give you that faith, for you don't trust anyone now. Not even yourself. That is why you're unhappy, cynical and disillusioned. Believe me, I was there and I know how you feel. I can only tell you that I understand. I promise that I will not talk to you again about it, but in my heart, I know that one day, you'll find out the answer to your life."

At that moment, Father arrived home and led Father Josaphat to his study, while I went back to my room, smiling inwardly. I felt lighter than I had for months, and thought I'd ask Father Josaphat for the address of St. Mary's Cathedral. I decided that on my next visit to Cairo, I would visit my new friend.

Two weeks later, I took the train to Cairo. I often visited Madame Louise and, as usual, I was made welcome by her and Tante Nara, who immediately fed me outrageous pastries, led me to their guest bedroom, and then left for their Atelier de Couture, leaving me to my own devices.

When I appeared with a bottle of wine in my hand at the side door of the Cathedral, a Franciscan monk opened the door. He was slight of build with snow-white hair and a little pointed white beard. He had incredibly bright blue eyes, which were now twinkling with merriment.

"Is this wine for me?" asked the monk. "If so, you are very welcome. I am Father Elziar. Are you here for the confession?"

I was confused and nearly lost my poise. "No, I am looking for Father Josaphat," I said. "Is he in?"

"Come in, come in," said Father Elziar. "I'll get him at once."

He scuttled away quickly and came back a minute later with Father Josaphat.

"What a pleasant surprise," said Father Josaphat. He bear-hugged me and sat me down in the small private lobby, while Father Elziar produced three tumblers and poured the wine.

"Elziar, my brother," said Father Josaphat, "this is Captain Markov's daughter. I told you about her. Let's drink to our new friendship." He turned to me. "I am so glad that you came to visit me, and now that you know the way, I hope that we will be often in touch."

This was the beginning of our lifelong friendship. Father Elziar was often part of our meetings. His wit and happy disposition made him always a charming companion, but it was Father Josaphat who had

136

become, over the years, my confidant and my friend. I shared all my problems with him, and I could rely on him at all times. Understanding and caring, he was always there for me, giving me sound advice when asked, steering me safely through infatuations and romances that proliferated my young life.

Father Josaphat's prediction about my faith was realized several years later, and I always suspected that he had somehow engineered the event, but whether that was his machination or not, I will always be grateful to him.

This is how it happened. In the spring of 1956, he arrived at our door, impatient to share his good news.

"Do you know that I've been given permission to take a small group on a pilgrimage to St. Catherine's Monastery in the Sinai Desert?" he said, barely able to contain his excitement. "I have come to invite you, and ask your parents for permission to let you go on a two-week trip with my little group. It will cost you five Egyptian pounds, and we will be leaving in a month's time."

He told me that Justian built St. Catherine's Monastery in the second century at the base of the *Gebel Moussa* (Mount of Moses) from where, according to the Bible, Moses received the Ten Commandments.

I found out that at the time there was no proper road leading to the Monastery through the Sinai Peninsula, and few people had visited it through the centuries. However, it received much exposure in the news at that time because of Cecil de Mille's *Valley of the Kings*, which was playing in all the theaters then.

I thought it was a neat idea since I was due for a short vacation at the bank, and my mother had no objection to my taking the trip in such "holy" company. However, Father worried about the political situation that was about to explode in a war between Egypt and Israel. But Father Josaphat found the necessary words to calm him down, and he relented, though not without misgivings.

Little did I know that this projected trip was to be a turning point in my life.

Fifteen

The church bell struck five o'clock when I arrived by taxi at St. Mary's Cathedral. The massive church was located on one of the quiet streets near Emad el Dine, its wrought-iron gates already unlocked for early services. Above the oval domes of the Citadel, Cairo's slender white minarets were turning pink with the rising sun. Then, from somewhere far away, a single pure voice rose clearly in the morning silence. *"Allaaah Akbaar"* (God is great). As if by magic, the air became instantly alive with answering calls from other minarets, inviting the faithful to prayer by sending their harmonious appeal to God. As if competing with each other, the voices soared higher and higher, a live symphony orchestrated by the distance between them.

Since childhood, these sounds remain etched in my mind. Even today, on hearing them, I am transported to the wonderful period of my life in Egypt. The kind hand of memory has erased the negative aspects of those years, keeping alive only the wonder and the beauty.

I made my way towards a small group gathered near the side entrance to the cathedral, where stood a battered taxi, its motor idling, all doors open. Father Josaphat and the driver, a middle-aged Greek with a bushy moustache, were tying boxes and suitcases to the roof of the car. Father Elziar beamed a blue-eyed welcome and introduced me to the two other members of our party: a middle-aged woman in a black dress and a youth of seventeen. The woman smiled and the boy mumbled a greeting. He glanced furtively at my shorts, and blushed.

The driver finished loading the boxes. Father Josaphat turned to me with outstretched arms. "Victoria," he cried, "we are about to embark on an unforgettable journey, you little unbeliever. We will be traveling in the footsteps of Moses and we will visit many holy places mentioned in the Old Testament. Here, give me your suitcase. We are all packed and ready." He turned to the driver, who was wiping the windshield.

"This is Elefteris Stavropulos," he said. "He will drive us to the monastery and then will come back for us after two weeks." Elefteris shook hands with me. He was sweating profusely and kept mopping his red face with a large handkerchief. *"Kalimera ginekamu"* (Good day, Miss), he said. "I will take you all safely across the holy desert, because I put balloon tires on my taxi." At that time, these so-called balloon tires were the most suitable ones for rough terrain.

Then Father Josaphat addressed the woman in black. "Albina," he said, "meet Vicka Markov. She is Russian, but she speaks Italian and understands your Slavic language, so you can communicate freely with her. Her parents, good friends of mine, have entrusted her to our care. Vicka is a special friend of mine and I know that you will like her." He turned to me. "Vicka, at the monastery, you will be sharing a room with Albina. She is, as you will discover, a very interesting person." Then he put his arm around the young man. "This is Giorgio, the youngest member of our party. He is to learn many useful things on this trip. His parents believe that he will benefit from this unique experience, which I am sure he will remember all his life." When Giorgio impatiently turned his head away, I surmised that the trip to Sinai had not been of his own choosing.

Elefteris carefully arranged the various protective saints hanging from his rearview mirror and crossed himself before we drove off. Father Josaphat murmured a short prayer and we started the first leg of our journey.

Father Josaphat sat in front with Father Elziar, whose sharp little white beard bobbed up and down as he laughed. Both monks were animated and happy to start on their long-awaited pilgrimage. They were wearing their usual Franciscan garb: heavy brown woolen robes, tied with a tasseled cord around the waist, a crucifix attached at one end. I wondered idly for a moment whether these robes were suitable for the hot Cairo climate. I decided that they were chosen more for their durability than for the personal comfort of the monks.

I examined the faces of my fellow travelers with curiosity. Albina, in her forties, her brown hair tied up in a neat knot, was not pretty, but when she smiled, kindness radiated from her plain face. Although Father Josaphat had spoken warmly about her, I was still apprehensive: a long drive through the desert was exhausting enough without the added boredom of a religious lady who, I assumed, would entertain me with suitably chosen passages from the Scriptures. So I thought when

I wedged myself between her and the silent Giorgio, who was sulking, his still plump baby-face set in an obstinate pout.

I sighed. It was just like Father Josaphat to involve me in a situation which he thought would transform me into a better Christian, and hopefully, for him, a Catholic. I glanced at him, promising myself to tell him later what I thought of his choice of companions. But for the moment, I armed myself with patience.

We drove along the south road leading to Suez, where we planned to take the ferry across the canal, at its most narrow point, to the Sinai Peninsula. It was a two-hour drive, mostly through desert on a one-lane road. All the windows were open to the warm, dry air. It brought with it an elusive draft of bitter fragrance from some distant prickly plants, hiding in the wavy mounds of golden sand. After a couple of hours, we saw an extraordinary sight. A freighter ship was sailing across the horizon and for a moment, I thought it was a mirage. When we approached closer, we could see that it was floating high on a narrow canal, which was practically invisible from a distance. This was the *Suez Canal.*

Before entering the small town of Suez, we were dazzled by the startling sight of flamboyant trees on both sides of the road, their crimson flowers carpeting the desert sand at their base. We encountered only a couple of cars, and the few houses on the outskirts of town were shuttered and visibly abandoned.

In Suez, we were struck by the absence of bustle, which was unusual in this important crossroad from the Mediterranean to the Red Sea and the Gulf of Aqaba. The year was 1956.

Although the Egyptian press was full of rumors about an impending war with Israel and its allies, this disturbing quiet brought home to us the fact that Egypt could very soon be at war.

However, Fathers Josaphat and Elziar were not going to change their minds about visiting the holy places. They calmly declared that God would be with us, and joined Elefteris at the ferry, negotiating for a cheap fare. After much haggling and big smiles, our taxi drove onto the incredibly small ferry, and at last, we landed in the Holy Land, driving off the ferry onto a narrow, potholed road, going east across the stony desert.

Before we drove off, Father Josaphat and Father Elziar got out of the taxi and deftly whisked off their robes, revealing colorful checkered shirts. They giggled, getting back into their seats, and we all joined in the laughter, gazing at the two bearded monks in their civilian outfits.

Looking back on our journey through the prism of years, I am astonished as to how we progressed in our rickety taxi through the desert. Elefteris drove like a cowboy through sparse, prickly bushes, occasional anemic trees and piles of rocks dotting the landscape. From time to time both Fathers stopped him and read from the Old Testament the part about Moses leading his people from the perils of Egypt.

In the early afternoon, we reached the shore of the Red Sea. This was the scheduled resthouse stop for pilgrims: a simple low structure of cement blocks provided for short stays. There was not a soul in sight, and the door to the building was unlocked. While Albina, with the two Fathers and Elefteris, collapsed onto benches in the shade, Giorgio and I ran barefoot towards the beach. The tide was out and the water very warm. We walked in as far as we dared, our feet treading on the soft, mossy bottom, while schools of tiny fish swarmed around, investigating our intrusion, nipping at our toes. Even after half a mile, the water remained at a low level, reaching only up to our calves. There was no question of any swimming in that soup, and we retreated to the beach, where Albina was already busy organizing our lunch. We were ravenous and welcomed the simple fare of Greek cheese, hard-boiled eggs, cucumbers and pita bread. Father Elziar produced a liter of red wine, which somehow managed to be cool, much to our delight. Soon Elefteris was pressing us to move on, as he expected to reach the monastery before sunset, and we all packed into the taxi, refreshed and rested.

Sixteen

We reached our destination well after eight of clock and St. Catherine's monastery was already shrouded in darkness. As we entered the deep valley between two giant mountains, twilight had already wrapped itself around the fortress walls while the granite mountain peaks were still bright against the deepening blue of the evening. We stopped to look up at the monastery nestling in the foothills of the holy mountain and we could still make out the outline of the dome and the minaret of the mosque. This mosque was built by the order of Prophet Mohamed to prevent anyone from harming the monastery and its inhabitants.

The two Fathers jumped out of the car and quickly donned their brown habits. As they fumbled with the heavy robes, I mischievously snapped their picture with my small camera, which earned me a disapproving look from Elefteris. Today, as I look at that snapshot, my heart overflows with tenderness remembering those two unique friends of mine.

As we knocked on the gates of the monastery, a voice from the tower commanded us to identify ourselves, and Elefteris embarked on a lengthy introduction in Greek. Our luggage ready, we waited to be admitted. At last, a creaky contraption was lowered from the tower and we crowded onto the narrow platform, hauled by ropes to the terrace of the monastery. Two silent figures in black robes waited for us. Elefteris handed them some papers. The older monk examined them carefully and, apparently satisfied, gave a slight bow and led us down to a lower level where there were rooms along the narrow balconies, running above a square patio. A weak bulb gave off a yellow glow, creating eerie shadows on the rough adobe walls. Father Josaphat and Father Elziar were to share a room with Giorgio, while Albina and I were to be housed in the next room. There was no question of dinner, and we reconciled ourselves to some leftovers from our feast on the beach. Then Elefteris disappeared, presumably to be housed somewhere else, as he was to depart early the next morning.

The window of our room had iron bars and the wooden door had no locks of any kind. The two cots were clean with threadbare blankets and in the early morning I was so cold that I was pulling the blanket over my head to get warmer when a knock at our door startled me. Fathers Josaphat and Elziar stood there with a frying pan and packages of food, inviting us to join them at the communal kitchen provided for visitors. Giorgio slinked behind them.

Apparently, the Fathers had brought lots of food for us to supplement the meager hospitality of the monks. I was thankful for their foresight as I enjoyed the tasty omelet prepared by Albina. Even Giorgio showed some signs of civilized gratitude as he cleaned his plate.

After breakfast, we were invited by the same voiceless monk to sign the visitors' book. We all signed, and I had the opportunity of examining the large book containing names of the infrequent visitors. I noticed that the first entries, in pale purple ink, were dated back to the early days of the nineteenth century. Also being an avid cinema fan, I was thrilled to see the signatures of Cecil B. de Mille and the cast of Hollywood actors who participated in the making of *The Ten Commandments*.

Later, we were shown around by the silent host, who, by now, was vocal as he told us about the history of the monastery. He spoke French with a Greek accent. He showed us the underground chapel, but much to our regret, we did not spend much time there. We were told that we were free to visit it when there were no services held for the monks, which was during the very early morning hours and in the evenings. I promised myself that I would go down alone and sit awhile in that small church which had seen many centuries go by. We visited the strange mausoleum full of white skulls of defunct monks and then, much to our surprise, our guide took us to a library full of ancient manuscripts. Usually, the library was off-limits except to scholars. It was a series of long rooms with open shelves filled with sheaves and rolls of yellowed documents. It was cold, but not damp, and that probably explained how these documents could be preserved for so long. There was not much light. The only illumination at that time was a pale light from narrow horizontal windows near the ceiling. The floors were covered with old, scarred stone slabs, and there were no doors between the connecting rooms.

He showed us a framed document bearing the seal of Prophet Mohamed, which decreed that a mosque should be built within the walls of the monastery, to protect it from enemies of Christianity. Our guide did not allow us to visit the upper gallery, where, apparently, only historians were allowed to examine the documents.

In the late afternoon, we sat on the flat roof near our rooms, watching the mountain peaks change colors in the setting sun.

Albina and I sat on the old bench, while Giorgio and the two monks perched on the whitewashed stone wall. Giorgio began to seem more relaxed. He lost his capricious pout and laughed when Father Elziar teased him about being spooked by the sight of the white skulls.

Albina and Father Josaphat were planning for the next day's walk to see and photograph some Hebraic writing cut into the sandstones along the road leading north from the monastery.

"Are you coming with us, Vicka?" asked Father Josaphat.

"Not this time, Father," I said. "I thought I would go down and spend some time in the chapel. There are so many interesting historical objects there, and I really would like some time alone."

"Excellent idea," said Father Josaphat. "The day after tomorrow will be a very special day, for we are going to go up Mount Sinai. It is also called Gebel Moussa, or Mount of Moses. We can either go up by the steps the monks have cut into the mountain over the centuries, or the easier way, made for elderly tourists with handrails to hold onto. That is, for quite athletic elderly, for it will take us several hours to get to the summit. There are no handrails on the original steps, but one can hold onto the sides of the steep rocks. About one-third up, there is a natural rest-place: a couple of flat rocks surrounding a deep grotto, where there is always water. But we will take a couple of bottles with us, for we will certainly need them."

"Which way are we going to go up?" I asked, hoping that Father Josaphat would want to go up the old steps. I was not disappointed. "We will go up the old steps, of course," he said. "You and Giorgio are young, but in spite of my venerable years, I am still able to climb mountains. I was a bit of a mountain climber in my young days and I am sure that Albina and Elziar would also want to go up like real pilgrims."

The next morning, from the terrace, I watched my friends start on their walking tour: Father Josaphat striding in front with a tall walking stick, his brown habit billowing in the breeze, followed by Albina and Elziar, with Giorgio ambling in the rear.

"What a slob," I thought. "He is not trying to be pleasant at all. He acts like a spoiled overgrown baby."

* * *

I was alone for the first time on this trip and it felt good to explore, on my own, the cool passages that led to the underground chapel. As I descended, the steps became smaller and narrower and I thought of all the quiet footsteps preceding mine in the centuries past. I became keenly aware of my surroundings, and the passages and turns of the spiral staircase seemed to be leading to a place where I really wanted to be. A feeling of awe took hold of me as I reflected how fortunate I was to be here in my lifetime, in a historical place where Christians, Jews and Moslems found a common ground to worship.

The heavy door to the chapel was unlocked as I slipped through. In the warm light of candles, ancient icons watched me, their dark eyes stern and steady. A large icon of St. Catherine, daughter of a king, adorned a niche, her young tormented face illuminated by soft candlelight. It was said that she preferred to be tortured to death rather than give up her vows to Christ.

So much faith! I thought. *How did she find that strength, being so young?* I sat on a nearby bench, its seat polished by the faithful, and tried to imagine what it would be like for a young girl to live a cloistered life. Could I give up the alluring promise of a normal life to pray and live in isolation? Had St. Catherine been looking for happiness? Did faith give her serenity, or did she die before she awoke one day to the bitterness of having denied herself a normal life? I decided to ask Father Josaphat, but I changed my mind. On second thought, maybe that would not be a fair question. Didn't even Jesus have doubts?

What am I looking for in life? I thought. *To be happy? What is happiness? To be loved? Maybe.* I was loved by Vuko, but did not return that love, and our relationship was miserable. When was I really happy? The answer came quickly, for even before I formulated the question in my head, my lips smiled at the memory of evenings spent with Pierrot, our heads bent over poetry books, reading to each other unforgettable lines by our favorite poets. I nearly laughed aloud at the memory of Pierrot's mother standing in the doorway watching in dismay as we shook out the last drops of cognac into the only teacup, which we shared.

So, was friendship happiness? Did friendship happen spontaneously or grow with time? I had friends then, but still something was missing. Once I believed that everyone was good and only sometimes, we did evil things. But now, I was sarcastically inclined and criticized everyone. Here I was, in this holy place, and I didn't feel a thing. Maybe I wouldn't speak to Father Josaphat about it. I would try to talk to Albina; she seemed like such a well-adjusted, serene person, while Josaphat would only make fun of me. I tried to remember some prayers, but probably nothing came of it, because I fell asleep.

When I woke up, I was still alone in the chapel and my contemplative mood deserted me. I looked with interest at the huge golden candelabra donated by Catherine the Great of Russia, and admired the marble coffin containing the remains of St. Catherine. It was the gift of Napoleon, and I was overwhelmed by the historical significance of this ancient chapel where, in centuries past, the greatest of this world had brought their homage from their far-off countries.

As I emerged into the sunlight, I followed my nose and found my companions already cooking lunch. Albina was stirring something appetizing, giving instructions to Giorgio, who was chopping onions. I offered to help and did not tell them about my visit to the chapel.

Seventeen

But I did not forget. That night, when Albina and I retired to our room, I lay for a while staring at the pattern of light and shadow on the bare wall across from my bed. Albina was not asleep and I thought it would be a good time to talk to her and ask her a few questions.

"Albina," I asked, "do you feel like talking?"

"Of course, my dear," said Albina. Her kind voice encouraged me to continue and I tried to formulate a question that was still not very clear in my mind. I started with telling her about my visit to the chapel; then, somehow, I slipped into my dissatisfaction, my loneliness and aimlessness that seemed to color my life at that time. I ended up saying, "I really don't know why I am telling you all this. What could you possibly tell me that I don't already know?"

There was no answer at first. I thought that Albina must have fallen asleep, and I cursed myself for being a fool, expecting anyone to be interested in my problems. Then a shadow materialized near my bed. She sat on the chair next to my bed and spoke quietly.

"How well I understand you in your pain and doubts. You wanted everything in life and were disappointed. With every loss, there was a void that could not be replaced. You probably think that you are being punished for not being what you were supposed to be and that is why you feel guilty and angry. Yes, you have lost wonderful friends. Some have died and others are no longer with you, and you have closed your heart and love to the rest of the world. You wonder why I know this and understand you? Maybe because there was a time in my life when I, too, was not able to find any answers to my doubts."

I was on my guard again. "You are going to tell me that I should start going to church and that will make me a better person? I heard all this from Father Josaphat and from my mother."

"No," said Albina. "There is nothing wrong with going to church, but you need to find out yourself how you can find fulfillment in your own life, without waiting for someone else to give it to you."

I was surprised, but kept my peace.

"Here is my philosophy," said Albina. "It is not an orthodox one, and has nothing to do with organized religion, although I do go to church, since I believe that all religions of the world are equally good and pure."

She stopped for a while, then continued: "When we are born, there is a spiritual part of our being which is God's gift to us. This part may grow if we choose the right path. Every day of our conscious life, we are given a choice in everything that we do. So we can either choose a positive solution to our problems or adopt a negative one. The Bible tells us that it is the struggle between the Devil and the Angels. Every religion speaks about this condition. But in our day-to-day reality—in our decision to act one way or another—we are either expanding our sacred gift, or destroying it, little by little. This gift has many names, but today, I will call it love. Love comes in many forms and it is always available to give and to receive. We are like radio receptors, for we can send out waves of feelings to other human beings who receive them and can return them to us. If our choice is hate, when it is received, it can increase and generate untold evil, but when we send out love, something magical happens, which is also a healing process. God determines who walks into your life and it's up to you to decide whom you let walk away, whom you let stay, and whom you refuse to let go.

"Remember that every person you meet will somehow change you forever, for you are receiving all kinds of messages from the waves of thoughts generated by others."

"But," I asked, "how can I protect myself from evil waves which are directed at me?"

"Well," said Albina, "here is a little experiment that you can try. Pick out someone who may have good reasons to resent you. Without appearing to do so, send out a wave of love and goodwill to that person. You do not have to say or do anything more. Soon you will see how that particular individual's conduct will change towards you. You might even become good friends. By sending positive, loving thoughts, you will neutralize the negative climate and nip it in the bud."

"But," I said, "how can I send out love if I don't feel it?"

"Aha," said Albina. "Of course, you cannot, but you are a creator because you are a child of God, so find a place in your heart that will generate love. If you like animals, you can understand that. You love an animal when you see one, don't you?"

"Yes," I said. "They are so innocent and vulnerable, it is not difficult at all."

"So is everyone. Or, rather, we all have multiple facets of good and evil and often our first reaction to what we think is a rejection is to protect ourselves with a defensive attitude, judging others and sending out waves of negativity."

"So that's why I was really happy," said I, "when Pierrot was by my side, for I never judged him."

"That's right," said Albina. "Friendship is love in one of its purest forms. Once you learn how to love and accept love, you will never be alone or unhappy. By not judging others, you will soon form a field of love around yourself. This is what religions are about, but they each say it in different ways."

Nothing more was said that night.

Eighteen

Next morning, we were up at dawn. Fathers Josaphat and Elziar tied their robes as high as they dared and we started up the ancient steps leading up the Gebel Moussa. As I looked up, my heart fell. The steps cut out in the mountainside were well used with time and there was nothing to hold on to, except the rough granite boulders.

The two monks carried bags of water bottles and I was relieved that I was not asked to carry anything. Albina only rolled her eyes when she saw that I was bareheaded, and gave me a straw hat with a wide brim. I was dressed in shorts and most unfortunately for me, a pair of leather sandals, which were definitely not the prescribed footwear for climbing mountains. I soon realized my mistake when an hour later, I was in real pain, but out of pride, I stoically kept my mouth shut.

Going up was harder than I thought, although we did not hurry and stopped occasionally to rest. Halfway up the mountain, we had a break by the fresh water source, near a cave. There we sat on the flat polished rock listening to the faint sound of running water. It was cool and pleasant as I leaned against the wall of the cave, looking over the valley with the monastery nestling below us, looking very small. By the side of the cave, a small path led to more vertical steps up to the top. They were wider and easier to climb, and to my surprise, a wealth of short fragrant plants grew nearby.

"Here," said Albina. She picked a fragrant plant and put it in my hat. "This is a special plant that grows near springs," she said. "You can still wear your hat with the plant inside. It is supposed to be medicinal and the monks use it for all sorts of ailments."

I put the hat on and forgot about the plant.

After four hours, we reached the summit. It was the size of a football field, leveled flat over the centuries by the loving hands of monks. A small primitive chapel stood in the center. A few icons decorated the church with a couple of primitive benches against the walls, because in the Orthodox tradition, these are used only for elderly people who are unable to stand. Outside the chapel, some stone benches were placed facing the vast valley. I turned around and caught my breath. All the splendor of the Sinai Desert unfurled below. We were surrounded by powerful red-granite peaks that crowded around the holy mountain from which Moses brought down the Ten Commandments.

The sun, on its way to the west, had already illuminated the backdrop of the eternal giants, lighting the crystal planes and angles in hues of purple, red and violet. Every detail stood out clear and sharp as we gazed speechlessly at the panoramic view below us.

At first, I thought it was the silence that woke me from my reverie, but it was not that at all. Hundreds of birds, mostly invisible, filled the air with songs and chirping. Birds were everywhere, nesting in sheltered crevices along the sides of the mountain. I sat stunned, overwhelmed with the sights and sounds, not realizing that my companions were busy at something else.

By a stone bench, Josaphat had made a makeshift altar, at which he placed a length of embroidered red cloth and a gold cup. I understood then why he was so insistent on carrying the cloth sack with the water bottles on his back during our ascent. He was about to say a Mass on the Mount of Moses.

I stood with Elziar, Albina, and Giorgio as Father Josaphat intoned the Latin words of the Mass, lifting the cup in both hands. We all knelt and my friend Josaphat celebrated God in the place where He had manifested Himself to the Jews through one of their great Prophets.

What does it matter, I thought, *whether we are Hebrew, Christian, Moslem or Buddhist? God is with us wherever we are. It does not have to be in a church.* I was sure my companions felt the same, and that made me feel close to them. I marveled to think that Moses had stood on the same stones on which we were kneeling, and he must have heard the songs of the birds that we were hearing today. A wave of peace washed over me. Was it the peace Albina was talking about? Had I missed something so important in my life through distrust and negativity? Why was I cultivating bitterness instead of finding good qualities?

When we prepared to go down, I was dismayed to find out that my flimsy sandals were in shreds and my toes were bleeding. I sat on the ground and dabbed my blisters with a handkerchief. A shadow developed near me. "Here," said Giorgio. "Put these on." He handed me a pair of thick socks, which he had just pulled off his feet. "My shoes are sturdy and I can do without them, but you cannot attempt to go down these steps with blisters on your toes. You are just like my sister, who always wants to wear something pretty, rather than practical." He helped me fasten my torn sandals with a piece of string that he produced from his pocket. I felt tears come to my eyes because of his kindness, but my malicious tongue could not resist a teasing barb. "What a perfect Boy Scout you are, Giorgio," I said. "Do you always carry string in your pockets when saving mindless maidens on mountain tops?" As soon as I said it, I stopped short, realizing that I had been sarcastic when in my heart, I was deeply touched. But Giorgio grinned good-naturedly and said, "I will disregard your last remark for the simple reason that I am indeed a Boy Scout and I am always prepared for emergencies when saving ungrateful maidens."

"The age of chivalry is not dead," I said, and smiled. "I am sorry for being unappreciative of your kindness, Giorgio, and here and now, I appoint you my knight. I must confess that I am a fairy princess who was spirited away by bad genies from my father's palace. My father, the king, will reward you richly for bringing me down this steep mountain."

"It's a deal," said Giorgio, helping me down the steps. "Just try not to look down beyond the next step."

This was the beginning of a friendship that lasted for many years. During our difficult descent, we talked like old friends. I learned that Giorgio and his twin sister had a rough time adjusting to the man who married their widowed mother. Apparently, their stepfather was a kind and decent man, but Giorgio rebelled at the thought of his mother marrying again. He had confided in Father Josaphat, who thought that a short vacation would give Giorgio an opportunity to examine his true feelings and come to terms with the fact that his mother was happy in her new marriage.

Contrary to my usual hasty analysis, Giorgio turned out to be a thoughtful and intelligent young man. *So much for my psychological conclusions,* I thought wryly. I had been appraising him without even talking to him, just as I did with so many others, endowing him with the negativity that was the reflection of my own bitter philosophy. Was I really so heartless, or was it a role that I liked to play? The role of an unhappy, disillusioned person, like the romantic heroes of the past century? In fact, after my talk with Albina, I had learned an invaluable lesson, which later served me throughout my life.

* * *

That night, when Albina and I turned the lights out, I continued my inner dialogue far into the night. In my mind I went back to the time when my world was not shattered by loss and disappointment. Images of happy times flooded my conscience: sunlit days, the pleasure of swimming in the turquoise waters of Mersa Matruh, my years of friendship with Mike, our long, happy talks, sharing our lives together, happy dinners with Russian friends, sounds of a guitar playing and someone singing. Then came the memory of cruel years of loss and disappointment. In the light of my new knowledge, I knew then that I had used my bitterness to shield me from being hurt again; that I was afraid to expose myself to happiness because I was afraid to suffer again. How much of it was just pretense? I wondered. *Where is the real me?*

I decided that only time would tell. I was right, for although nothing magical happened, I knew then that that was the turning point in my life, and that I could never again revert to be the person I was before I went on a two-week trip to St. Catherine's monastery.

Nineteen

When we returned to Cairo, rumors of an impending war loomed over the city. Everybody was worried, and my parents summoned me back to Alexandria, where I learned that Egypt was mobilizing. We were subjected to tests of the wailing air raid signals and told to cover our windows with dark curtains.

People gathered on street corners, and the British and French consulates were mobbed by people asking for visas. The Jewish members of the European community were particularly worried. They even abandoned their houses and left with whatever they could take away with them, fearing the worst. Our house was filled with our many friends, all discussing the possibility of a war.

The shareholders of the Suez Canal Company were apprehensive that Colonel Nasser would nationalize its assets, but no one really believed at that time that this could happen. When it did happen, it proved to be an international disaster, which not only affected the British and French interests, but also led to a virtual standstill of a once thriving sea route. The short, but violent, war that followed resulted in the bombing of the ships along the Suez Canal, blocking with debris the narrow passage through the desert.

Home in Alexandria, I was plunged at once into the feverish atmosphere of the impending war and had no time to think about my recent trip to Sinai. I put away the few souvenirs I had brought back with me, including Albina's hat, and did not think about it anymore.

Soon, the British and French families in Alexandria and Cairo found themselves under house arrest. Within days, they were expulsed from Egypt. We were unable to even say our goodbyes, while members of the Jewish community, especially Egyptian nationals, were under threat of arrest and their bank accounts confiscated.

This was the end of an era, and a new chapter in my life started, one of unexpected and romantic events, but also one of much pain and sorrow.

My friendship with Father Josaphat had consolidated into a relationship that supported me all the following years. As for Albina, I did not forget her advice, although we never met again. I tried to adopt her philosophy of life and it never let me down. She also left me a special gift. Many months after our trip to St. Catherine's monastery, I found a box where I had stuffed Albina's hat. As soon as I took it out, a waft of aromatic herb assailed my senses. The plant was tucked into the crown of the hat and as I sat still, my astonished memory transported me back in time. I was once again sitting on a stone bench on the summit of Gebel Moussa, sharing a moment of perfect joy with my friends.

I smiled and sent out my love and gratitude to Albina.

Twenty

While WWI had its share of displaced persons, when many countries lost their rulers, nothing could equal the catastrophic upheaval of WWII. Today, these tragedies that affected large empires are historical facts found in every school textbook, but not much has been written about smaller countries of minor political interest.

Only too often, former rulers of such countries had to flee their homeland, seeking asylum wherever they could.

Egypt, in the World War II post-war era, was a haven for several deposed heads of state. Young King Farouk, following the generous precepts of his father, King Fouad, welcomed, with open arms, a number of sovereigns who had lost their crowns. To name a few, Queen Marie of Rumania, with her son Simeon; King Victor Emmanuel and his wife, Queen Maria Jose of Savoy; and King Zog of Albania, with his Hungarian-born Queen Geraldine, all found shelter in many of King Farouk's luxurious palaces.

The royal personalities did not come alone. Their close entourages were, unfortunately, obliged to fend for themselves for housing and daily survival.

It was at this point that we met the Juka family.

Father was asked at the Governorate to help, in any way he could, the recently arrived family of Mr. Juka, the former Prime Minister of Albania. Apparently, Mr. Juka had rented a house in our vicinity, but was ailing, and Father set out to pay the family a visit. I tagged along, curious to meet young Albanians.

When we arrived, the door to the dark, dingy apartment opened. A smiling young girl of about nineteen greeted us warmly in perfect French, and ushered us into their shabby living room with the same gracious ease she would have taken us into a palace drawing room.

Two young men got up when we entered and stood at attention while she made the introductions.

She said, "I welcome you in the name of our father. My name is Lume and I represent my mother, who is not able to meet with you today." Then, with a warm smile, she turned to one of the young men. "This is my eldest brother, Burhan. He was able to join us from France only yesterday." Burhan, about my age, twenty-nine, was of medium height with laughing eyes and a pleasant, easy manner. He said he was studying at the Sorbonne University in Paris.

Lume put her hand across her other brother's shoulders and said affectionately, "And this is the benjamin, of the family Fiqret. Our elder sister, Saffet, is not at home, but we expect her momentarily." Fiqret was about eighteen years old. He shook hands with us and murmured politely that he was enchanted to meet us, but did not say anything else. His intense dark eyes were alert and he kept brushing away a lock of unruly hair from his brow. I thought he was very handsome.

After introductions, Lume invited my father to step into her father's room, and then came back, carrying a tray with sweets and black coffee. I watched her tiny, precise movements as she served coffee, all the while making small talk.

Before our coffee cups were empty, I was answering questions asked by the three of them, and suggesting possible venues for finding a job for Burhan, who aspired to be a teacher. Apparently Saffet, a graduate archaeologist, had already secured a position with the Greek Roman Museum, and Fiqret was to enroll in the Egyptian University, where he wished to take courses in Arabic. There was so much to learn from them, and I enjoyed the contrast between the two brothers, and also their sister. Burhan was soft-spoken with an elegant way of expressing himself. He had spent all his school years in France and, before the evening was over, he confided that one day, he intended to go back to Paris, where his girlfriend, Marguerite, was waiting for him.

Fiqret lost no time informing me that he was only interested in politics. It seemed to me at the time that he was the most affected by their exile, but that was before I became closer to Lume and learned about the stoic abnegation and sacrifice she concealed beneath her serene manner.

To my astonishment, Fiqret was strongly influenced by the extreme conservative politics of Petain and Daladier of the Vichy government, who allowed the Germans to occupy Paris. I was about to argue with him, when Burhan, with a mocking smile, contradicted his brother and without raising their voices, they started a heated discussion.

Lume, apparently accustomed to her brothers' arguments, sat near me and shared impressions of her new life. As I listened to her quiet voice, I was astonished at the composure and sweetness of this young girl, who must have gone through some agonizing experiences as she fled her country. She did not choose to speak of the dramatic flight from Albania, but told of her life in Tirana, the capital of Albania, where she had attended a Catholic convent. Her eyes glistened with tears when she remembered the kindness of the nuns and how she chose, one day, to become a Catholic, much to the dismay of her parents. She smiled a little as she said, "My parents are Moslem, but they accepted the fact that this was the only way for me."

Even then, I could see a unique spiritual strength that later on manifested itself in Lume's unusual life. She told me also that since her mother was in poor health, she, Lume, volunteered to keep house for the family.

Some time later, Father joined us and I could tell that he was deeply moved by his encounter with Mr. Juka. After we had taken our leave, I asked Father about his meeting with the former Prime Minister. Father sighed and said, "This is such a sad situation, Vicka. This man has sunk into a deep depression. He blames himself for failing to prevent the coup d'etat planned by the Communist party of Enver Hodja." Although he did not say so, I knew Father was thinking of his own despair when he and Mother were forced to leave Russia.

I squeezed his hand. "But Father, maybe things will change, and one day the Albanian people will feel differently."

"No, my dear," Father said. "Mr. Juka is in his sixties and I am afraid he has lost all hope and will not be able to survive his grief."

Father's words were prophetic. Mr. Juka died of a stroke one month later.

We did not attend the funeral. It was a private affair, but soon after, I visited the bereaved family. Lume and her two brothers became frequent visitors to our home. Saffet never joined us. She was always absorbed in her work, and in later years, when she moved to New York, she worked on her doctorate and published several textbooks on Albanian history.

In Lume, I found a friend unlike any other. Although she frequently shared with me the incongruities of her new life, she laughed them off as unimportant, and she never complained. We both liked to take long walks and she listened patiently to my daily joys and pains and just laughed softly, commiserating with me. I felt so much better after unloading my frustrations into her friendly ears, and she always advised me to be more patient and less impulsive. However, she, herself, was very vulnerable and would trust anyone, especially those who pretended to have spiritual aspirations

In Alexandria, as nearly everywhere else at that time, small encounter groups of metaphysical orientation flourished, and I learned to steer clear of them. My philosophy of life already had been forged by the practical, street-wise likes of Mike, Pierrot and Ernesto, tempered with the spiritual strength of Father Josaphat and Albina.

To me the first red light of Lume's enchantment with a so-called spiritual fraternity was her enthusiastic support of a society called Moral Rearmament. The motto of this group was Absolute Purity, Chastity and Integrity, and it drew her like a moth to a bright lamp.

This group was Swiss-born, presided over by a Mrs. Burckhard, wife of a cotton magnate. Mrs. Burckhard was well known for her contributions to charity and her love of gossip. She welcomed Lume as a devoted acolyte, whom she immediately promoted to be her Vice President. Lume was appointed to lead otherwise boring encounters on days when Mrs. Burckhard had to attend important social functions.

Membership in the Moral Rearmament included annual seminars in Geneva, Switzerland, which largely accounted for its popularity. I was not tempted enough but Lume insisted that I attend one of the group meetings downtown, where I had a lot of fun listening to members spilling their guts, describing efforts to remain pure. Mrs. B., who led that particular meeting, had me in stitches as she counseled, with a straight face, the best way to extinguish the ardor of one's offending partner, by throwing a glass of cold water on the unfortunate sinner. Needless to say, I was not interested in joining the society, but Lume, convinced of the good work she was doing, led her group to Switzerland, extolling Purity, Sincerity, Chastity and Integrity to the faithful audiences.

My friendship with Burhan was on a different level. He was quite different from Lume and Fiqret. He was not interested in any form of spirituality, but loved literature, music and art. He was a fountain of information on French culture and a delightful companion. He stayed in Egypt until the mid-fifties and then joined his girlfriend, Marguerite, in Paris, from where they eventually emigrated to the U.S.A. Burhan and I kept our friendship intact throughout the years until he passed away in 2007

With Fiqret, it was another matter. He was a fiery activist for the French conservative party and never changed. He remained an eternal student, living in Paris, attending political meetings, and calling anyone who did not agree with him "idiots." He had a crush on me when he was eighteen, but later was disappointed in me when I said I liked Sartre and Simon de Beauvoir, and he labeled me as having "leanings towards the left."

Lume's involvement with the Moral Rearmament lasted several years, and it was harmless enough, but led to an unfortunate decision, which nearly destroyed her.

Mrs. B,, who was fond of Lume, thought it a good idea to introduce her to Omar, a young Egyptian lawyer who was looking for a wife.

At one of the encounter meetings, he told Mrs. B. that he was yearning to marry a cultured and pure girl from a good family.

Mrs. B., a matchmaker at heart, decided that Lume would be a perfect wife for Omar, and assured him that she knew exactly such a girl.

Without first finding out more about Omar's undistinguished background, she started working on Lume and Mrs. Juka. Lume made no secret of the fact that her dearest wish was to join Mother Theresa in her work in India, but Mrs. B. convinced her that Omar was in need of spiritual rehabilitation. Unfortunately, this was not the only rehabilitation that Omar needed, but he was determined to improve his career by marrying into an excellent family, and Lume seemed to fulfill the requirements. He played Mrs. B.'s game and faithfully attended Lume's meetings, biding his time.

By that time, both Burhan and Fiqret had left Egypt. Mrs. B. had no trouble convincing Mrs. Juka to influence her daughter to accept such a suitable husband. Under their pressure, Lume decided that it was her destiny to change Omar to absolute Purity, Chastity, Sincerity and Integrity, and agreed to marry him.

The marriage ceremony was conducted Moslem-style by a Mullah. It was held in a rigged colorful tent where only male guests were invited.

The bride, in another tent, surrounded by women from Omar's family, wore a pretty dress and a bewildered smile. Her frail mother, who did not speak Arabic, sat nearby with Mrs. B. and myself.

I went home, bewildered and sad. I blamed Mrs. B. for putting unfair pressure on my young friend. Mrs. Juka did not look happy, either, but I suspected that she encouraged her daughter to marry, hoping that Lume would stay near her, instead of following her vocation to serve the poor in a far-off country.

Twenty-One

After the wedding, I did not see Lume for quite a while. In the European communities, there was an atmosphere of uncertainty. As I mentioned before, these were the mid-fifties and the newspapers reported rumors of an impending war with Israel. People in the streets gathered in small groups, asking each other, "What now?" A shadow of doom hung over my hometown. Father was preoccupied, but still believed that outside events would not touch us.

I wanted to see Lume, as I had an uncomfortable feeling that all was not well with her. I hesitated, however, not having any proof of my fears except a nagging intuition. With that thought in mind, I decided to put off my visit until I heard from her.

For Christmas, I was planning to attend a late supper party preceded by the traditional attendance at the Midnight Mass. At home we usually celebrated the Russian Christmas on January 7th, according to the Orthodox calendar, but on December 24th, I always joined my friends and was not missed at home. That night, as I was ready to leave, it suddenly occurred to me that maybe there would not be another Christmas for our tight little group, and that soon we all might be dispersed in different directions.

But my usual optimism came to my rescue and I brushed off black butterflies of negative premonitions. However, there was no kidding myself: That night, I felt very lonely, for the truth was that no matter how many friends I had, I did not have a special partner whom I loved. Many of my friends were already married, some with children, but there was no one who touched my heart sufficiently to make me contemplate getting married. I had dated several men, but quick infatuations wore off as soon as there was a question of commitment, engagements, and invitations to dinner with the prospective mothers-in-law. Secretly, I yearned for a great love, immense as the sky, that would sweep me off my feet, and a happiness that would immerse me in a feeling that I felt only in my restless dreams. So, that night, I just squared my shoulders and decided that lonely or not, I was not going to compromise and settle

162

down with someone who was not exactly what I hoped for, and that was it! In my melancholy mood, I did not suspect that on that magic Christmas night, destiny would present me with a challenge that would change my life.

* * *

I saw him for the first time at the midnight mass in St. Mark's chapel.

Following a long-standing tradition, the alumni of St. Mark's Jesuit College for Young Men returned to their beloved school on Christmas Eve. As usual, we accompanied those of our group who kept this custom faithfully, and also we wanted to hear a famous Italian tenor sing "Oh Holy Night." Every year, a different celebrity would be invited to sing at the chapel, and it was quite a social event.

When we ascended the wide steps leading to the chapel, we were surrounded by a swarm of pretty social workers collecting donations for the *Petits lits blancs*, the Children's Hospital. In exchange, we were given small bunches of white daisies. As we slipped through the heavy door into the overcrowded chapel, the Mass had already begun, and there was standing room only. Separated from my group, I inched forward through the festive crowd of worshippers, nodding and smiling at acquaintances. I felt at home in this small church, which was familiar to me since my childhood. I soon found a place by a column to the side, where I could see the solemn ritual of the Catholic Church, but still my mind was wandering. I tried to collect myself as I watched unguarded faces praying in the glow of candlelight.

I still could not shake off my despondent mood and thought that maybe I should have stayed at home. Suddenly, my restless eyes fell upon a tall man slightly to my left. He was completely oblivious to his surroundings, a tiny frown of concentration on his handsome face. Dark eyelashes concealed his eyes as he stood very still, lost in his secret world.

Something arose in me, desperately willing him to open his eyes and look at me. But he did not lift his eyes, and continued to pray. An intense feeling of sadness possessed me, as if I had just lost something precious. A part of me desired to know him, not to let him escape, while my rational mind ridiculed the sudden emotional storm playing out within me. This remote stranger was completely unaware of me and I was behaving like a silly teenager. Would I ever know him? Would he pass out of my sight without even noticing me?

Then, my sense of humor plugged in and I mentally chastised myself for being overly romantic, but somehow my logic failed me. Unable to control my inner turmoil, I finally closed my eyes and tried to pray.

I came back to reality as murmurs and coughs died down and an air of expectancy filled the silence. It was midnight. A single bell sounded above, and a clear vibrant voice rose towards the graceful arches of the chapel. *"Minuit Chretiens, c'est l'heure solonnelle"* (Oh Holy Night). There was no accompanying choir as the simple melody glorified the birth of Christ.

I was so moved by the beauty of the moment that sudden tears ran down my face. All sophistication left me as I fumbled for my handkerchief, but could not find my purse. Then a hand in a dark sleeve materialized by my side, holding my small black purse. A quiet voice asked, "Is this what you're looking for, Mademoiselle?" A pair of gray eyes looked at me.

My heart gave a jolt. I gazed speechlessly at him, unable to say a word, until my good manners took over.

"Oh, thank you very much, Monsieur," I said. "I didn't realize I dropped it." His eyes smiled as he said, *"Joyeux Noel,"* and disappeared into the crowd.

When I looked at my purse, it had a white daisy tucked in the clasp.

As I came down to the waiting cars with my chattering friends, my heart was singing.

That night I dreamt of gray eyes.

Twenty-Two

A couple of weeks later, I had an unfortunate accident. It happened on the beach at Mandara. The wonderful climate of Alexandria allowed year-round swimming and although there were some rainy and windy days, most of winter was spent on the beach, swimming, socializing, and playing what we called "racquets." The racquets game was played on the beach with heavy plywood paddles, sending tennis volleys between opponents. It was played on the firm wet sand near the water line and there were usually two or three matches going on. The balls were not supposed to touch the ground, and we played in pairs or in foursomes. I was a fervent player, though not as good as I imagined, and never missed an opportunity to play with better players.

That weekend, I was paired with an exceptionally good player, a newcomer, and we were all very impressed to learn that he was the bodyguard of King Zog, exiled from Albania. Husky, of middle height, he was an ideal partner, catching all the difficult volleys, although I was trying very hard not to miss any sent our way. He took care of most of the backhand balls that I missed, and during a particularly tricky move, I ran forward trying to hit the ball while he delivered a powerful blow, which, unfortunately, struck the back of my head.

I fainted at once. When I came to my senses, I was lying on a gurney in the emergency room of French Hospital. My head was throbbing and something sticky was oozing on my face. I tried to open my eyes, but was blinded by the overhead lights.

"What do we have here?" said a voice. "Mademoiselle, can you open your eyes?"

A nurse removed a towel, and gentle hands probed my head. "Ai," I whimpered, "it hurts."

"Well, Mademoiselle," said the voice, "you're going to have a very big bump on your head. No, I won't hurt you again, but I will give you a shot, which will make you feel better." I felt a slight prick of a needle. Through the fog, I saw the doctor's face as he bent over me, a straight nose and concerned gray eyes.

165

I am dreaming again, I thought. *He is here with me because I wished to see him again.* I was drifting away in a fog. "Thank you," I murmured. "Thank you for the daisy. You know, I kept it."

The nurse laughed. "She is reacting to the injection," she said. "There, there, you received such a hard blow. You'll feel better soon." She cleaned the blood from my face, and I tried to open my eyes.

"Well," said the doctor. "What a pleasant surprise. You are the young lady of the Midnight Mass."

I quickly closed my eyes again, distraught that he should see me in this state, probably looking like a wet chicken.

"I am so sorry," I mumbled, "to give everyone so much trouble. I will be all right. I can get up and my friends will take me home."

"No, no, Mademoiselle," said Gray Eyes. "We are not finished yet as we still have to find out whether you have done some real damage to your head. We are calling your family, and I am sure someone will come to comfort you." I did not hear the rest of his sentence for I fell into a deep sleep.

I spent that night at the hospital. It must have been the effect of the drugs when at night, I felt a cool hand linger on my burning forehead. Did I hear a murmur, or was I dreaming again?

The next day, my parents brought me home. I had a big lump on my head and a quiet joy in my heart. I did not see him again before I left; yet somehow, I was certain that life would bring us together again. Before I left, I learned that his name was Dr. Philippe Van Dorgen.

A week later, completely recovered, I told myself that I needed to thank the doctor for taking such good care of me. I went to the hospital, and asked two young assistant nurses where I could find Dr. Van Dorgen.

"Oh, Dr. Philippe?" said one of them. "He left a few days ago for Brussels." The other girl giggled and said, "What a pity that all handsome doctors are already married. No wonder his wife called him to come back!" The two girls walked off, still laughing.

The shock of what I just heard left me stunned. I felt hurt and angry for imagining myself in love with a stranger, who just happened to be married. What a fool I was. The good doctor was probably kind to all his patients, and I mistook his professional manner for something more. *Oh God,* I thought bitterly. *Will I never learn to curb my imagination?* Albina was so right when she said, "Wait, my dear friend, wait. Happiness and love will come to you at the right time. Don't be impatient, and above all, don't try to invent someone that you can love and admire. An illusion is exactly what it is, an illusion, and it can only hurt you in the long run."

But Albina was far away and I decided to seek out Lume, from whom I had not heard for a very long time, and decided to visit her in her new home, during Omar's working hours.

* * *

When I arrived at Lume's new apartment, I was shocked beyond words when she opened the door. Her tearful face was swollen as she gazed speechlessly at me. She just put her arms around me, saying, "Oh Vicka, oh Vicka, what have I done!"

I led her to a sofa and sat down, holding her close while she sobbed. Little by little, she was able to speak and told me her story in bits and pieces.

Apparently, Omar behaved in the only manner he knew. He raped her on their wedding night and every night after that. A week after they were married, he resumed his habitual life of returning home late, after drinking with his friends, and expected her to serve him food at any late hour.

Lume said, "Omar forbade me to leave the house alone, unaccompanied by him, and threatened to deport my mother if I complained to you or Mrs. Burckhard."

She started sobbing again as she continued her story.

"Now that I am married to him, I have absolutely no legal right, as the Moslem law gives him absolute power over me. Oh, what have I done? I hate this man and nobody can help me now!"

I knew, of course, that by Moslem law, she was entirely at the mercy of her husband. At that time, the only recourse for a divorce request from a wife would be if the husband did not provide her with sufficient money to buy food. But times were changing, and the Egyptian civil law was now favoring battered and ill-treated wives. I thought that I just had to find an Egyptian woman lawyer who would take Lume's case. But, unfortunately, Omar was an associate in a large law firm and would fight Lume in order not to lose face.

I promised Lume I would consult with a lawyer friend and left with a heavy heart. The weather seemed to match my mood, as dark rainy clouds announced an impending storm.

Twenty-Three

Peace in the Middle East was deteriorating at a fast pace. When the Egyptians suffered a fiasco in their negotiations with the United States concerning financial aid for the construction of the Asswan Dam, they appealed to the Soviet Union for help. This was readily given, with dire consequences for my father's standing in the Governorate.

Both Alexandria and Cairo were soon flooded with Soviet consular and trade missions, much to the approval of the leftist members of the Egyptian government. Appointments of officials with socialistic tendencies followed, and my father's department at the Governorate underwent drastic changes. Previously, the Egyptian military government upheld the former King Farouk's decision to outlaw Communist activities sprouting around universities. Now, this was no longer politically correct, and the special department at the Governorate was reinvented along KGB lines.

My father's position became precarious, as he was responsible for enforcing measures against Communist activities, cooperating with English, French and Israeli authorities in that respect. There was a sudden shake-up in the Governorate departments. Several of the younger pro-Socialist-oriented officers replaced military Egyptian officials.

Father was warned by his friends at the British Consulate that it was time to leave Egypt, but he clung to his belief that loyal service of thirty years would keep him out of harm's way. I thought differently and pressured my parents to apply for immigration visas, either to Australia, where my old friend Mike was urging me to join him, or Canada, which would have readily accepted us.

My uncle Lev, in Washington, D.C., repeatedly invited us to join him, but going to the United States presented an insurmountable difficulty. Both my parents and sister, Jenny, were born in Russia, which had a small immigrant quota, but I was born in Egypt, and my waiting time was seven or eight years longer. My parents, both in their sixties, would have had to rely on Jenny's earning skills, which, alas, were nil. In addition, Father and Mother spoke little English, and since I could not go with them to the United States, we regretfully resigned ourselves to either Canada or Australia.

The feared war with Israel loomed on the horizon and an exodus of European nationals began. Alexandria had a large Jewish community, mostly stateless families who had lived for generations in Egypt without any problems, and they were especially at risk in case of a war with Israel.

Then came a day I will never forget, when Father came home earlier than usual.

We could tell at once that something terrible had happened. His face was drawn and he suddenly looked much older. He told us that he was officially informed not to leave town. Apparently, many of his European colleagues were already arrested that same day and he feared that it would soon be his turn.

We sat around our dining room table, weighing all possibilities in the event that Father would be arrested. My heart was breaking seeing my parents' life shattered again after three decades, and I realized, for the first time in my life, the responsibility that fell upon me to find a solution.

Father urged us to leave Egypt in case he was arrested. He believed that he would soon be set free, as his impeccable record would prove that he was never involved in any activities against the Egyptian government.

Mother promptly said that Jenny and I should leave as soon as possible while she would remain in Egypt with Father. Jenny said she wanted to stay with Mother.

I said I would never leave anyone in Egypt, and argued that I would get in touch with Father's friends at the European embassies and ask them to use their influence with the Egyptian Military Command to absolve Father of any absurd accusations.

I put on a resolute face and spoke confidently, but I had no idea at all where to begin.

We went to bed late, emotionally exhausted, hugging each other. That night, nobody in our house slept. I lay tossing in my bed, trying to think of a solution and rejecting one plan after another. *Where do I go first? Whom should I see? Maybe a friendly Egyptian official? No! I should go to Cairo, and in the morning, ask Father for some names.*

I wished I could speak with our friend Oliver Trent, the British Vice Consul, but hadn't his wife told me the other day that they were waiting for orders to leave in case of war? I wondered whether Father knew any high official at the Italian or Belgian consulates.

I tried to sleep, but cold fear gripped me as I envisioned Father locked up in an Egyptian prison. Who could protect us? We were stateless and completely at the mercy of the Egyptian authorities.

At dawn, a loud banging on our front door startled us. Several armed army officers with drawn guns forced their way into our apartment, brandishing a document which they read aloud. The gibberish nonsense stated that my father was accused of treason against Egypt, and the officers were empowered to search our home for incriminating documents. Father was held back, ordered not to interfere, and we stood helplessly by, watching them ransack our home.

They threw piles of files and papers out of cabinets, laughing and commenting that some were written in Cyrillic Russian. Two of the officers could read French and they examined dossiers and manuscripts, tore books apart, and viciously ripped the lining from our living room sofa. After several hours of bedlam, they finally left with several manuscripts in Russian, promising to be back soon.

It was already late morning. Our next-door neighbors came fearfully to ask if they could help us put the front door back on its hinges. They hugged us and brought us food, but nobody could eat.

That night, Father had a heart attack. I was awakened by Father screaming in pain, "Mother, Mother, help me."

We found him unconscious on the floor in the bathroom. We immediately called Dr. Nazarian, who arrived soon, and Father was taken in an ambulance to the hospital. Mother went with him.

Twenty-Four

Left alone, Jenny and I tried to cope, each in our own way. To calm herself, she started to restore order in our home, and as soon as I could, I went to the Governorate to find out what I could learn about accusations against my father.

At the Governorate, I waited a long time in a drafty corridor before I was ushered in to see the officer in charge of the investigation. This was an arrogant young man in his early thirties, with an inevitable moustache on his sneering face. When I walked in, he examined me from head to toe, leering impudently at my breasts.

"Mademoiselle Markov?" he asked, slowly stretching every word. "Why are you here? Are you looking for a job? I have always a place for a pretty secretary."

I tried to control my voice as I explained that I wanted some explanation of yesterday's raid at our home. I spoke as calmly as I could. I knew that losing my temper would only make things worse. I was at the complete mercy of this upstart young official and he knew it, too.

I spoke about the long years of my father's faithful service to Egypt, and how much he loved this country which had given us shelter.

"My father could never be a traitor to Egypt," I said. "He cooperated at all times with the policies of the government during the period of monarchy, as well as during the years of the Revolutionary government."

The officer stopped smiling. He banged the desk with his fist. "That was during the time when you foreigners thought you owned us, kept us, the rightful owners of this land, as second-class citizens while you exploited the riches of our land. You robbed us of our birthright. You, the Jews, the English and the French. These times are over, Mademoiselle! No longer will we permit foreign officials like your father to have the audacity to tell us with which countries we are to conduct our diplomatic relations. Today is the era of international Socialism and the enemies of the Soviet Union are our enemies. Your father had been a traitor to his own country, the Soviet Union, and today he is a traitor to Egypt, for he has been cooperating with the so-called Allies who are now threatening us with war.

"I don't know why your father sent you, Mademoiselle," he added coldly. "He should have come himself instead of sending you."

"My father is at present in intensive care at a hospital," I said. "He suffered a severe heart attack early this morning. He did not send me. I came here on my own initiative and I intend to hire a lawyer to defend my father against your absurd accusation."

"Well, well," he said. "It looks like you are one of those modern women who think that they can defy military authority." He paused for more effect.

"Let me tell you one thing, Mademoiselle Markov. Take care, take great care not to antagonize me. And remember, it's very easy for a young girl to get into trouble. As for Captain Markov, if he survives, he will probably be indicted for treason as soon as he leaves the hospital."

Fear like a cold hand gripped my stomach. *All is lost for us,* I thought, *and this awful man knows it.* Then without thinking, I blurted out, "My family was thinking about immigrating to the United States for quite a while, and we are waiting for our papers to arrive."

He smiled. "It is common knowledge that your parents and your sister never applied for Egyptian nationality," he said. "But how about you? You were born here and yet you never asked for naturalization papers. Don't you want to be an Egyptian citizen?"

"Of course," I lied. "I love Egypt, but since we always traveled with our Laissez Passer passports, I never needed official papers, because I was born on Egyptian soil."

"Well, maybe this is a good time to become an official Egyptian citizen," he said, with a meaningful look. "With all the rights and privileges of an Egyptian woman."

My blood ran cold. "Of course," I said. "I will think about it."

"It will be my pleasure to help you with the formalities for your Egyptian naturalization," he said as he walked me out the door.

* * *

As I sat in the rickety bus, which took me to the central tram station, my mind was racing furiously. How could I extricate myself from being forced to accept Egyptian nationality, which would certainly prevent me from ever joining my family wherever they went? I bitterly blamed myself for antagonizing this stupid jerk. I reasoned that we simply had to leave Egypt as soon as possible. There had to be a way.

The bus was jerking and bouncing on every pothole. *This is awful!* I thought. Without European influence, Alexandria was changing from a glittering international center to a poorly maintained native city, with uncollected garbage piled up at every street corner.

I tried to remember the text of the formal letter we had received from the U.S. Embassy in Cairo. It stated that Father, Mother, and Jenny could receive immigration visas for the States but, regretfully, Victoria Markov, born in Egypt, would have to wait seven years before joining her family.

How would the family survive without me? I thought. Probably Jenny would be able to find some work, but how would they fare without my support? Father sick, and Mother's sight worsening, as her cataracts had matured to a point where she was nearly blind. No! Mother and Father would never agree to leave me alone in Egypt.

By the time I reached French Hospital, I had decided that the next day, I would take the first train to Cairo and visit the U.S. Embassy.

Twenty-Five

Father was in the intensive care unit at the hospital. Mother was sitting at his side, watching him as he slept, a hissing oxygen mask on his face.

"How is he?" I asked Mother.

She squeezed my hands. "It is too early to assess the damage," she said. "The next twenty-four hours will decide whether he will survive. It's his aorta." She stopped trying to control her tears. "How are you? Jenny was here all morning. Have you eaten? Why didn't you come earlier?"

I led her to a chair outside and told her about my visit to the Governorate, editing parts of my interview with the officer, so as not to have her worry even more. I told her about my plan to go to Cairo, where I would probably stay for a couple of days. She was nervous about me going alone, but I reassured her that I would immediately tell Madame Louise of my arrival, and have Ernesto or Dimitri meet me at the Cairo Main Station.

"Don't go alone to the Embassy, Vicka," she said. "You know how unsafe it is now for white women on Cairo's streets."

I promised her I would not go alone. I held her in my arms. I was now taller than she was. She was still that courageous fighting Zhenia, my father's partner, and also my best friend. She was in her early sixties, her hair silvery-white, but her eyes were as bright blue as ever. Now, they were filled with tears as she kept vigil by Father's side, watching his every breath.

As we sat talking, Dr. Nazarian approached us.

"Don't despair, Dr. Markov," he said. "Although Captain Markov did suffer a serious heart attack, I believe he will pull through. However, it will mean that he will have to stay in bed for a long time, and I am sure you can give him the best care when he goes home." Mother started to say something, but I interrupted her.

"Dr. Nazarian," I said, "can you arrange for Father to remain in the hospital as long as possible?"

Mother looked at me in surprise. "What are you saying, Vicka? Of course I can take care of your father, and he will certainly be more comfortable in the familiar atmosphere of our home."

"No, Mother," I said. "Not at this time." Unwilling as I was to worry her, I was obliged to tell her and Dr. Nazarian the ominous news that Father could be arrested as soon as he left the hospital.

"Well," said the doctor, "that certainly would be the wrong thing to do. Tell me all about it and maybe I can help."

We went to Dr. Nazarian's office, where I told him and Mother, in detail, of my visit to the Governorate. The doctor listened attentively, with a frown on his kind face, and then remained silent for a while, digesting what he had just heard. When he spoke again, I could tell that he had the situation well in hand.

"Captain Markov will remain in the hospital as long as it takes for you to arrange immigration visas for your family," he said. "I will take care of that myself. At this stage, I don't think that you still have the luxury of choosing the country that will accept you. It is not important where you will go, but one thing is certain, you must get out of Egypt as soon as possible. Let me see if I can arrange for you to go to Cairo tomorrow with one of our doctors from the hospital. I have someone in mind, who I am sure will be willing to take you along."

I could tell by Mother's face that she was relieved to have such sound advice. We had known Dr. Nazarian for more than twenty years, and he had been our physician and our friend, and I, too, trusted him absolutely.

He picked up the telephone. "Operator," he said, "please connect me to the doctor on duty in the west wing." He waited for a moment. "Hello, Doctor," he said. "This is Nishan Nazarian. I am glad I caught you before you left. I want to ask you a personal favor. Are you still planning to drive tomorrow to Cairo? Yes, I know. Yes, yes, of course. Dr. Amram is leaving next week with his family, and you'll barely have time to complete the formalities. Yes, very kind of you. No, it's not a medical emergency. I would like you to take along with you a daughter of an old friend. She needs to be in Cairo for a couple of days or maybe more. No problem? Well, that's great. I will send you directions to her house at once with one of the assistant nurses. At what time are you planning to pick her up? Eight-thirty? Fine. Much obliged. Thank you very much. Goodbye." He hung up and smiled at me.

"There, young lady. Now be sure not to be late tomorrow morning when Dr. Van Dorgen will pick you up."

* * *

At home, an array of conflicting emotions rocked my world. I was terribly worried about my father and hoped that Dr. Nazarian would be able to keep him in the hospital as promised. But would he survive his heart attack? I did not even want to think how this would affect Mother.

I had to think about taking the necessary documents for the trip to Cairo. My trip with HIM—with Dr. Van Dorgen! I realized that I was pushing to the back of my mind the fact that somewhere deep inside me, something was singing with joy. He did say Van Dorgen, didn't he? But the doctor with gray eyes had left more than a month ago. Left to join his wife, unaware that I had fallen in love with him. Well, since he knew nothing about my fantasies, I need not be embarrassed to see him again. Should I be? In truth, I should not even continue thinking about him but concentrate on tomorrow's visit to the U.S. Embassy. *Oh, God, please help me! Here I am, fantasizing again, while Father is so sick, and I am now responsible for arranging for our departure from Egypt.*

I rushed around our apartment, getting the necessary documents ready to take with me, snatching some clothes from their hangers, and making lists of people I had to see. Jenny was not at home, probably on her way to the hospital. I was glad she had the support of her many friends. We had seldom acted like loving sisters, but these days, we clung to each other in our hour of need.

I called Madame Louise to tell her I was coming. As soon as I heard her heavily accented voice, I calmed down. "Hello, my little girl," she said. "Of course, you are welcome to stay with us as long as you can. No, Ernesto is somewhere in the South of France, spending my money with his disreputable friends, but Mimi is here and will be happy to see you. What time are you planning to arrive? Never mind. If you are late, I'll leave you something in the refrigerator. Nara will roast a chicken for lunch, which you like so much. *Ciau piccina, a domani*" (Bye, little one, see you tomorrow).

I felt reassured and stronger. How lucky I was to have such wonderful friends like Madame Louise and her sons.

As I came down at eight-thirty the next morning, a small green Fiat was waiting. A tall figure disentangled from the driver's seat and came over to greet me.

"Mademoiselle Markov, it is a pleasure to see you again," he said. "What a series of coincidences brings us together," he added with a smile. "May I call you Victoria, or is it Vicka?" he asked, his eyes laughing.

"Of course, Doctor," I said. "Everybody calls me Vicka."

"No, no," he protested, "not Doctor—it's Philippe. Now we are nearly old friends, are we not?"

I nodded my head, speechless for the moment.

As we sped along the two-way desert road towards Cairo, I tried to put order into my thoughts. I lectured myself not to be so gullible as to fall for the typical approach of a married man to a woman who was going alone with him to another city.

I have to remember at all times, I told myself, *that he is married. All I have to do is keep my mind on the business in hand, and be as friendly and social as I would have been with any other pleasant acquaintance.*

Philippe asked if he could be of assistance to me during my stay in Cairo. I told him about our predicament: Father's heart attack, and my visit to the Governorate. He seemed concerned and suggested that in Cairo, I call him at his hotel, should I need his help in any way. He gave me his card with the name of the hotel where he would be staying.

He said he was curious as to why my family lived in Egypt, and though I was still on the defensive, I told him about the circumstances that brought my parents to Egypt and before I knew it, I was talking about my own life. He drew me out with tactful questions, and I felt his genuine interest and encouragement when I spoke about people dear to my heart. I told him that I really did not need any help, as my close friends in Cairo would be there for me. He did not insist, but said, "I am glad, for these are bad times."

It dawned on me that I was a little short with him and tried to make amends by asking him about his visit to Cairo.

"As a Belgian national," he said, "I am required to appear personally at the Ministry in Cairo in order to obtain a special permit to replace a colleague who is leaving Egypt. This is just a formality as I have been asked before to stand in for the doctor in question. Up to now, French Hospital had several European doctors on their staff, but lately there has been an exodus, and I agreed to come over again until permanent resident doctors were found."

Not a word about his wife. "How about your family?" I asked as diffidently as I could.

He did not reply at once. When he did, his voice was low. "Nobody," he said, "is waiting for me."

I looked at him, unable to repress a question in my eyes.

"It's a long story," he said. "You have been so genuinely open with me that I feel I can tell you about my life, too, but this is not the appropriate time or place. I want to get you safe and sound to your destination."

Sure, I thought. *He wants the right atmosphere to spin the story of a misunderstood husband, who is looking for consolation in the arms of a gullible victim, yours truly.* After some small talk, I settled down in my own unhappy thoughts while Philippe concentrated on driving.

An hour went by and I was getting hungry. As if reading my thoughts, he asked me whether I had breakfast before leaving.

"Yes, a cup of coffee, as usual," I said.

"Well," he said, "that is certainly not good enough. How about if we stop at the next roadside restaurant and risk our lives eating some of their food?"

"It's a deal," I said.

We parked in the sandy parking lot near three anemic palms, alongside a primitive shack that boasted two empty tables. Presuming that my companion did not speak Arabic, I asked the Bedouin owner what he had to eat.

"I just made some fresh falafel," he said, "and my wife baked some flat bread on hot stones. They're good." He smiled, showing snow-white teeth.

"Great," I said. "Can you make us some hot black tea and two portions of falafel?"

We sat down, watching cars speed by, and soon our host brought us generous portions of delicious falafel wrapped tightly in flat bread and two glasses of sweet black tea, Bedouin style.

"Is this Arab a Bedouin?" asked Philippe.

"Yes," I said. "They are nomads and seldom come into towns. They travel from place to place in the desert where they stop from time to time, allowing their goats to feed on desert plants. At present, more of them come into towns as they are slowly pushed out of the desert by developers who, unfortunately, build cheap housing, making deeper inroads into the desert. When I was a little girl, I met my first Bedouin family, and…"

Soon I found myself telling Philippe about my childhood, and prompted by his questions, I talked on and on. He asked me about my family and wanted to know what I thought of the war, of life and destiny, and we somehow ended talking about predestination.

"We're not done yet," said Philippe as we got back on the road. "This is such an interesting subject, and it is extraordinary how your family managed to adapt to living in such a different culture. I want to hear more about you and your family."

"Well, this will be your turn to talk about yourself," I said, smiling inwardly as I thought that it would be an opportunity to find out how clever a liar he was. Since he did not say a single word about his wife, or that he was married, I thought I would find out soon enough that he was as bad as any married jerk looking for outside fun. With that, I smiled sweetly at him.

"We certainly will talk more," I said. "You piqued my curiosity. Now I want to know more about you."

"How about dinner tonight?" he asked.

I quickly weighed Nara's roasted chicken against a whole evening spent in his company and said, "I would love to," cursing my own weakness, as my heart grew larger in my chest.

We were now approaching Cairo. The Pyramids appeared hazy on the horizon, in their eternal vigil over the desert.

"I always get a jolt of thrill when I see them from afar," said Philippe. "You are probably accustomed to seeing them by now."

"No," I said. "I am still awed and humbled when I see them, especially when approaching them from the desert."

We passed Mena House, a Victorian sprawling hotel where Howard Carter and Lord Carnavon stayed when they astonished the world by discovering the King Tutankhamun tomb in 1922. The hotel was surrounded by well-tended lush gardens, and were it not for numerous cars parked on the side, one could, with a little imagination, be transported to the beginning of the century.

"Would you like to have dinner tonight at Mena House?" asked Philippe. "It's only half an hour's drive from the center of Cairo. I will make reservations as soon as I get to my hotel, and maybe ask for a table on the open terrace where we can talk."

I liked the idea and agreed readily.

Twenty-Six

Philippe deposited me at the century-old apartment house, where Madame Louise occupied the whole second floor. Her "Maison de Couture Louise" was located in the left wing. She employed dozens of young dressmakers busily turning out stylish outfits for Cairo's high society ladies, and for Queen Farida and the Royal Princesses, Fawziah, Faiza and Faika.

Her own home occupied the right wing. In spite of twelve-foot-high ceilings and tall windows, the apartment was usually dark, illuminated only by old-fashioned candelabras giving off yellow light. Dark velvet drapes covered the windows and only the kitchen and the bathrooms windows allowed the sun in. All four bedrooms were huge, with high four-poster iron beds, piled high with lots of embroidered pillows. I was usually assigned to such a room with the bathroom at the end of the dark corridor.

When I arrived, Madame Louise was still at her workshop, and Aunt Nara greeted me warmly. This pleasant woman was the wife of Tio George, Louise's brother. The story was that George did not believe in long commitments and took off for greener pastures a couple of years after they were married, and Nara remained with the family, cooking and supervising the servants. The two sons of Louise, Ernesto and Dimitri, still lived with their mother. Ernesto, his mother's favorite, was a charming scoundrel. He led a "*dolce vita*" life, spending his mother's money lavishly, and was often absent from home, flitting between Monte Carlo and Nice. Periodically, he would reappear like a meteor; kiss everybody, charm his mother out of more money, and boogie off again to unknown destinations.

Dimitri (Mimi for short) was a gentle soul. As I mentioned before, he was gay and made no secret about it. He had studied tailoring in France and on his return, opened a successful tailoring business, "L'Homme," at Place Tewfikieh. Both young men treated me like a sister and I loved them sincerely, though my parents were not very comfortable with such non-conventional friends.

Although Ernesto and Mimi did not adhere to the social standards of their times, they were undoubtedly the most loving sons and nephews. They frequently took their mother and aunt out to dinner and to dance at the best Cairo cabarets. I had sometimes gone with them, and it never failed to touch me to tears to see them dance after dinner with their colossal overweight parent. They led with style the elderly women in tango, fox trot and waltz. Nobody laughed at them, for they held them tenderly and even twirled around the massive Aunt Nara before leading her to our table, and kissed her hand when she sat down.

Soon after I arrived, Madame Louise walked in upon us in the kitchen. She clutched me to her massive chest, and gave me a resounding welcome kiss. When Louise asked me, "So what's new, my little girl?" I dissolved into tears. All my pent-up emotions and misery of the preceding days spilled out as I told her all that had happened to us, and why I came to Cairo.

Aunt Nara only wiped her tears and shook her head, while Louise held my hands. She said, "Let it all out, sweetheart. Cry to your heart's content. You needed this. Now, blow your nose, and let us see which way you have to go."

"Well," I said, "tomorrow I am planning to visit the United States Embassy, and find out whether there is a way for me to be granted an immigration visa. This is going to be difficult, for I was born in Egypt."

"Difficult or not, you have to try, little girl. Mimi will accompany you, of course."

To my own surprise, I said, "Thank you, Madame Louise, but I will be going with the doctor with whom I came to Cairo."

"Oh, she said. "First of all, tell me who is this man you came with? Do your parents know him?"

"No," I said, "but Mother agreed to let me go with him because our doctor knows him."

"Hmm," said Madame Louise. "Was he respectful at all times?"

"Yes, yes," I said impatiently. "He was. That is, I knew him from before, but not really,"

"Nara," said Madame Louise, "bring us the brandy bottle. This will probably be a long talk."

I gulped down the brandy and decided to tell her the whole truth.

"Madame Louise," I said, "I am in love with this man. He doesn't know it, but the worst is that he is married. That's it, the whole truth." I then told her every detail, starting with Christmas night, to our trip to Cairo, and then added defensively, "I am going out to dinner with him tonight," and watched their faces as I said it.

Aunt Nara raised her expressive eyebrows and said loudly, *"Dio mio!"* while Madame Louise remained silent for a while. Then she spoke: "Since you are so much in love with this doctor, and he has been respectful with you, I think that you should give him an opportunity to tell you about himself before you decide what kind of man he is. You are a smart girl and you will be able to judge him by the way he will speak and behave. Wipe your tears, put on a pretty dress, and enjoy yourself tonight."

Twenty-Seven

Philippe was already waiting for me when I came down at eight-thirty. We drove along Cairo's glittering streets, alive with people strolling along wide sidewalks. Ambulant merchants were selling everything, from carpets slung across their shoulders to native brew carried in big brass urns. A melting pot of nations going about their business; young people holding hands, families with children, people dressed up to go to theaters, all mingling with natives, some in turbans, and some in red fezzes with a single black tassel, the official Egyptian headwear.

To me, this was a familiar scene, but Philippe was avidly drinking in the colorful pageant, very different from Alexandria, where the Europeans dominated the busy streets.

"What will happen when there will be a war?" he asked. "Will it ever be the same again?"

"We are sitting on the edge of a live volcano," I said. "Egyptians are ready to shake off the European invasion, and I don't know what form their anger will take. Combined with an impending war, this could mean the end of a peaceful era."

Soon, we drove through the large gates of Mena House. Snatches of music were coming from the wide-open windows, lit by muted lights glowing in the dark.

A *suffraghi* (attendant) in a white robe and wide red belt opened the car door for me and we walked up the old wooden steps.

Once inside, we were thrown back some fifty years. The foyer was enormous with a wide circular staircase leading to the second floor of the hotel. Framed photographs of ancient Egyptian art were prominently displayed, lit by concealed lamps.

As we were led to the restaurant, we heard soft piano music playing in the background. Discreetly lit tables were separated by tropical plants, creating islands of privacy, and a polished dancing floor beckoned in the semi darkness. Our table was on a terrace open on three sides to the moonlit garden and the warm night.

As I sat across from Philippe, my heart was melting in my chest. He looked at me, very intently, and I could not take my eyes off him. *Here I am, alone with him,* I thought, *but I must remember not to betray my feelings.*

So I put on my social face and tasted the wine. It was cold and fruity. We talked about things that were not important to us. I don't remember tasting the food. I only remember how his eyes darkened when he looked at me. I quickly reminded myself that maybe he looked at every girl this way, and tried not to feel the joy. I felt we were making small talk, just marking time until dinner was over and we could—what? What could he say to me about himself, about his life, about his wife?

Suddenly, I didn't want to hear him; I did not want him to break the magic of the present moment, when the past and the future were no longer important.

As the waiter cleared the table, we sat quietly facing each other. *How strange this is,* I thought. *Here I am, agonizing to hear the truth about him. How ironic it is that he is completely unaware of my interest and, just because I talked so unguardedly about my own life, he wants to return the favor and spin a tale of whatever will make him look good.*

Our silence was broken by the opening strains of a dance orchestra.

"I would like to ask you to dance," he said, "but not before I tell you something about myself."

"Of course," I said. "Are you going to tell me you are an international spy, and enroll me as an assistant?"

Philippe smiled at my joke, but his expression remained serious.

"Today," he said, "you asked me who was waiting for me at home. Although technically my answer was correct, what you were really asking me was whether I was married. The sad truth is that although I am married, my wife is in a coma from which she might never recover."

I already knew he was married, but my heart came to a standstill for a few seconds. So I blinked my anguish away and assumed a listening attitude, propping my head with my hand.

He took a sip of wine and continued:

"Ours was a happy marriage. My wife, Marie Louise, was a nurse in Pediatrics and we were thinking of starting a family when she became very ill and was diagnosed with multiple sclerosis."

A shadow of pain touched his face as he struggled to dominate his emotions. I sat transfixed by the sober words and the unspoken pain he must have been feeling. I put out my hand, wanting to stop him.

"No," he said. "Let me go on. It is important that I tell you all."

That statement surprised me, but I didn't interrupt as he went on.

"We had her tested, hoping for a miracle, but in just a few months, the terrible disease transformed my beautiful bride into a human shell. Her young constitution fought valiantly the encroaching disintegration of her functions, but finally, it affected her brain and she no longer recognized me, or her parents. After three years, she slipped into a coma. That was five years ago.

"At the beginning, I spent my days by her bedside, but seeing no progress, I sank into depression. My mother was still alive then and she persuaded me to continue my medical practice, and in order not to lose my mind, I started taking assignments in other countries. I worked in South Africa and in the Republic of Congo. A year ago, I accepted an offer to join French Hospital in Alexandria. Every few months, I would return to Belgium, but it was to an empty house. My mother died two years ago, and Marie Louise was still waiting for her release, suspended in her impersonal hell."

When he finished, we both were silent. Philippe had already regained his composure and my astonished mind was refusing to absorb what I had just heard. I felt ashamed of my previous doubts about him, and deeply touched by his trust.

He continued, "No matter how I tried, I still was not able to erase the image of Marie Louise in the hospital asleep in her coma, hoping for a miracle. Only recently, I finally was able to accept the fact that I had lost my wife forever. There is little hope that she will ever wake up, but as long as that remote possibility exists, I will be there for her."

Philippe stopped for a moment, gazing into space, and I thought he had no more to say. But he tasted his wine and continued.

"Slowly, I came back to life again. I plunged into short affairs that left me empty with a bitter aftertaste. But the truth was that I was emotionally starved for real feelings."

I was uncomfortable hearing about his adventures, but I also felt sorry for him, so I held my peace and hoped my little smile was not too pitiful.

He stopped talking, his expressive eyes softening, and said, "Then something happened, which I can never explain. When put into words, it will sound banal, but to me, it was a miracle. I wonder, do you believe in miracles?

I managed a "Yes. Why?"

"Well, that ironic look on your face speaks volumes," he said. "It seems I have already spoken too much about myself, and now you know everything about me. That means, Mademoiselle, that you owe me a dance."

We joined the slow-moving crowd of dancers. Philippe put his arms around me and I melted against him, feeling the light touch of his face against my cheek. His skin was smooth and warm and I could discern a faint hint of lavender. We did not speak as he guided me around the floor, and probably it was my imagination when I felt his arms tighten around me.

After the dance, we walked slowly back to our table. The moon had risen and the garden below revealed paths leading to benches nestling under tall bushes of night flowers.

"Let's take a walk," suggested Philippe, and we went down the Victorian staircase into the fragrant night.

We sat on one of the benches. We were not alone, for we could hear snatches of quiet conversation, somewhere in the semi-darkness.

"Would you like to hear the rest of my story?" he asked. "Since I cannot see your expressive face in the dark, I will not know when you mock me."

"I promise that I will not laugh or judge you," I said.

"Please do not say anything until I finish. This is very important to me. It happened on Christmas night. Being alone that night, I decided to attend the midnight Mass at the chapel of the Jesuit College. Alone in the crowd, I felt anonymous and my thoughts went back to the happy years when there was no pain or sorrow. I tried to recapture the person I was before my life was shattered by hopelessness. I prayed for Marie Louise, I prayed for myself, and I desperately wished for happiness—to be alive again and to overcome the inertia that had dominated my life. I prayed as I had never prayed before. I forgot where I was, lost in my thoughts. After a while, when I opened my eyes, I noticed a young woman standing near me. She, too, was alone, oblivious of her surroundings, praying for something important to her. A single tear glistened on her charming face. A surge of tenderness welled in my heart and I wanted to kiss away her tears. She was unaware of me. I noticed that she had dropped her purse. Impulsively, I picked it up and handed it to her with a polite sentence, which conveyed absolutely nothing of my sudden emotions. Yet, I desperately wanted to give her something to remember me by, if only for a second, so I tucked a small flower into her evening purse.

"I walked away, rebuking myself for being romantic, ashamed of my schoolboy conduct, but I kept thinking about her, wondering who she was."

I clenched my hands, trying to slow down my beating heart as his words echoed my own feelings of that Christmas night. I longed to touch him, to say something, but I had promised not to interrupt, and he continued.

"In the following two months, my mind often went back to the impression she left with me, with a kind of tenderness that one has towards someone you have lost forever. Until that day in the emergency room, where destiny brought you again into my life. When I finally recognized that you were the wet and bloody patient, I felt a surge of hope that life could still hold for me the miracle of love. I discovered that you had not forgotten me, as, in your half-drugged state, you remembered the white flower I gave you. That night, I slipped into your room and sat at your bedside watching you sleep, wondering if you held the key to my happiness. I promised myself that the next day, I would speak with you and ask to see you again.

"Then that night, I received a telegram asking me to return at once to Belgium, as Marie Louise's condition required my presence. When I arrived, I found that she had descended deeper into the coma, and I had to make arrangements to transfer her to another nursing home. That brought home to me the fact that I would be needed to care for Marie Louise as long as she lived. That I was not free. Although she will never recover, her organism still clings to life. She is the woman I loved and married, and I can never abandon her. The tragedy is that her heart is still strong and she may live for many years." Philippe's voice died to a whisper and stopped.

I was silent for a long time. What could I say? That I had also fallen in love with him? Would that change anything? He was not free to love me, and the happiness would only be possible when someone's life would come to an end. I could not imagine wishing someone to die. Would that be the price of our love? Philippe must also have felt the same way, for there was such hopelessness in his voice.

He spoke again. "When Dr. Nazarian asked me to take you along to Cairo, I began to believe in miracles, and that we were destined to meet again. All day today, I tried to read your mind, hoping that I was not mistaken that there was something magical about my attraction to you, and that you had not been indifferent to me."

Since I was silent, he said huskily, "Maybe I should not have spoken at all. Please forgive me."

I could not speak. I believed him. His words touched softly all my dreams.

"Please hold me," I said. "Hold me tight."

His arms wound around me. I could feel his face buried in my hair as we sat for a while, not saying anything. There was no need for words—those came later.

Then he kissed me. Again and again, and held me as if he never wanted to let me go. His kisses tasted of a dream I never forgot.

* * *

On our way back to the city, we spoke very little. He drove with one hand and I sat close to him with my head on his shoulder.

I did not want to think. I just wanted the time to stop, for I knew that there would be plenty of time for thinking and sorrow.

We arranged to meet the next day. I quietly let myself in, took my shoes off and sneaked to my room. My head was spinning and I still could feel Philippe's kisses on my face. I wanted to relive every moment of that evening, and I was glad I had already packed all the necessary documents in my attaché case for the next day's visit to the American Embassy. I did not want to think about Philippe's wife—I thought I would do that later, but that sleepless night, I wanted to savor every moment of my joy. I fell asleep at dawn, giddy with the thought that I was loved by Philippe.

Twenty-Eight

The United States Embassy was located in a spacious villa surrounded by lush gardens. I asked Philippe to wait for me in his parked car outside and I rang the bell at the tall iron gates. A military guard came out and asked me the purpose of my visit. He let me in and I entered the solid-looking front door to the foyer, where white-robed *suffraghis* scurried around, carrying cups of morning coffee to the embassy personnel. A redheaded young man in shirtsleeves came out and asked me, "Can I help you, Miss?"

"Yes," I said. "Could I speak to someone about our immigration status?"

"Do you have some documentation?" he asked

I produced the correspondence I had brought with me, and he disappeared behind one of the closed doors.

After what I thought was an eternity, he emerged again and ushered me into a room where a blond man was sitting behind a cluttered desk.

This one was older, with wire-rimmed glasses and an equally easy manner. He held my papers in his hand.

"What seems to be the problem, Miss Markov?" he said. "It looks like your parents and your sister are eligible for immigration visas for the States. All you need now are the official visas, which, at your request, can be processed within a month. This way, they will be on their way to the good old U.S.A."

I could see that I was dealing with a pen-pusher, not anyone in authority, and I said, "I have something very confidential to say to the official in charge of your political section. Please ask him to see me."

The young man smiled condescendingly and said, "Why don't you tell me, Miss, what this is all about? We all deal with political matters. Maybe I can help you."

But I stood my ground. "Please announce me to your superior officer," I said. "I have to speak to him." All of a sudden, to my great shame, I started crying. Tears poured down my face, which I hurriedly

191

tried to wipe away. To make things worse, the door suddenly opened and a gray-haired man walked into the room without knocking. "Hey, Fred," he said, and then stopped, looking at me sobbing into my hankie.

"What the...?" He looked askance at Fred, who got up hurriedly.

"Well, sir," he said, "I was about to announce this young lady, who wants to speak with you, sir. Apparently, she has something important to tell you."

"Then why on earth is she crying?" He held my chair while I got up. "Come with me, young lady," he said. "Wipe your tears and tell me what this is all about."

Mr. Wright, as was his name, listened attentively while I told him in detail what had happened to Father.

"I don't think I know your father," he said, "but allow me to make a couple of personal calls." While he spoke on the phone, I tried to compose myself, and I asked God to help me. When he put the phone down, his manner became more personable and kind.

He said, "I am told that your father has done some excellent service for the European community and our Consulate in Alexandria. We are always ready to help such valuable people as Captain Markov. However, what you are asking is something out of our hands. Had your father been in need of an emergency visa, there would be no problem. Unfortunately, in your own case, there is no valid reason for your inclusion into a Russian quota. In addition, your parents will not be alone, for I understand that your sister will be traveling with them, and she will be able to take care of them upon arrival in the United States.

"You will be eligible for immigration in about six years, and in the meantime, I think that it will be the best decision to have Captain Markov take advantage of his immigration visa as soon as possible."

I walked slowly back to the waiting car, my heart heavy with disappointment. Philippe read my face. "Bad news?"

I nodded my head. "Nothing's changed. They won't change established rules for me. I have to wait for my quota, and I know Father will never leave without me. I simply don't know what to try next."

"Let's talk more about it," said Philippe. "We can go for lunch somewhere and look at all possibilities." We drove to a Greek restaurant, where we found a table outside, under a wide awning, and I started to relax a little.

"The most pressing problem is to get your parents out of Egypt as soon as possible," said Philippe, "and maybe there will be a way for you to join them sooner from another country."

"How can they survive without me?" I said. "Both Father and Mother will be completely helpless. They don't speak English, and my sister, Jenny, has never worked in her life. She is not as independent as I am, and she always lived a protected life at home. I cannot let them go off without me. I just *must* find a way to go with them."

"I think we should return to Alexandria as soon as possible," said Philippe. "Give me a couple of hours to settle my business at the Ministry, and in the meantime, you can get ready for me to pick you up. There is something important I have to tell you."

"What is it, Philippe? Tell me now. Please. You look so concerned."

"Well, I don't want you to worry, Vicka, but while I was waiting for you outside the Embassy, an unmarked car driven by an officer parked behind me. He came to my car and asked me for my papers. He also asked me why I was waiting for the young woman who walked into the U.S. Embassy with an attaché case. I had to tell him your name, and that you went there about immigration visas."

"They must have been following me after my visit to the Governorate. Yes, let's return to Alexandria as soon as you are ready. I will be waiting for your call."

* * *

We started on our return in the late afternoon. This time, we did not stop for a rest, each lost in unhappy thoughts. The traffic was light, and his hand held my cold fingers. We had no need to speak. During my sleepless night, I had struggled with conflicting emotions of hope, conscience and despair. My head still reeled from the memory of his words and kisses, but the cruel reality was that he was married. I shuddered, thinking that I could be waiting for his wife to die to fulfill my dream. I knew that I could never put myself in that position, and I felt that neither could he. Now my most pressing problem was to convince my parents to leave Egypt without me, and then try to find a way to follow them.

With my mind in turmoil, I must have pressed Philippe's hand hard, for he slowed down and parked off the road.

He put his arms around me and we sat there without speaking for a while.

"Do you want to talk?" asked Philippe. "I have so many things to say to you, and maybe tonight, we can do that after your visit to the hospital."

"Yes," I said. "We can meet tonight, but now I need to plan carefully my parents' safe departure to the United States. Then I need to consult some of my father's Egyptian friends as to how to delay the formalities of a forced Egyptian citizenship."

As I said that, a guilty jolt reminded me of Lume's plight. The tragic events of my father's condition had made me forget all about her, and now the memory of her tear-stained face brought back my concern for her. As we resumed our drive, I told Philippe about her predicament.

"This is terrible," said Philippe. "That friend of yours needs legal help, but since her husband is a lawyer, there is little hope that she will be able to divorce him."

He thought for a while. "Maybe there is another way, Vicka. If your friend still has her valid Albanian passport, she could be included in the group of European nurses who are leaving in a few days. I have a friend at the Belgian consulate, who, I am sure, would help me. But we have to be very careful. Your friend, Lume, should not let her husband suspect that she is leaving him. Let her walk out of the house in just her clothes, not to arouse any suspicion, and you could prepare a small suitcase to take with her on her trip. But I am talking ahead of myself. When I see you tonight, I might have some news for you. Don't tell Lume anything yet, not to raise her hopes, before I see you."

We drove straight to French Hospital, where I found Father asleep, but without the oxygen mask. Mother was at his side with smiling eyes.

"He is better, thank God," she said, hugging me. "Dr. Nazarian said that he will improve, but needs to stay very quiet. Tell me, what have you done in Cairo?"

"Mother," I said, bracing myself for her opposition, "you have to accept that I may not be allowed to immigrate with you at the same time. You must convince Father that I will be able to take care of myself, and that I will join you as soon as I can."

Mother's lips trembled as she tried to control her emotions.

"We will never leave without you," she said. "There must be a way. Only today, Leonid Sisoyev told Jenny that he was leaving for the United States. How could he go? He was also born here, just as you were, at Mustafa Barracks Hospital. I remember, because you both were born on the same day."

"That's incredible!" I exclaimed. "I will call him today and find out how he managed to obtain an immigration visa so quickly."

I hurried home. Jenny was anxious to hear about my visit to the U.S. Embassy. I told her about the disappointing news and then questioned her about Leonid's incredible good luck. I called him immediately and was told how he was able to be included in the Russian quota with his widowed mother.

"I still can't believe it," he said. "When I was called to the U.S.A. Consulate for an interview, I told them about the refugee camp at Tel El Kebir, where my parents lived for a year, and how I was born in a military hospital. Well, there was that young lawyer who said that maybe there was a chance for me to be included in the Russian quota. He said that immigration law allows children born in refugee camps to be included in the parents' national quota. They checked my birth certificate and decided that this law should apply in my case."

"But, Leonid," I said, "they turned me down when I visited the Embassy this morning."

"Well," said Leonid, "they didn't ask you the right questions. You should go back as soon as you can and tell them that there is a precedent, and you can mention my case."

"So all I have to do now is produce my birth certificate to be granted an immigration visa at the same time as my parents?"

"That's right," said Leonid.

"Oh, my God!" I said. "I can't believe it! I'll call the Embassy first thing in the morning. When are you leaving?"

"Next week. We already have our plane tickets and Mother is busy packing. I told her we will not be able to take too many things, but you know how Mother is. But we're getting there. I left our new address in

New York with Jenny. Well, good luck. I have to run. See you in the new world!"

"Good luck, Leonid. Have a safe trip."

Jenny and I were very excited by the good news. We decided not to tell Mother anything, though, until we had confirmation from the Embassy that my case would be re-examined.

* * *

I wanted to be alone. I needed to collect my scattered thoughts. I went out on the sheltered balcony and sought refuge on the old couch, where I used to daydream in happier days. My world was coming apart. I had tried to deal with each pressing problem at the time, while in my mind, I already knew that there was no happy resolution for Philippe and me.

I trusted him, but I realized only too well that it was up to me to make a decision. The pattern was already set and I had to make a choice.

Although Philippe wanted me to stay, I could not abandon my parents until they were safely established in the United States.

Philippe was morally tied to his sick wife—you do not divorce a living corpse.

Could I live happily with him waiting for her to die? Impossible. I knew I could not do it. I did not even want to envision the effect of such a decision on my parents.

Tonight, I needed to have a clear head when we would meet to talk, and I knew I had to be strong when I told him about my decision.

A wave of sorrow washed over me. I remembered his words of love, his kisses and my own overwhelming response to the happiness his presence gave me.

How ironic, I thought. *I have waited all these years for that unique love, and when it happened, it falls on me to end it.* I felt very lonely that night as I saw my dream of love fade away.

* * *

My decision not to give in to Philippe's eloquent arguments was not easy, but once I made up my mind, I felt better. No longer did I feel I was taking away something from Marie Louise, and I gave myself entirely to the magic of my love for him. We met every day, but mostly in public, and I wisely avoided situations that could get out of control, for on rare occasions, when we were alone for a short time, his kisses left me breathless and hungry for more.

I thought La Pergola restaurant would be a good choice for us to talk. Its open windows looked out on the Bay and there was soft recorded music, which allowed for conversation. There was no wind that night, and a shielded candle at our table lit the angles of Philippe's face. I could feel his anxiety as he held my hands. He waited for me to speak

I drew in a deep breath. "Well," I answered his unspoken question, "I have unexpected news."

I told him about Leonid's good fortune, and how it gave me a reason to believe that I might come under the same legal category for an immigration visa.

"Tomorrow morning, I will call Mr. Wright," I said, "and in light of the new information, I will ask him to reconsider my application for inclusion in the Russian quota. He will probably need to have some time to examine my case, but at least this will be a step in the right direction."

"Do you have any idea," asked Philippe, "how long it will take to issue American visas, so that you can make arrangements for traveling?"

"Not really," I said. "But I will certainly ask him."

Philippe looked at me, his face tense with emotion.

"I just can't lose you now," he said. "Not now, not ever. I will follow you, and when your parents will be established, you could come away with me."

He stopped when he saw the expression on my face.

"You know, Philippe, that this is impossible. How can we plan any future life together as long as your poor wife is still alive? Could you do it? I don't think so, and neither could I."

He was silent, holding my hands tightly.

I continued, "Do you think I could tell my parents that I am planning to join you as soon as they are settled, to go live with a man who will marry me as soon as his wife is dead?"

"I love you," he said. "I want to spend the rest of my life with you, have children with you. I loved Marie Louise with all my heart, but she is gone forever, and what is left is a mere shell. It is just a matter of time."

"No, Philippe," I said. "Please don't. While a part of me never wants to let you go, I still realize that we would not be happy under these circumstances."

"Would you wait for me? I know I will always love you."

My eyes filled with tears. "I will always love you, too," I said, "but please do not make any promises now. I learned that we don't control our destinies, and what we have had together has been a gift. But we have to part very soon, and I don't think it would be fair to make promises. If we are meant to be together, then destiny will work another miracle."

He tried to speak, but I put my fingers to his lips.

"You know by now that I will never be able to abandon my parents. It is my turn to take care of them. Neither can I ask you to abandon Marie Louise, who is asleep but is still your wife."

"Please, don't make up your mind now, Vicka," he said. "Let us find a way together. Now that I've found you, I just can't accept this as a final decision."

I was emotionally exhausted and felt my resolution crumbling. "Yes," I said, "but not tonight. Tomorrow. Yes, tomorrow. Now all I want is to be close to you, so let's dance."

We stepped onto the dance floor. I dissolved in his arms and closed my eyes.

Twenty-Nine

The next day I placed a long-distance call to the American Embassy in Cairo.

I had to go through two secretaries before being allowed to speak to Mr. Wright. He sounded slightly surprised when I identified myself, but when I told him about the new development in my case, his tone became warmer and he promised to look into the matter.

Lume was still on my mind, and I went to see her, hoping that Omar would not be home. She was anxious to see me, and I immediately outlined Philippe's daring plan to get her out of Egypt.

As I anticipated, Lume was afraid that the plan would fail and she would be stopped from leaving. She was terrified that when Omar found out that she was abandoning him, he would turn violent. I calmed her down as well as I could and thought that at this stage, we should seek Mrs. B.'s help in arranging a Swiss visa for Lume. Much as I disliked the woman, I believed that in view of Lume's plight, she would be willing to help. Lume agreed to call her and much to my relief, Mrs. B. promised immediately to use her influence, as soon as I would give her more information. Lume looked visibly relieved as I kissed her good-bye.

At the hospital, I found Father in better shape. His oxygen mask was removed and he was conscious, with Mother hovering over him. He looked strong enough for better news and I lost no time in telling both my parents that there was a good chance that I would be able to leave Egypt with them. Father had tears in his eyes and Mother embraced me, asking me over and over again to repeat in detail what Leonid had told me.

Father asked me to make a list of important files he wanted me to pack into the heavy trunks in our storeroom. I was surprised, since I thought we would be flying out of Egypt, but Mother told me that Dr. Nazarian said that due to Father's recent heart attack, he should travel only by sea.

At that point, Jenny arrived and although we still did not have any certitude that I would be granted an American visa, we started planning for our departure from Egypt.

It fell to Jenny and me to pack our large library and put our apartment up for sale. We were to find out about sea travel and prepare books and manuscripts to be censored by the authorities.

I did not tell Father about my earlier visit to the Governorate, and, of course, he did not know that I was identified as his daughter when I visited the Embassy. But I chose not to tell him anything that might worry him. When I came out of Father's room, I was stunned to see Philippe outside talking to Mother.

"Vicka," said Mother, "I was just thanking Dr. Van Dorgen for giving you a ride to Cairo, and I told him of our good news about your being able to come with us to the States."

I could tell from Philippe's face how much this information affected him, and I tried not to look at him.

"Hello, Doctor," I said. "Here we meet again."

"It is a pleasure meeting a fellow doctor from Russia. During our drive to Cairo, your daughter spoke of your ordeal during the Russian revolution. I admire greatly your courage during those terrible years."

I could see that my mother was charmed by Philippe and I wondered whether he had planned beforehand to meet Mother. I was afraid that my parents would find out about my secret, as I did not intend to tell them, at least not then, about our hopeless love. So I hurriedly took my leave and left. Philippe caught up with me in the parking lot.

"This is so sudden," he said. "I just can't think straight. I want to talk to you, to plan for our future, and I feel we have no time. Please, when can we spend some time together? Can you arrange to give us a few precious days, which may be all that we will ever have?"

We got into his car. He put his arms around me and we sat close together, oblivious of the world outside.

"Let me think," I said. I knew then that I had to make a responsible choice that could affect the rest of my life. I became aware that my mind had already been made up.

Philippe waited, silently. The set of his features reminded me of that Christmas night when I first saw him lost in his own dream.

"You are right," I said. "We need to be together for a few days. Since I will have to go to Cairo several times in the next month, I will think of something and we can then decide where we want to spend a few days together. I love you and I really don't know whether there will be a tomorrow for us, but these days will be ours as a beginning or an end."

As I spoke, I could not believe my words. *What happened,* I thought, *to all my principles and determination?* But I chased this nagging thought away as Philippe's lips closed on mine.

* * *

In the next days, Jenny and I started to liquidate the contents of our apartment. We found out we could bring to the United States only $20 per person. No gold coins or gold jewelry. We heard horror stories of passengers being searched at the last minute, and discoveries of gold sewn in the soles of shoes. These unfortunate people were dragged off to Egyptian jails. However, traveling by boat, we were allowed an unlimited number of suitcases. Madame Louise, on hearing about those draconian conditions, told us that she would outfit Mother, Jenny and me with sufficient wardrobes to last us for a year. Mimi arrived one day with three enormous suitcases filled with fashionable outfits. I remember how, in the first years of our life in the United States, Jenny and I enjoyed the luxury of being dressed in the latest fashion, and I often blessed Madame Louise for her last gesture of friendship and love.

* * *

Lume's papers were ready in record time and she was issued a Swiss visa in her maiden name. The day of her departure, I drove in a taxi to her front door, where she was already waiting, dressed in a simple white dress. I had outfitted a small suitcase for her, and Mrs. B. had given her some money and the address of friends in Zurich. We drove straight to the airport, where a group of doctors and nurses from French Hospital surrounded her as they boarded the Swissair plane.

Today Lume lives in the United States. She never remarried.

* * *

Before the month was out, an official letter arrived with the seal of the United States of America. With trembling fingers, I slowly cut open the envelope. Was I accepted, or was it a polite form of regret? I unfolded a single sheet of paper.

It said:

> *We are pleased to inform you that your case has been reviewed and you have been included in the Russian quota. Please present yourself, at your convenience, at our Embassy in Cairo for further instructions.*

Filled with joy and dread, I hurried to French Hospital. Father was by now able to sit in a chair and was chatting with some of his Russian buddies. I found Mother in the corridor with her eternal cigarettes. I grabbed her in my arms and cried, "Mama, we are all going to the United States. I have been accepted in the Russian quota." Then we both went to tell Father our good news. His friends left and we could talk and plan our departure. Father was concerned that he had yet to surrender his gun at the Governorate, and we decided we would do that on the date we visited the Maritime Travel Agency, "Tavoularides," where the manager was Father's long-time friend.

There is no medicine like good news. Soon Father rallied well enough to permit short walks outside the hospital. With Dr. Nazarian's help, he was still sleeping at the hospital, and apart from one or two trips to town with me, he remained there until our departure.

Thirty

When Father and I took a taxi to the passport office, it was crowded, and long lines stretched behind every window. Father was still very weak, but he waited stoically in line with me for the best part of an hour until we had our passports stamped. The official wrote something beneath the stamp and smiled grimly as he handed them back to us. It stated in French, "*Sans retour*"—Without return.

We then proceeded downtown to the shipping agency to pick up our passage tickets for the Greek cruiser, *Ulysses*, that was to take us to Piraeus, where we would board the transatlantic *Olympia* for our nine-day voyage to New York.

We carried with us Father's attaché case containing a large amount of cash to purchase our tickets. Before our account at the Barclays Bank was sequestrated, we were able to withdraw enough money for our expenses. The leather case also held our precious American visas, plus Father's large police gun, in its leather holster, which was to be consigned to his office the same day.

Our taxi driver was waiting for us and we asked him to take us to the shipping company on Sherif Pasha Street, in the center of the busy downtown area.

Father was nervous because we were carrying his revolver. He no longer worked for the Governorate, but had had no opportunity to return it before. During those dangerous days, it was a criminal offense to carry firearms, and people were pitilessly jailed for less than that. However, we hoped that we would soon consign the gun to the Central Precinct before anyone would spot it.

We arrived at our destination and went up the ancient elevator to the third floor of the massive building built at the turn of the century. Greeted by the friendly manager of the shipping company, Father sank into a comfortable chair and turned to me with a smile.

"Sweetheart, let me have the attaché case."

I gave him a blank look. "But you had it...?"

We gazed at each other in horror, unable to speak. While I thought that Father was holding the case, he believed I was carrying it. When we got out of the taxi and paid the driver, neither of us noticed that the case was left behind.

Father leaned back in his chair and closed his eyes. I knew the loss of the case meant that we had lost everything. The case contained our passports, our only identification now, with the rest of our money, our American visas and, more ominously, the service revolver.

There was little hope of the taxi driver ever returning the contents of the case. Even the most honest of men would be too frightened to admit that he had a revolver which could land him directly in jail.

Too impatient to wait for the elevator, I rushed down the stairs and into the busy street. All taxis were yellow, and there were dozens of them speeding in all directions, while I looked around in despair. The sidewalks were crowded with shoppers and peddlers who jostled me. I prayed to God, unable to remember any proper words, hoping He would understand my turmoil and helplessness.

I jumped as a hand grabbed my arm, and I looked into the laughing face of a friend, whose office was in the business district.

"Hey," he said, "what the heck are you doing here instead of packing your belongings?"

I could not contain the tears that streamed down my face as I told him in a few jumbled sentences what had happened.

He questioned me as to whether I remembered anything about the taxi or the driver, but all I could tell him was that we had flagged him up on the street and asked him to wait for us at the passport office.

My friend hailed a passing cab and told the driver to go to the passport office. This was our only clue, weak as it was. Arriving at our destination, we saw a long line of yellow cabs, all identical, all the drivers looking like clones of our fateful driver. We got out of our taxi and started walking towards the waiting cabs.

All of a sudden, one of the drivers thrust his head through his window and shouted, "Mademoiselle, Mademoiselle, where do you want to go this time? I'll take you!"

I thought I would pass out from anxiety. We rushed towards the taxi and my friend quickly opened the back door.

There, flat on the floor, half-concealed under the back of the driver's seat, was our precious attaché case, still bulging with its priceless contents.

I will never forget the expression of disappointment on the driver's face when he saw us pull out the attaché case, as he realized that he had failed to spot it earlier. However, since he did not know what he had missed, after we gave him a generous tip, he happily drove away, while I suddenly remembered that God had indeed heard me, although I had forgotten the proper words of prayer.

I went back to the shipping company, where I knew a moment of pure joy when I handed over the case to my dear father, who just held me in his arms for a while, wiping away my tears.

Thirty-One

By the time Philippe picked me up for our trip to Cairo, my mind had already been made up. I decided I had the right to make my own decisions concerning my personal life without seeking anyone's advice or approval. Since destiny had given me no choice, I felt I owed myself a few days of happiness. I refused to think about the future without Philippe, and that future loomed very near.

As planned, I went to the American Embassy, where I was given four large envelopes with the impressive seal of the United States. Mr. Wright saw me to the door and wished me good luck.

"How much time do we have?" asked Philippe as we drove through the shady streets of Shoubrah.

"Five days," I said. "Five whole days! I told my parents I needed to stay in Cairo a few more days."

"Then let's return at once to Alexandria," said Philippe. "During that time, I want to have you all to myself. We could stay at my chalet on the beach and make plans for the rest of our lives."

I squeezed his hand, too happy to speak, letting my heart expand in my chest.

We reached Philippe's chalet in Mandarah in the late afternoon. After quickly loading the small refrigerator with food and wine, we sat on the balcony overlooking the deserted private beach, sipping our cool drinks. A fragrant breeze wafted from a neighboring garden, as we watched the sun slowly sink into the sea.

"This is the beginning of our life together," said Philippe.

I said nothing. I could not lie to him, for no matter how hard I tried, I was not able to believe that somehow, destiny would bring us together again. *How ironic this is,* I thought to myself. *Only a short while ago, before meeting Philippe, I was an incurable romantic, believing in happy endings. Now, why have I no hope of ever seeing him again?*

Philippe put his arms around me.

"I know you are afraid of being hurt," he said. "I know you trust me, and although we will be separated for a while, I promise I will come back to you. I also know you will wait for me. There is no doubt in my heart. Life in the United States will not be easy at first, but you're strong. I don't want you to promise me anything, but you must know that one day, I will come to you. After you leave, I will apply to go to the Congo again. We'll be in touch all the time, and I want you to write to me about your new life."

Held in his arms, the future happiness seemed possible and real.

There was no moon that night and the dark sky was scintillating with a myriad of stars.

We walked to the water's edge, our bare feet digging into the still-warm sand. I used to love swimming at night in the calm bay. Many parties held on the beach included swimming in the caressing night waters, often warmer than the air. Now, Philippe and I swam towards the natural barrier of smooth rocks.

"Look at that blue star," said Philippe. "It's Sirius, and the small one next to it is his companion."

"And there is the Big Dipper," I said. "How lucky we are to be able to see all that glory in the sky."

"Do you know," he said, "back home we seldom see stars at night because of the fog," but I was not listening.

I felt his arms around me as he held me closer. His mouth found my lips and my body dissolved. We clung to each other. I felt dizzy with longing as he kissed and caressed me, whispering my name over and over. I tasted sea water on his mouth, and his shoulders felt smooth and cool under my hands. I was living again that dream in which he loved me all night.

We spent five intoxicating days making love. Philippe was full of hopes and plans. I listened to him, hoarding every moment for the rainy days. I lived my love to the fullest, not trusting any dreams or future plans. This was my time to love, to live my magic dream that would stay with me always.

We parted on the sixth day, not planning to see each other before my departure. I begged him not to see me off. But Philippe was full of hope for our future, and laughed with happiness, certain that this was only the beginning.

The week before our departure, I filled the time with last-minute arrangements and goodbyes to dear, dear friends. The small Russian community had dwindled to only a few. Most had gone to live in Switzerland, and only a handful, like us, left for the United States.

Loaded with large suitcases, we boarded the *Ulysses*, a beautiful Greek-owned ship bound for Athens, where we were to await the transatlantic *Olympia*, which was to take us to New York.

I stood on the top deck, watching the familiar outline of my beautiful city of Alexandria merge into a faint mirage on the horizon. Philippe had kept his word and did not come to see me off, but as we lifted anchor, I thought I saw his tall figure standing beside a small car in the parking lot. He lifted his hand and waved, and my courage left me and I wept like a child.

My parents were also saying their farewell to a country that had given them shelter for more than thirty years. Each of us had special memories, but for once, I wanted to be alone as I said goodbye to the golden sands of Alexandria. We sailed past the fortress of Kait Bey, built on the ruins of the Alexandria lighthouse, and I remembered the carefree days of laughter and fun spent sailing in those waters.

* * *

After a couple of days in Athens, we left for our nine-day crossing of the Atlantic. We had two comfortable cabins, and I shared mine with Jenny. Both my parents were looking forward to their life in the United States, and Father seemed quite recovered. He had with him his small Russian typewriter and spent hours in a sheltered corner of the deck banging away his impressions of our trip. Mother looked younger, and Jenny quickly made friends with a Swedish couple in the next cabin.

During our crossing, I had ample time to do a lot of thinking and planning. I knew I was going to a country where I could have unlimited possibilities to work and study, but my first concern was to get any job as soon as possible to support our family. I'd had plenty of experience as a secretary but I wanted to use my knowledge of languages to get a more interesting and better-paying job. Settling in New York was a possibility, but I really wanted to go to California, where the climate would be more suitable for Father's health. There was a thriving Russian community in San Francisco, a Russian Orthodox cathedral, as well as many cultural activities which my parents would certainly enjoy. Upon our arrival, we were to be met by one of Father's cousins who lived in Pittsburgh, where we were to stay for the first few weeks. I was planning to borrow money from this cousin, so that we could leave for San Francisco as soon as possible. All this I jotted down in a notebook, where I had a list of people I would contact. I wanted to organize everything up to the last detail, although I was aware that I tried not to think about whether I would see Philippe again. But my nights were full of dreams. I was in his arms once again, his low voice whispering in the dark. Memories washed over me like warm waves, or was it the gentle heartbeat of the huge vessel rocking me to sleep? I knew then that I would wait for him, but would he come to me?

During the days, I would come to my senses and resolve to take one day at a time, following whatever pattern life designed for me. In that mood, I welcomed the sight of the Statue of Liberty as it emerged from the morning fog on July 14, 1958. I was determined to begin a totally new life. I was no longer a carefree person sheltered by loving parents. I was now in charge of our life in the United States and I intended to succeed.

Father and Mother stood nearby, his hands around her shoulders. They were talking quietly, lost in a world of their own memories. A wave of tenderness washed over me. History was repeating itself. Thirty years ago, he had stood with Mother on the deck of another ship, which brought them from a snowbound country to the golden sands of Egypt.

Thirty-Two

Our life in the United States was a series of adjustments for our parents, Jenny and myself. Father and Mother quickly adapted to our new life and changes, mainly because they were received with open arms by the Russian Community in San Francisco. Father was already well known for his articles in the New York and San Francisco Russian press, and he basked in the warmth of his admirers and friends. Those happy years of fulfillment, after our arrival in the United States, were also the last years of his life. In spite of his failing heart, Father valiantly chose not to complain, although he knew only too well that his days were numbered. Jenny and I found employment and although our monetary situation was pretty tight, we were able to live modestly well. I worked for the international branch of Bank of America, and Jenny had a job she liked at Blue Cross, processing medical claims.

Secretly waiting for Philippe, I still had to participate in the social events into which we were plunged from the first day of our arrival in San Francisco. The Russian Center was humming with activities such as concerts, balls, plays and musicals, and celebrated the many festivities and holidays with parties and receptions. My parents and Jenny loved it all, but I just went through the motions, while my inner life was with Philippe, who wrote long letters full of love and hope.

The first few months of my life in San Francisco turned out to be the hardest for me, for I was unhappy in my work, feeling that I was not recognized for the various skills I had previously acquired. I resented being relegated unceremoniously to the rank of a beginner, doing menial clerical work with not even a hint of how I could improve my situation.

At home I had to present a happy countenance so as not to worry my parents, and when I saw them content with their new life, I thought the effort was worthwhile. But while working on mechanical jobs at the bank, in my mind I escaped back to the magical times when I was loved by Philippe. As I typed endless lists, I remembered how it felt when his arms were wrapped around me. Banging away at the typewriter, I wondered if anyone suspected that I was far away, lost in my memories, my face against his chest, tasting the happiness that engulfed all my being. These fantasies kept me from nonstop weeping.

In our wonderful new country, I had had no time to make friends. I did not want to share how much I missed the wonderful days of my life in Alexandria, and the feel of warm sand under my bare feet in the transparent waters of the Mediterranean. San Francisco was cold in the summer and I had to wear my dark-blue coat which dear Madame Louise had made for me. As I stood in the cold wind waiting for the bus to take me home, I clutched at the warm collar of my coat, sending my love and gratitude across the globe to Madame Louise.

Then one day, my small world crumbled around me.

In September of 1960, I received a larger-than-usual package from Congo. As I opened it, I noticed that the writing on the package was not Philippe's, although the address was the same. At first, I could not grasp what the letter was about. I had to read it a second time before the contents reached my brain. The one-page letter from a hospital in Congo, stated that Dr. Philippe Van Dorgen, had died as a result of a snake bite. This had happened suddenly in the night and they were unable to save him. The package contained my letters to Philippe. There was also a clipping from a Brussels newspaper, announcing the death of Marie Louise Van Dorgen after a long illness.

Numb with grief, I tried to cope with my feelings, but at home nobody noticed that I was going through my own private hell, as Father's condition worsened rapidly with a series of heart attacks. I desperately needed a friend, but I had none. I realized at that point how alone I was; in spite of many new acquaintances surrounding us, they were all my parents' friends, because I kept to myself, living in my own secret world. Now Philippe was gone and all that remained were my memories, but I could no longer return to them.

* * *

When I thought that things could not get worse, I was mistaken. A few months after I received the letter from Congo, Father had a stroke and died two days later. Mother tried courageously to bear her loss, but the light had gone from her life. A month later, she died quietly in her sleep.

This concentration of pain and grief were enough to plunge me into a hopeless depression. But fortunately for my sanity, I could not afford the luxury of staying at home with my sorrow, as I had to attend to all the formalities connected with the funerals. Jenny, traumatized by our loss, was unable to help me, and it fell to me to deal with whatever had to be done.

This experience was a catalyst in shedding my weaknesses and insecurities, as I emerged from the depth of depression. I took stock of my present situation and decided not to react, but to plan carefully my future course of action.

I started by enrolling in a series of courses at the bank. These studies paid off and I was transferred to an interesting job, processing lost and stolen travelers checks, which brought me in contact with the FBI, and I started enjoying my work. I also attended evening classes at Dominican College in San Rafael, and acquired a used car to drive across the Golden Gate Bridge.

Jenny advanced in her work at the claims section of Blue Cross, and had her own circle of friends. Now that our parents were gone, our differences became more marked and we gradually drifted apart, and only saw each other at breakfast time. One morning, in September of 1963, Jenny told me that she wanted me to meet a man she had been dating. "He is quite a bit older," she said, "but I like him very much, and he is so very different from anyone I know."

When I met Vladimir, I was delighted with Jenny's choice. A veteran of World War II, Vladimir was a physicist and a mathematician. He walked with a slight limp from a German bullet but declined to talk about it. He lived in Monterey, California, where he taught Russian at the Defense Language School. The way he looked at Jenny left no doubt in my mind that he was head over heels in love with her, while Jenny seemed to bloom from his attentions.

They decided to get married at the end of December, and leave for Montere at once. I started looking for a smaller apartment, but before moving, I intended to send Jenny off with a New Year's celebration party. I had three months ahead of me to plan my party. During that time an unusual meeting took place, although at the time I did not attach any importance to it.

At the bank the head of my department asked me to show the ropes to a new employee, an attractive lady in her mid -thirties. Her name was Marietta. She spoke excellent English with an accent. When I asked her where she came from, she said, "I am of Armenian origin, born in Turkey. When my father died, my mother and I immigrated to the United States. How about you? You also have an accent, but I can't place it. Are you from Poland?"

"Oh no," I said. "I am of Russian origin. I was born in Egypt after my parents were exiled from Russia. I studied in Egypt and in 1958 we immigrated to the United States. Both my parents died in 1961 and my sister Jenny and I still grieve for them. Quite recently my sister met a wonderful man and they are to be married in December."

Marietta and I soon became good friends. It turned out that she lived quite near our apartment and she invited me for a cup of coffee.

The following Sunday I went to visit Marietta. She welcomed me like an old friend and ushered me into a small parlor furnished with old-fashioned, heavy furniture. Gleaming copper artifacts from Turkey decorated the mahogany sideboard. The shutters were closed, but the sun filtered through the wooden slats, illuminating the beautiful rug. The air was redolent with incense and baking cookies. In a corner, a tiny red light burned in front of the image of the Holy Virgin.

"Mother," said Marietta, "I want you to meet my new friend from the bank. Her name is Vicka."

Only then did I notice a tiny elderly lady sitting on a straight chair, with her back to the window.

"Good afternoon, my dear," she said. "Come and sit next to me. Marietta, bring us some coffee and cookies."

As I sat next to her, a pair of startling black eyes examined me. She exuded an aura of tranquility, her hands folded in her lap. Then she took my hand and held it for a while.

"You did not come alone," she said. "Who is that tiny lady with white hair and blue eyes who followed you? It must be your mother, for she brought her love with her." She patted my hand. "She is gone for now, but she is still watching over you."

I was amazed and a little frightened.

"Mother died two years ago," I said, "but you described her very well. I heard that some people do have the ability to see the spirits of departed people, but to tell you the truth, I am rather skeptical about such a gift."

Mrs. Boghossian smiled. "Even as a child I was able to do that. Clairvoyance is not uncommon and should be used very carefully. Unfortunately, ignorant people use this ability to make money, with the result that they lose their gift. I told you about your mother's presence near you because she wants you to know that she will always be close to you, though invisible."

I was stunned into silence, not knowing what to say. Inwardly, I was blaming myself for having told Marietta too much about my life.

Marietta brought a tray with small cups of fragrant Turkish coffee and a plate of sesame cookies. When I lived in Egypt everybody drank Turkish coffee, and I was delighted to see that Marietta had made it properly, with a thick froth floating on the surface. Made correctly, the coffee is brought to a boil three times, and the foam is distributed equally between two or three tiny cups before filling them with coffee.

I sighed with pleasure. Mrs. Boghossian nodded in understanding. She said, "My daughter told me you lived in Egypt. Maybe this coffee will remind you of days gone by."

We sipped our coffee in silence. The rich, strong taste brought a rush of nostalgic memories. I let them wash over me, lost in remembrance, while my companions sat very still. When I finished, I automatically swirled the dregs in my cup, turning it upside down on the saucer. As soon as I realized what I had done, I tried to explain.

"I apologize, Mrs. Boghossian," I said, "for reverting to my Egyptian habits of reversing the cup on the saucer. We always did that among friends, pretending to be able to read our destiny at the bottom of the cup."

Mrs. Boghossian laughed and said, "I know. It is always done among friends. But in addition to reversing the cup, you should be turning it three times on the saucer, so that the cup adheres tightly to the saucer. When you do that, you should be thinking of what you would like your future to be."

I promptly turned the cup three times to show I was a quick learner. Then we talked about politics, the price of meat, and Marietta's new job.

After an hour I was about to rise and leave, when Mrs. Boghossian laid a restraining hand on me. "Don't leave just yet," she said. "Let me have a look at your coffee cup."

She took the cup that had stuck to the saucer. "Well, well," she said. "You are about to encounter a strong love."

She pried the cup from the thick residue and held it upside down, counting the drops that rolled down on the saucer. Three in all.

"What I will tell you," she said, "will happen within the count of three. It can be three days, three weeks or three months."

I settled back, enjoying the familiar ritual of having my future read in a coffee cup. A long time ago, I also pretended to read my friends' futures this way. It was fun, especially when I knew all their little secrets.

Mrs. Boghossian peered into the cup, turning it in her hands. She spoke slowly, distinctly, her face a study in concentration.

"I see a great tragedy, but it is like a black cloud floating away from you and will not affect your life. Something else is awaiting you. Your life is about to change completely. Your destiny will be tied to a stranger who will come to your door. He will never leave. You will marry him very soon. I see you together living in a place with many trees. You will see many horizons with him. You will be very happy with this man for many, many years. At present your heart is full of another man, but I do not see him beside you. That is all."

"Why, thank you, Mrs. Boghossian," I said with a forced laugh. "What a lovely prediction."

"Don't thank me, my child," she said. "I am happy to see that fate has a good life in store for you. Your destiny is with a man you have not met before, but you will know him when you see him." She added with a kind smile, "Life is full of surprises."

I hugged the mother and daughter and took my leave, pretending to believe in fortune telling.

That was September 1963.

On November 22nd of that year, President Kennedy was assassinated. All life seemed to be put on hold as we walked around, stunned by our national loss. During that time, Marietta and I became good friends, often meeting at our lunch break. I visited Mrs. Boghossian a couple of times, but we never spoke about her predictions. By that time I had completely forgotten the incident with the Turkish coffee. She shared with me her collection of succulent Middle East recipes, which I still treasure, and I enjoyed hearing about her life in Turkey.

I was delighted that I would be living alone, for, in spite of Mother's urgings, Jenny and I never succeeded in getting along. As planned, I had decided to celebrate New Year's 1964 with a farewell dinner for Jenny at our apartment. We were to be ten couples, and it was a potluck affair.

Our dining room table was extended into the living room to seat ten couples. These were all Russian friends, mostly married couples, with the exception of our neighbor, Vera. Since I had no seating companion, my brother-in-law promised to bring a bachelor friend, but there was no partner for Vera. I appealed to Ilya, a married friend, to provide Vera with a suitable stand-in, and he volunteered to bring along a friend. He said, "There is this guy whom I have known for years. He is a Russian who arrived from Venezuela only a few months ago, and he might be free. He is divorced and is reputed to have a nasty temper. Still, he will do if we can't find anyone else for Vera."

"Great," I said. "Tell him to bring a bottle of champagne and some smoked salmon. Also tell him to come at ten o'clock." Then I called Vera and teased her about getting a mystery partner.

Vera was all excited. "Who is he? How old? Is he handsome? Oh, I know, he is probably as weird as they come. I have been so unlucky in my dates lately."

On the eve of the party, I was very busy with last-minute preparations. My sister had arrived from her honeymoon that very same afternoon and was not much help, and neither was her husband. They were at that silly stage of holding hands and kissing, while my promised partner turned out to be a former monk. While I was spinning like a top, he was trying to get me aside for a heart-to-heart talk, explaining why he decided to quit the church.

I am afraid I was rather impatient with him. What I needed most at that moment was some help with getting more ice, moving my record player out of the way, and picking up more chairs from my landlady.

But he followed me from the kitchen to the dining room and back, spinning the tale of his woes.

From time to time he would ask me, "What can I do? Please tell me." He did not wait for my answer but would continue his spiel of misfortunes, without noticing my lack of interest.

At ten o'clock my friends seemed to arrive at the same time. There was a moment of bedlam, when all kinds of food ended up piled up in the kitchen. There was a lot of work to be done before it all came together. The girls helped while the men, typically enough, stood around greeting each other, catching up on the latest gossip.

The doorbell rang again. I ran to open it. It was Ilya with his wife, Olga, and a stranger. As I welcomed them, I got a quick look at the stranger, and liked what I saw. A strong nose and a stubborn chin on his tanned face bespoke a decisive nature, while bright-blue eyes danced under generous blond eyebrows. Ilya said, "Vicka, I would like you to meet George, who is a newcomer from Venezuela. He is usually very pleasant, but lately he has become quite boorish. I hope that tonight we can cheer him up."

George, in the process of bowing over my hand, as is our Russian custom, smiled and said, "How can I be boorish in the company of such a lovely lady?" He had not quite finished his sentence when he dropped one of the bottles of champagne he was carrying. It shattered and splashed all over the place.

As I looked aghast, he quickly asked, "Where is the kitchen?" I pointed in the right direction, where he disappeared. He surfaced immediately with a mop and a roll of paper towels and proceeded expertly to clean up the foaming wet mess.

"See," he said, "nothing happened. I have another bottle." He gave a big smile and his eyes twinkled. "It is your fault for being so attractive. I am usually very adroit at carrying two bottles of champagne while kissing the hand of a pretty hostess. Aren't you going to invite me in? Ilya brought some dancing records. Since you are going to be my partner, may I have the first dance?"

"Wait a moment," I said when I could catch my breath. "First of all, you are not my partner at all. Your partner is my friend Vera. Oh, here she is. Vera dear, I want you to meet George, who is very good at smashing champagne bottles. He is also an expert at fast talking, something he must have picked up in Latin America."

Vera zeroed in on to the pushy stranger and ignored my irony. "So you are the mysterious George," she said. "Let's go to the bar and have a couple of drinks. Vicka is very busy now." She gave me a conspiratorial smile. "By the way, dear, your partner is looking for you. He says he has not finished telling you about himself."

But the stranger with laughing eyes thrust the other bottle of champagne into Vera's hands, saying, "What a good idea. Let's all have a drink. It has been a bad year for everybody and we must chase the old year out. Why don't you get us some glasses, Vera, so we can toast 1963 on its way out?"

A reluctant Vera disappeared into the kitchen and we both laughed. Suddenly I felt very much at ease with this unconventional export from Venezuela. We started talking, asking and answering questions, oblivious to the bustle around us. Eventually I joined the party, with George following me closely. At dinner we sat next to each other and talked, but I remember nothing about the rest, except Vera's snide remark, "With friends like you, I don't need enemies." I was told later that everybody had a good time, that the food was fabulous, and that there was dancing and singing until the wee hours of the morning.

When everybody left, I made some breakfast while George washed the dishes. Then we packed a picnic basket and went to the beach. We slept on the sand for a few hours, then resumed our talking. There was much to say. George spoke about his childhood, about his parents and the difficult years of Russian exile in Poland, where they were barely tolerated. The school years, the terrible day in 1939 when Germany occupied Poland. He spoke of being torn from his family to labor in prison camps; of bombs, cruelty and loneliness. He found humor in special situations when he was, at last, able to escape. The memory of kind people who helped him turned his blue eyes dark, and I knew then that I would never let him go.

He wanted to know all about me, and I told him. I talked about Philippe, and he held my hand when I finished. Then he told me about his unhappy marriage. We alternated asking questions, comparing our destinies during the difficult years of world turmoil.

It was turning cold, but we were not ready to leave the beach. We wrapped a blanket around our shoulders and sat watching the pink clouds. He put his arm around me and tucked the blanket around us. I leaned against him, feeling secure and safe. I watched out of the corner of my eyes how the setting sun lit the angles of his pensive face. It felt so right to be with this stranger, and I was surprised to remember that I had met him only hours ago.

He said, "Most of my life I was waiting for you, but every time it turned out to be someone else. How can we be sure? I don't know, but I feel that I have come home at last." He kissed me tenderly and there was no need for words.

He said, "Let's make a pact. Our lives will begin a new chapter today. Let us not dwell on our past unhappiness, but rather on the present while planning our future."

The sun was setting and we had polished off the sandwiches and drunk all the flat champagne, and it was time to go. We drove home, happy to be in each other's company.

The rest is history.

At that point I was too stunned with what was happening to my feelings to remember Mrs. Boghossian's prediction. Marietta brought it back to my mind when I returned to work. It was lunchtime, and I was sharing with her my impressions of New Year's Eve.

"I met an incredible man," I said. "He just walked into my life and changed it."

Marietta opened her eyes wide. "Oh my God! This must be the stranger Mother saw in your coffee cup. Tell me! Is he handsome? Did you just fall in love with him on sight? Have you seen him again? Did he declare himself?"

"No, Marietta, it is not like that. Although he is good-looking, that is not what attracted me. It's something deeper than mere looks. It's what he is, which comes from a simple way of expressing himself, and of speaking about his life. When we talked we seemed to understand each other without unnecessary explanations and posturing."

I stopped and laughed. "Here I am trying to explain something so special. Words are so inadequate to describe how close I felt to this stranger."

Marietta giggled. "Did he kiss you? Did you swoon in a passionate embrace?"

"No, my romantic friend," I said. "He only hugged me and gave me a chaste kiss when we finally said good-bye." I lied, of course, but thought that I did not have to tell her about our dinner that night at the Fairmont in San Francisco, when we danced cheek-to-cheek and he kissed me.

"So when are you seeing him again?" asked Marietta. "I must tell Mother about it. She will be happy for you."

"Well," I said, "I was not going to tell you at first, but we decided last night that we would spend all the coming days of our lives together."

And so it was. Today, forty-six years later, I can confirm that we have spent all our days together. Those happy years went by quickly, and today, although endowed with quite a few wrinkles and gray hair, I don't see them when I look at the laughing blue eyes of my husband and my friend.

Looking back on our long life, I am still amazed at the boundless energy and imagination which drove George to make every moment count, in our daily life and in the discovery of the many countries we visited. When we met I had just turned forty and George was one year older.

Soon after we married I went to work for a private school, where I taught French. At the same time I continued my studies in French and Russian literature, and those were fulfilling years for me.

George continued working for a large engineering company in San Francisco. At school I enjoyed three-month vacations and we traveled extensively to Europe, South America and Australia. Due to George's ability to communicate in Spanish, we were fortunate to make many friends in Latin America. Although George spent a large part of his early life in France, he felt more at home in the many countries south of the border. Not speaking Spanish, during our first year together, I was relegated to the status of a decorative plant when we traveled in those exotic and interesting countries. Therefore, I quickly made up my mind to learn that language – pronto. I started taking courses in Spanish, and after three years of shamelessly distorting grammar and mispronouncing words, I was able to communicate freely, if not perfectly, with our Spanish-speaking friends. My newly-acquired skills benefited greatly from a major decision in our life, which occurred, typically enough for us, as an unplanned and rapid event.

It all started in the summer of 1979, when George and I crossed the frontier at Tijuana and drove south, down the Baja Peninsula, along Mexican Highway 1.

After twelve exhausting hours of negotiating dangerous curves in the mountainous road, trying to avoid potholes and wandering cows, we found ourselves in the quiet city of La Paz, on the shore of the Gulf of California, also known poetically as the Sea of Cortez. From there we planned to take the ferry to mainland Mexico to visit Guadalajara and return home via Nogales.

However, destiny decided otherwise. That day, after checking into Las Gardenias, a charming, clean motel, we decided to walk down to the Malecon, a long, palm-studded avenue skirting the Bay of La Paz. Here we found an abundance of small restaurants, and we chose Las Palmas when we noticed several Mexican families already seated comfortably around small tables, happily eating something succulent, while an appetizing fragrance of cooked seafood wafted in our direction.

"Looks good to me," said George, as we were installed at a small table right on the beach, while I burrowed my sandaled feet into the warm sand. An eager waiter appeared with a handwritten menu and George proceeded to translate it. The prices were so ridiculously low that I decided to pick the most expensive item.

"Camarones Imperial," I decided, "should be good. However, I would like to know what camarones are?"

"Camarones are shrimp or prawns," said George, "but we will have to ask the waiter what 'Imperial' is.

We found out that Camarones Imperial was a fragrant shrimp dish redolent of garlic and herbs, with just enough hot red chilies to suit our taste.

So while enjoying our food and sipping the good Corona beer, George and I decided, on the spot, that it would be a great idea to build our second home right there in La Paz.

There was no need to cancel the reservation for the ferry, as it turned out that "due to unexpected problems," the ferry was not operating until further notice

We immediately started exploring the business center and soon were able to locate a real estate agency, and it was then that we found out that in Mexico, nothing is done in a hurry. To make a long story short, it took us two months and three trips by air to La Paz before we found a suitable building lot for our dream house. By that time we were completely inoculated and acclimatized to the idea that there is never any need to hurry or get upset at the slow motion of all business dealings, as there is nothing one can do about it, so better slow down and enjoy life.

While our initial plan was to have a small casita, the result was an apartment of four units for rent and a penthouse for us. This turned out to be an ideal solution for us and for fifteen happy years, we blissfully lived between La Paz and our home in Santa Rosa. George enjoyed himself immensely during those years, managing our rental business. As for me, a new world opened for me as I learned Spanish and made lifelong friends.

Today, my friend Gloria is the nearest I have to a daughter. I learned from her all about the traditional values that hold Mexican families together, and the unbreakable bonds of grandparents to grandchildren. During that time we became accepted into the small, conservative circle of La Paz society. These were families who were often descendents of the English pirates who settled in that pleasant remote part of Baja, with such names as Fisher, Miller and Douglas. The descendents of these adventurers formed the solid nucleus of wealthy merchants and tradespeople, sending their children to universities in mainland Mexico or in the States.

I have been able to publish a memoir of the fifteen years we spent in La Paz, and although we were already in our retirement years, that time was the happiest and most productive years of our lives.

I have been blessed with wonderful friends all my life, and although destiny had not given us close relatives, the warm friendship of our many friends has created a circle of love around us.

* * *

After our definitive return from Mexico to Santa Rosa, it was time to fulfill a promise I had made to my dear father. He had asked me to visit our family nest in Russia. Now that the Communist era was happily a thing of the past, I began to make preparations for that long trip. It was very important to me, as I was the last living member of that old family tree, and I needed to pray and meditate on the destroyed remnants of the Pokrovskoye estate, in the Province of Kursk.

Lev Markov and his bride Victoria, on their wedding day 1889

Nicholas, Sonia and Anatole Markov, 1898.

Anatole Markov in full dress uniform of the Savage Division, 1915.

Dr. Eugenia Markov at New Year's celebration in Baiburt, 1918

Eugenia von Eggert, medical student, 1913.

Vicka Markov, 5 years old in Alexandria, 1926

Vicka Markov at Siuf, Alexandriam 7 years old, 1928.

Anatole Markov with daughters, Jenny and Vicka, 1930.

Captain Anatole Markov in uniform of the Anglo-Egyptian Police, 1935.

Vicka and Vuko 1942

Vicka with Father 1943

Markov family, Anatole, Eugenia, Jenny and Vicka, 1944

Vicka at St. Catherine's Monastery, 1956

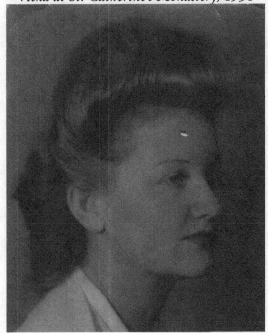

Jenny 1945

Vicka Markov - 1945

Anatole Markov

PART III

One

On May 31, 2005, I checked in at the Lufthansa counter for my trip to Russia and as I was going through the security gates, my mind was already in Russia, creating various scenarios. I was awakened from my daydreaming by an unpleasant *ping-ping*. Before I knew it, I was being dragged aside to a cubicle. After I explained that I had an artificial knee and the attendants determined that I had no gun on my person, I realized that my purse and the carry-on had disappeared. I was instructed not to move from my chair while the attendants scurried in all directions, trying to locate them. I helplessly watched the other lucky passengers as they snatched up their belongings, while I hoped that I would not miss my flight.

Every black bag looked exactly like mine and I was thankful that I had tied my precious dollars around my waist. I did not even want to think of what had happened to my clutch containing my passport and reading glasses.

Then an attendant rushed at me and shoved my hand luggage into my lap. She ordered me to go "quickly" while I was struggling to put on my shoes, which did not contain any explosives, after all.

On the plane, once safely in my aisle seat, I offered a quick prayer of thanks for getting me to that point without any damage. I glanced at my next-seat neighbor and said "hi." I was rewarded by a friendly grunt from a cute Japanese girl, who was devouring a breakfast burrito. I was relieved to have been given such a tiny neighbor for the long flight to

Frankfurt. Then, after some small talk, she immersed herself in a book and I closed my eyes.

I turned my mind to the overdue pilgrimage to the land of my parents and ancestors. I was both excited and apprehensive. Here I was, all alone, having left my dear husband and my cat at home in Santa Rosa, California, going for the first time to the country which my parents left in 1920, having had strong disagreements with an *experimental* philosophy of Communism, which was to hold Russia in bondage for eighty years.

My father, who had waited all his life for Communism to end, died in 1961. A talented writer, whose books and newspaper articles were full of hope, he instilled in me respect and love for a country I had never known. Several years before, I had sent a box of his published memoirs to Kursk, where he was born. Now, at the sunset of my life, I was about to fulfill his dream for me to visit the cradle of our family in the city of Kursk, the fertile territory south of Moscow. My cousin Sergey, who lived in Moscow, was going to meet me on my arrival.

Armed with advice from all my good friends as to what would be of invaluable help on my journey, I mentally went over the list of recommended items such as Kleenex, toilet paper and numerous small gifts for unknown recipients. I smiled indulgently over this presumably unnecessary list, not even suspecting for a moment that I would later bless my friends for their invaluable advice.

Soon the shades were pulled down, we settled for the night and I dozed off.

We changed planes in Frankfurt and finally, three hours later, my plane was approaching the Sheremetievo airport. Looking down at the green landscape seen from above, my heart was beating fast. *Here I am at last in Russia*, I thought. *How pleased my parents would have been to know that I was returning to a country free of Communism.*

Rushing along with the other passengers towards the baggage carousel, I wondered whether my cousins would be able to find me. Sergey was my fourth cousin, descended from my great-grandfather's brother. Although we were remote cousins, in reality, he and his wife, Tanya, were the closest in spirit to me, and it took only two weeks for my husband and me to adopt them forever when they visited us in the States in December of 2004. It was at their insistence that I decided to take that long trip to the motherland, and I was going to stay with them in their apartment in Moscow.

I worried in vain, for there among the anxious crowd behind the glass partition, I saw Sergey, towering above all the rest, smiling and waving at me. Soon I was engulfed in his arms. His gray eyes were moist as he crushed me in his arms. Sergey looked much younger than his sixty years; his handsome face was unlined and he boasted a thick mane of silver hair.

"Tanya is waiting for us at home," said Sergey. "She went home early to prepare for your arrival. Now, let's get your suitcases and get out of here!"

Sergey was a metallurgical engineer, semi-retired, still working in a consulting capacity with Swedish and German companies, and was also involved in a scientific oceanography project with Anton, Tanya's son from a first marriage. Sergey had watchful gray eyes and was a good listener. He was an organizer and there was not a detail of their life which he had not thought over. He had planned the whole three weeks of my stay to the minutest detail. Only later did I understand the extent of his planning of the time I was to spend in Moscow, St. Petersburg and Kursk.

The weather was cool, and I was ready to enjoy and discover Russia. Sergey's Ford was parked in the open-air parking lot. The vast area was filled to capacity with all kinds of vehicles, mostly made in Russia with a sprinkling of German luxury cars. I was loaded into Sergey's Ford with my two suitcases and off we went on the Garden Highway, one of the three highways circling Moscow.

Sergey, very proud of his city, wanted me to absorb a lot of details all at once, and decided to take the long way home so that I could get the feel of Moscow. My first cultural shock was seeing all the names and directions in Russian, which I could read, of course, but apart from that, everything was pretty much the same as we had it in the States. Well, to tell the truth, not quite the same, as two cars were overtaking us at the same time, making illegal maneuvers. Sergey skillfully avoided bashing into them, without even a swear word, with which the Russian language is particularly rich.

The cell phone rang. It was Tanya, reprimanding Sergey for not bringing me home right away. So we took the nearest cut-off and, after plunging into the downtown traffic and taking a couple of turns, we arrived at the street where they lived.

While the broad streets were in perfect condition, this could not be said for the small side streets where the citizens parked their cars. Broken potholes and puddles of recent rain made it difficult to navigate, but Sergey managed to steer like a pro, and in no time, we were standing before an old apartment building. The front door was of scarred solid wood with two keyholes and some buttons which, when punched, revealed an iron door. After some manipulation, the door opened inward to a dark entry hall with a stone stairway leading to the first floor. A dank odor assaulted my nostrils. Sergey supported me while I attacked the first high step, clinging to the shaky banister. We stopped at the first landing, and here I discovered an elevator, a steel box with a temperamental door which closed up on the unwary passenger, and did not cooperate when I tried to put my hand out to keep it from slamming shut. While we were shuddering to the third floor, my dear cousin lectured me about the dangers of trying to stop the elevator door. When we arrived, I was wise enough to hurry out on the dark landing, happy to be in one piece.

The apartment door was flung open; that is, the two doors—the outer and the inner one—with locks that would be the envy of New York apartment dwellers, and I was smothered in Tanya's arms.

Tanya was a doctor of biochemistry, teaching at the Mendeleev School of Chemistry. She was absolutely beautiful. Of average height, her honey-blond hair framed her lovely face and intelligent hazel eyes, which darkened with every emotion. She was in her early fifties, but looked much younger, and was feminine, warm, kind and very efficient. Tanya managed her little world with an economy of effort, spoiling her dictatorial husband, whom she adored.

Tanya had that wonderful ability to calm the atmosphere around her, and as I entered their apartment, I felt I had arrived where I was most welcome. The round table in the kitchen overflowed with Russian hors d'oeuvres and brown bread nestling in a basket, while a crystal jar of red caviar invited the eye towards a bottle of iced vodka, promising numerous toasts for the tired voyager.

I was shown around the small apartment. It consisted of two rooms, one a fairly large one with a tiny balcony, and another, a guest room which was to be my bedroom for the stay. A large couch was opened to a bed and, *voila*, I was hanging my clothes in the family closet out in the hall. Near the entrance hall was a row of shoes, as all the floors were polished wood parquet, and I submitted obediently to the new custom, shuffling in a pair of borrowed slippers. An enticing aroma of fresh bread reminded me at once that I was hungry. I tried to absorb the details of the plans that Sergey had made for me: the first week in Moscow, the second week in St. Petersburg and the five-day trip to Kursk with three of my relatives whom I had yet to meet in person. Then the doorbell rang and I was happy to meet Irina again, their daughter-in-law, whom I had already met in the States when she came to visit us while on assignment to New York.

Irina was thirty-five, petite, blonde, and seemed to be always in a hurry. She was Masha's mother, a rosy-cheeked twelve-year-old who materialized at her mother's side. She appeared to be older than her age, until you saw her laughing, limpid blue eyes, ready for fun at any time. She stayed by her mother, as if in a protective stance, while the latter poured out the reasons for not having met me at the airport.

Irina was a product of the new Russia. She was a professor of virology (study of viruses) and her life was a whirl of assignments, both in Russia and abroad. She was married to Anton, who had a doctorate in oceanography. He researched the life of different seas, but not the oceans, he told me. So his travels took him to different seas of the world, where they were fighting a losing battle with the pollution of the seas.

Two

I met Anton on my second day in Moscow when he popped in to say "hi" to his mother, Tanya, on his return from Bulgaria. Anton was an oversized specimen of a man, his young face framed by a well-kept auburn beard. His brown eyes were kind and curious as he greeted me. He had not yet been home but his first visit was to his parents, as he not only adored his mother, but also was his adoptive father's best friend and co-worker. Although Sergey was semi-retired, he was also a member of Anton's research team on an unofficial basis.

When he left, Tanya told me all about the young couple and their problems. Apparently the marriage was shaky, as they were not giving enough time to their daughter, Masha, who was mature enough to have told them that she needed more of her parents' physical presence than they were giving her. Anton blamed Irina, who felt that she had to fulfill her professional agenda by achieving yet another step in her career—a full professorship—in order to keep up with her husband. Tanya got very emotional while telling me about her son and his wife. I got the feeling that Tanya was definitely taking sides with her adored son.

She was obviously backing up her giant Barbarossa of a son, while I listened without comment, feeling sorry for the hustled Irina, who was torn between her career and her family. Obviously Anton's shortcomings were not discussed, and it was the same story the world over: the daughter-in-law was never good enough for the cherished son. I was glad that Masha, at least, seemed to be her mother's best friend.

My first white night in Moscow was a disaster. The light through the flimsy window shades told my tired senses that it was daytime. I knew that it was the season for the "white nights," when complete darkness never falls over that part of the world. The grandfather clock in the room struck 2 a.m. I couldn't sleep, although I was very tired, and I took trips to the unfamiliar bathroom along the dimly lit corridor, the pleasant fragrance of waxed floor assailing my nostrils.

At six o'clock I was all dressed up and staring at the portrait of some distant relative on the wall from across my bed. Seven o'clock, 7:30,

8:00, 8:30, and finally at 9:00, a smiling Tanya appeared at my door, worrying whether it was too early for me.

I followed her gratefully to the kitchen and tried to familiarize myself with the electric teapot, a definitely different gas stove, and the location of all items needed for breakfast.

This was a working day for Tanya, but in spite of my protestations she insisted on giving me an "American" breakfast. She deftly produced a two-pound slab of bacon, which she cut into half-inch cubes. She fried the cubes in a skillet and when it was half-full of melted pork fat, she threw three eggs in and stirred them around, while I watch speechlessly, my mind working overtime, trying to calculate the amount of cholesterol I was about to ingest. I must have said something which might have sounded like "Oh boy!" when Tanya piled it all on my plate and said smilingly, "Don't worry, sweetheart, the eggs are not as harmful as they thought once, and they will give you plenty of nourishment."

Sergey appeared at the door in an Afghan kaftan, while Tanya kissed us good-bye and disappeared behind the two doors.

Sergey ate kasha with milk, and when he was finished, asked, "Where is my breakfast, woman?"

So, since I had not touched my "American" breakfast, I asked whether he would like to try the bacon and eggs.

"Tanya starves me," he said, eyeing my offering, "because that idiot of a doctor told her I have a heart condition."

Then one of the three telephones started ringing. Two of them were cell phones and they all had different chimes. When on occasion I was left alone, I was told to answer them and write down the numbers. That resulted in me rushing from the hallway to the bedroom or to the kitchen and back, and invariably, I was too late to catch some of the calls.

By the time Sergey emerged from his telephone conversation, I had his American breakfast heated, minus one egg, which I devoured because I was very hungry.

Sergey ate it all up and complimented me on my cooking skills, but said he was still a little hungry, so he pulled various goodies out of the big refrigerator. There were several kinds of salted and pickled fish, some red caviar, a couple of tomatoes and the remains of a crumbly cake. He said it was a Georgian cake and one didn't need a knife to cut it. He showed me the technique by pinching off a great lump of the crumbly sticky stuff, which he polished off, washing it down with a pint of milk. He then produced a plastic box filled with different prescription medicines, some of which he swallowed religiously.

"You know, Vikulia," he said, "I am a very disciplined man, and when the doctor tells me that I have to take pills, I follow his advice to the letter."

In the evening, Tanya returned home from work. It was the end of the school year and graduation time at the Institute, with all the busy chores that it involved. There were meetings and last-minute reports, late decisions and sessions with her many students. Still she optimistically brushed off her problems and cheerfully started to prepare dinner, listening as her husband outlined for me his program for the next day.

Born and bred in Moscow, Sergey was eager to show me the many wonders of this ancient city. The next day, we drove along the ancient Kremlin walls, which have surrounded Moscow since the fifteenth century. Kremlin was also the present seat of the Russian government, where Mr. Putin had his office.

We took many photographs and admired the architecture of stately mansions that had escaped the destructive hand of Communism. The Moskva River had several bridges, and we walked across some of them to get the feel of history. We stopped for a long time in front of the magnificent churches, and entered the Cathedral of Christ the Savior, which was recently restored from the foundations up, since Stalin had demolished the old building and turned the ground into a swimming pool. Now, with the help of the people of Moscow and many donations from abroad, the Cathedral rose in all its glory, every detail duplicated. It took but a few years for artists and artisans to replicate the icons and the mosaics destroyed by the Communists, a testimonial to the great faith of the Russian people.

On the third night, I still could not shake off the jet lag. The feather bed was too warm and the pillows were probably stuffed with rocks. Thank God for the small neck pillow I bought at the drugstore back home, which, if folded twice, felt as if I were back in my own bed in Santa Rosa.

The next evening, Tanya organized a family reunion. Three of my relatives were invited to see me: my grand-niece Elena, from my Aunt

Sonia's side of the family, my third cousin Ludmila, and my fourth cousin Lisa. I had previously met Ludmila, a.k.a. Lulya, in 1990 in Mexico. She was a botanist, specializing in rare plants, and at the time I was happy to have met at last one of my family from the Soviet Union, but I was disappointed when she turned out to be a dyed-in-the-wool Communist. At the time my best intentions turned to annoyance when she argued bitterly that Gorbachev was a Western lackey trying to please the rest of the world at the expense of the Soviet Union. I think she was disappointed in me and labeled me as having "sold out" her country. So I was not looking forward to meeting Lulya again, but decided to be tolerant, at least for the time being.

When Lulya arrived for the evening's festivities, we all welcomed her warmly and she even smiled. Her mouth was a bleak study in sepia, showing only two remaining front teeth on a dark cavernous background. She was brandishing her gift for me: a bottle of Georgian champagne.

The fourth cousin, Lisa, turned out to be very pleasant. She was an engineer working for the telephone company, and I was interested to hear about her life. She was married with two sons, but complained that they were unemployed most of the time.

Another relative, Elena, was supposed to come too, but called to cancel at the last minute, complaining of high blood pressure. Her voice, rather low and hoarse, seemed full of love and emotion, but Tanya and Sergey told me right away that Elena was completely drunk and that it was just as well that she did not appear. Lisa, who diagnosed Elena's flow of apologetic love as drunken drivel, confirmed that Elena was unusually partial to gin and tonic.

We had a pleasant time, enhanced by vodka and the usual trimmings. A succulent berry and almond tart crowned the evening meal. Lulya behaved herself and I was ready to decide that she was a born-again Russian, when Lisa whispered in my ear, "Don't be surprised by anything, Lulya is a KGB agent." *Great,* I thought, *here I am scheduled to go to Kursk with three women I have just met, one of whom is a drunk and the other one a KGB agent.* However, I decided that I would deal with the matter in due time and in the meantime, I solved the immediate problem by downing another glass of iced vodka, followed by a slice of smoked salmon.

Three

Due to my émigré status, I had many relatives scattered across the world. Most of them had left Russia in the 1920s and, as a result, were absorbed by a number of friendly countries. Thus, my Uncle Boris ended up in Guadalajara, where he married a Mexican girl who gave him five children, while Uncle Leo settled in Iran, where he prospered as an architect and even built the palace for the old Shah of Iran in the early thirties. Leo's children later settled in France, Belgium, England and South Africa. I corresponded faithfully with all of them and at one time or another was able to meet them all.

Not all my relatives left Russia. Aunt Sonia, father's sister, was unable to leave, as her husband was imprisoned and she waited for his release. After ten years in prison, he was shot for the unpardonable crime of being born into a noble family. So Sonia, unable to leave the Soviet Union with her young daughter, remained behind, and reconciled herself to living out her life in the hated regime. She never remarried and bore her fate with stoicism, nurturing a hope in her heart that things might change. She lived long enough to see the end of the Soviet Union, when, with tears in her eyes, she hung the Russian white, blue and red flag from the window of her bedroom. By that time, she was in her nineties. She lived in Moscow with her daughter, Irina, also a widow, and a granddaughter, Elena, a single mother of a twenty-year-old son.

However, Sonia was not the only one of the family who had remained in Russia. Her cousin, Eugene, brother to Boris in Mexico, stayed in Russia by choice. He was the only one of the clan who espoused the Communist ideology. During the bloody Civil War, he elected to join the Red Army against his brothers. By mutual agreement, Eugene's name was never mentioned among the family members, although everybody was aware that he lived and prospered in the Soviet Union, and that he had married and his daughter's name was Ludmila—Lulya for short. It was this same Lulya who came to dinner at Sergey and Tanya's apartment.

I had met Lulya ten years before, and she even spent two weeks in our home. It happened this way.

My husband, George, and I lived at that time in La Paz, Mexico, where we had built a second home to enjoy the warm winter months. My cousin Olga, daughter of Boris, called me one day from Guadalajara, all excited and happy. Stumbling over a mixture of English and Spanish words, she told me of an unexpected visit from her Aunt Lulya from the Soviet Union.

She said that Lulya was a scientist, sent to Mexico on assignment from the Botanical University in Moscow, to study the native Mexican plants. She added that Lulya wished very much to meet me, and wondered whether we could invite them both to La Paz.

George and I were delighted, and curious, to meet Lulya, since we were aware that the political climate in the Soviet Union was changing, and it was an opportunity to hear how things really were at that time.

One week later, we met Olga and Lulya at the La Paz airport. While Cousin Olga, her lovely smiling face full of joy, looked like an exotic flower, Lulya's, sadly enough, was more like one of prickly dusty cactus, which she was supposed to study.

As I tried to embrace her, she thrust me back with her outstretched hand and gave me a frosty smile. She looked older than she actually was, the impression strengthened by her dark-gray outfit. Her pale-blue eyes, calm and cold, examined my summer print dress with disapproval. She wore her wispy blond hair in an untidy knot at her neck.

George, the gentlemen par excellence, tried to kiss her hand, as was our Russian custom, but she violently jerked it back, much to the amusement of several people nearby who witnessed this.

We accommodated Olga and Lulya in our guest bedroom with a private bathroom, and I left the two ladies to settle down in their room while I went to the kitchen to prepare the evening meal. Soon Olga joined me and we worked together, eagerly catching up on the latest events in our respective families. Seeing that Lulya was not about to appear, Olga wanted to share with me her impressions of our cousin from the Soviet Union.

"I have to tell you something very funny," she whispered. "You have been to our small house in Guadalajara, and you know that we only had cold water, but since we learned that Lulya was coming, my brother remodeled the bathroom and installed hot water so that she would be more comfortable. Can you imagine what happened?" She widened her big eyes, giggling: "She never used the hot water, or the cold water for that matter! Do you know," she added, lowering her voice, "she never bathes, and she never even changed her dress since the day she arrived." Apparently she stayed with Olga for two weeks.

Seeing my shocked expression, she added, "I tell you, cousin, maybe she didn't like our soap, but let us see if she will use the lavender soap you put in that cute bathroom."

Unfortunately, the lavender soap was not to Lulya's liking either, and she remained true to her habits throughout their two weeks' stay in La Paz, never changing her gray dress, although, hanging in the guest closet, I did see a number of skirts and blouses which she never wore. As a result, it was necessary to revert to tactical maneuvers in order to keep her away from odor-sensitive noses. I resolved the problem by giving her a permanent place of honor at our table, near a large window, which proved to be an excellent solution.

As to our curiosity about the state of affairs in the Soviet Union, it was stunted from the beginning. Lulya told us firmly that first evening, "It is obvious to us all that Gorbachev is trying to ruin the country. Russia does not need any *perestroika* [reconstruction]. Our Union is very strong and everybody is well provided for. There is no unemployment and if there are unsatisfied people, they are suitably dealt with!"

She looked sternly at George and me. "What I cannot understand," she said, "is why are you both living in a capitalist country such as the U.S.A. when your real place is in the Soviet Union where you belong?" She produced several pamphlets from her attaché case. "Here," she said. "I brought you something that will show you how progressive we are in the Soviet Union."

"I'm afraid that this kind of literature is wasted on us," said George. "Why don't you save it for more credulous prospects, dear Lulya. I propose a toast," he said with a mischievous smile. "To *perestroika*." Lulya drank her wine, but did not raise her glass.

Two weeks went by quickly. I took the two visitors around the small town and showed the native plants to Lulya. She took some snapshots with her expensive camera and that was the extent of her scientific research. I tried to question her about her botanical assignment, but her vague answers about looking for some undiscovered plants on the Baja Peninsula coincided perfectly with her lack of interest in the many native plants growing around our small town.

We parted with no regrets, but with considerable relief, probably on both sides.

As I kissed Olga good-bye, she whispered with a laugh, "Pray for me, as I will be sitting next to her for two hours."

* * *

My trip to Kursk had been wisely arranged by Sergey, who decided that I should travel on the night train, rather than waste eight precious daytime hours of my three-week visit. In addition to Lulya, I was to be accompanied by two of my newly found relatives, Lisa and Elena. I was looking forward to spending more time with Lisa and Elena, in spite of Elena's reputation for hitting the bottle, for I thought I could handle that. As for Lulya, I decided to be as tolerant as I could, meeting her again after more than ten years.

In the meantime, since our projected trip to Kursk was still two weeks away, Sergey arranged that we spend a week in St. Petersburg.

According to our schedule, we left for St. Petersburg on the night train. Masha, the twelve-year-old granddaughter, accompanied us, and we had the whole compartment to ourselves. We were supplied with clean sheets and blankets, and Sergey showed considerable agility in hoisting his six-foot-plus frame up to the upper bunk, while Masha, agile like a monkey, climbed up and immediately changed into her colorful pajamas.

"I am hungry, *Babushka* [Granny]," she said.

Tanya immediately opened her basket of goodies and produced fruit and bottles of orange juice. Since it was past ten o'clock, all I wanted was to stretch out on my narrow bunk, but it was nearly twelve o'clock before Masha had her fill of apples and bananas. A pretty attendant brought us glasses of tea in silver glass-holders, which apparently was a tradition on all Russian railways.

In the morning, everybody said it had been a comfortable ride, while I kept my counsel, having spent a sleepless night on a pillow with an attitude.

245

The bathrooms on Russian trains were kept very clean. However, they were considerably smaller than the ones on airplanes, and I kept blessing my best friend in the States, who instructed me to take along a month's supply of toilet paper.

Once in St. Petersburg, we had to walk miles across the huge vaulted station, built God knows how many centuries ago, in order to arrive at the glassed-in area where reservations for hotels and temporary accommodations were made. Sergey disappeared and we had to wait for nearly an hour until he reappeared, triumphant, accompanied by a capable young man who grabbed our luggage and led the way to his car. Apparently we had just rented an apartment for a week in a central area of the town.

As we rode along the wide avenues of the city built by Peter the Great, I was awed by the beauty and symmetry of the architecture of the mansions and palaces. This historic city still stood untouched in spite of the German attacks during World War II, and where on the shores of the River Neva, every bridge and every monument was a work of art. Across the Neva arose the high spiral of the Petropavlovskaya fortress prison, a testimonial to the cruel fate of many Russian patriots who were unwise enough to disagree with the powerful rulers.

The next few days were a whirlwind tour of St. Petersburg. Tanya and Sergey tried to show me every historical palace and monument. I followed them everywhere, and that meant a lot of sightseeing on foot. Unfortunately, the city buses were not designed to accommodate senior citizens with knee problems. Getting on one of the modern wonder buses made in Germany was a major problem for me, for stepping on the first step of the bus required some hefty shoves from behind. Once inside the bus, Sergey, in his zeal to make me as comfortable as possible, would bellow at the top of his baritone voice: "*Tovarischi* [Comrades], make way for an eighty-year-old woman."

Invariably, this appeal had little effect, for nobody listened to him, but made me determined to ask him for a new approach to courtesy, without having to stress that I was born eighty years ago.

The endless walks, the going up and down gigantic marble steps and uncooperative city buses finally caused my right knee to go on strike. It happened in the most undesirable place: the summer residence of Catherine the Great. I found myself in a beautiful public park, unable to step forward or backward, with a strong urge to lie on the ground and die.

Sergey tried to distract me with a soothing "Just a few steps more, dear cousin, and you will see the Amber Room, which was a gift to Catherine the Great from the German emperor. See, the line is not so long. We will be able to get inside in a mere twenty minutes." My knee was swelling by the second and I was swooning from pain, so I collapsed onto the nearest garden bench and said, "I'm O.K., Serezha [diminutive for Sergey]. Go and join Tanya and Masha, and I will sit here until I recover."

Sitting in front of Pushkin's monument, I tried to forget my throbbing knee. I concentrated on the marigolds planted around the base of the sculpture at the feet of the poet, who, half-reclining on a bench, was gazing thoughtfully into space. My mind was racing in a panic. I knew that my swollen knee was going to throw a wrench into all the plans that were so carefully made by Sergey, and I did not even want to think what it would do to the long-awaited trip to Kursk. I was aware that my cousins had spent a lot of money preparing for a perfect visit for me, which they intended to be unforgettable.

As I entertained those dark thoughts, I realized that I was not paying attention to what was happening around me. Most of the tourists had gone from the little clearing in front of Pushkin's memorial, and a cyclist was circling the bench on which I was resting.

I tried to reassure myself by touching the money belt, which I had tied around my waist. It was invisible under my clothes, and I decided not to be afraid. Then I pretended to admire the landscape, while I examined the cyclist as he was cruising the circular paths. He looked like he was in his late thirties, with a mane of short unruly hair. His jeans and a checkered blue shirt looked clean and so did his athletic shoes.

With his dark complexion, he could have been from Georgia, I thought, and wished I knew what that little stud in his ear meant. Was that a fashion statement or what? My observation abruptly ended as he finally dismounted alongside my bench and said, "Good afternoon, lady. You are English? Yes? Maybe American? My name is Grigori. I am also a tourist, a Russian tourist, and I am, how you say, a gypsy. I travel to learn about the world." To put me more at ease he added: "I am like a hippie."

Since he did not snatch my purse, my fears were somehow abated and I managed a weak "Hi." Sergey was nowhere to be seen and I could see a group of tourists enter the clearing, their leader doing his thing in a nasal Dutch accent.

Grigori sat himself at the opposite side of the garden bench and that calmed my nerves. I figured that since I had nowhere to go, a friendly attitude would work to my advantage.

"I am an American of Russian origin," I said in Russian. "And you are the first Russian hippie I have met."

Grigori laughed spontaneously. "Well, I am not exactly a hippie like you have in America, but I think I am a free spirit because I don't like to stay long in one place. A week or a few days and away I go!"

Since that sounded like a long session, I asked, "So what do you do for a living?"

"Oh, this and that," said the Russian hippie. "I take small jobs here and there and I sometimes stay with a friend. I make a little money, just enough to survive, and then I move on. So I learn about different towns and I have only recently arrived in St. Petersburg. I bought this bicycle secondhand and it allows me to move around."

Fat chance! I thought. *He probably stole the expensive racing bicycle.* But I started enjoying myself talking to the Russian "hippie." Our conversation soon turned to world politics and, before long, after we had settled the bigger problems, we were chatting like old friends. Grigori seemed to be interested in many subjects. He was a soccer fan, but confessed his ignorance of baseball. He loved modern music, but did not approve of rap singers. He enjoyed going to the ballet, and looked forward to attending the performance of *Sleeping Beauty* at the Mariinsky Theater. He expressed his opinions freely, and we jumped from one subject to another, when suddenly, he really floored me by broaching the subject of mysticism.

"There is that extraordinary man," he said, "whom I met some time ago. He is a spiritual leader and a magnetic personality. This avatar is able to have out-of-body experiences and lately, he revealed to me and to a select few that he is the new Messiah."

Seeing my ironic smile, Grigori's eyes flashed with indignation as he said, "I can assure you that your skeptical attitude will change once you meet this exceptional human being. I will even tell you more. It was revealed to him in his meditations that the end of our world will happen very soon. All unbelievers will be destroyed."

"How interesting this is, Grigori," I said. "Do you have any clues as how to avoid being destroyed in that universal cataclysm?"

His dark eyes glowed when he said, "Only those who believe in him can be saved. I tell you what. I can arrange for you to visit him. I am confident that once you meet him, you will want to be his disciple."

You bet, I thought. I had just spotted the rapidly approaching figure of Sergey, who was probably worried to death seeing that his aging cousin had picked up a stranger.

Sergey's grim expression made me feel like a teenager creeping home after curfew, and I could not help but smile at my protective cousin.

"Is there a problem, young man?" asked Sergey, belligerently towering over Grigori, who was appropriately sitting in a lotus position on the bench.

"No, Serezha, of course not," I intervened, enjoying the situation. "I want you to meet Grigori, who is a Russian hippie. He has been very kind and entertaining. Did you know that we should postpone our visit to the Mariinsky Theater tomorrow, as there will be the end of the world?"

But my cousin hoisted me to my feet, and before I had time to say something witty, he said, "Let's go, Vicka. Step carefully and we'll make it to the tour bus." He glared at my new friend. "Good-bye, young man."

Grigori, who had scrambled to his feet, was hurriedly mounting his bike, his handsome face suddenly worried. He mumbled about being late for an appointment, and quickly disappeared on his expensive racing bike.

Sergey's kind face was a study in reproach. "Did you know," he asked me, "that you have put yourself at risk talking to strangers? This was obviously a thief looking for an easy prey, and he might have assaulted you and taken your money."

"Serezha, dear," I tried to reassure him, "what would that matter since tomorrow we are having the end of the world?"

Four

The incident with my knee triggered a series of calamities with my health.

After we returned to our rented apartment in St. Petersburg, I developed a severe sore throat, which heralded a vicious flu. Tanya took my temperature and ordered me to bed. She prepared countless cups of good-tasting tea for me and covered me with an extra comforter. At that point, I was drifting in and out of sleep and could not care less what I was ingesting, as long as I could lie quietly with my swollen knee propped up by a bolster.

I found enough strength to turn down the offer of a family-sized chamber pot and learned how to crawl out of bed and make my way to the bathroom, leaning on a museum-quality cane, which Sergei bought for me. This trip was fraught with dangers, for often the small German-made wash-machine in the corner of the bathroom was doing its thing, with a coiled tube dangling in the toilet, discharging a soapy Niagara to the peril of the uninitiated visitor. In addition, the toilets in Russia are invariably small in size and consequently, very low, and soon I realized that I had a tactical problem, but after some wet practice I mastered the technique of shoving the foaming tube out of the toilet into a pail, with minimal damage to the environment.

As our departure day neared, my flu symptoms disappeared and I was well again, except for a persistent, hacking cough. "No problem," said Tanya, slapping hot mustard packs on my achy chest. "Don't worry, my sweet cousin, you will be ready to go to Kursk without any sign of the flu. These mustard packs have helped your mother and grandmother, as they are much better for you than any chemical crap that they give you in the States." I gratefully coughed a "Thank you, Taniusha," and set my mind to a positive attitude.

We returned from St. Petersburg by an express train, which got us to Moscow in a record five hours—a definite improvement over the sleeper train. We were served sandwiches and hot tea, and the reclining, soft seats made the trip very pleasant.

When we arrived at the huge Moscow railway station, I envisioned, with some panic, the long walk through numerous levels and marble stairs, all in different stages of disrepair. Leaning on my beautiful cane with its carved handle, I hobbled along as well as I could. Sergey, loaded down with three suitcases like a pack mule, was striding bravely in front of us, while Tanya hovered around me, struggling with small packages of inevitable gifts for relatives and friends. After arriving at the top of a long stairway, I was looking with despair at the immense hall leading to the distant exit, when a pair of strong arms took hold of me from behind and a rough, deep voice said, "Don't you worry, *Babushka* [Grandma], I will get you safely to your car!" I was lifted bodily onto a low cart, probably used to carry heavy luggage, and pushed gently onto a folding chair tied to the platform. A huge porter with a red face and bushy moustache was smiling benevolently at me. "See how comfortable you are, *Starushka* [old lady]? Isn't it better than hobbling? At your age, you should not be walking such a long distance."

Back in Moscow, we followed the program arranged by Sergei, and two days after our arrival, we had tickets to hear the opera *Evgenii Onegin*, by Tchaikovsky, at the Bolshoi Theater.

When I was a child, my mother often spoke about the Bolshoi Theater, and of the Russian Opera, which I heard only on records. I loved *Evgenii Onegin* and knew, by heart, most of the arias, and of course, like most Russian-bred children, I read and learned the unforgettable poems by Pushkin. So going to Bolshoi with Sergey was a real treat for me. Seen from outside, the ancient theater with its massive columns was rather disappointing, as it was surrounded by steel and wooden structures for the planned repair work. Apparently it was to begin that very month, and I was lucky to have been able to attend an event there before my departure for the States.

However, once inside, the grandeur of the place worked its magic on me, and in my mind I heard my mother's enthusiastic tale of how she, as a young student of medicine, would buy the cheapest tickets for the gallery, where she and her friends would sit crammed one against the other and absorb every musical phrase with shivers of enjoyment. Every phrase, every aria would evoke sighs and tears of delight, as they listened to their beloved opera.

Sergey and I sat in the eleventh row and I was thrilled to admire the beautiful gilded woodwork decorating the vast theater. I ignored the modern crowd around me, mostly tourists from European countries. My imagination actively populated the balconies and the seats with the ghosts of another era. Ladies in long skirts with high waists, beautifully coiffed and bejeweled, accompanied by men in dark suits. A few children, in their best outfits, proud to attend with their parents. The Emperor's box, in the center of the first balcony, now was empty, but my imagination filled it with an array of ladies in dazzling dresses, diadems in their hair, and men in colorful uniforms, ribbons and medals across their chests, standing behind the ladies.

My reverie was broken by a nudge from Sergey. The dimmed lights set a quiet tone and the sounds of the beautiful overture took my breath away as I closed my eyes to better savor the heartbreaking sounds of *Evgenii Onegin*.

The enormous gold-spun curtain rustled as it unfurled slowly upon the old garden of the Larin estate, where Mrs. Larin sat making jam, and I drowned in the familiar sounds of my favorite opera. Maybe the performers were not the best, but to me, it did not matter. I was at the Bolshoi, in my mother's footsteps, listening to immortal music, and I was utterly happy—almost in a trance. During the intermission, I was still under the spell of Act I, which not even Sergey's remark about the gilded curtain could spoil. Apparently, in spite of the many changes that Russia had gone through, not every sign of the old regime was abolished, and the heavy curtain of the Bolshoi still displayed a pattern of the Hammer and Sickle woven in a repeating pattern from top to bottom.

"It is too expensive to change," sighed Sergey, "although many old-timers still hope that it is a sign of the return to the past. Knock on wood," he said smilingly. "The old guard is dying out—not quickly enough for my taste—but only an idiot would want the Soviet regime to return."

* * *

By our scheduled departure time for Kursk, my flu was completely gone, but I still had to use the cane for my swollen knee. We were to board the night sleeper leaving Moscow at 10 p.m., and, accompanied by Tanya and Sergey, I set out, clutching my small bag, my irreplaceable pillow and a bottle of champagne, Lulya's gift.

Elena and Lisa were already waiting for us. It was my first encounter with my cousin Elena. She turned out to be very pleasant and friendly. Of generous proportions, and with a loud voice, she soon established a protective attitude towards me, supporting my elbow while we made our way to our compartment. She was clutching a big shopping bag filled with cans of what I thought were soda pop. As soon as we were settled down, Elena fished out one of the tall cans labeled "Gin and Tonic" and announced in a happy, throaty voice, "Let's start celebrating, girls. I am thirsty!"

Lisa gave me a conspiratorial look and said in an artificially high voice, "Why don't we wait for Lulya, so that she doesn't feel left out?"

Elena waived her off with a dismissive hand. "Don't worry, I have plenty more of these little darlings. I seldom leave the house without a couple, for I never know how long I will be out!"

To Lisa's "No, thank you," and my "Later on, maybe," Elena sang out: "You don't know what you're missing, girls," and proceeded to pop the can. She must have been pretty thirsty, for she downed the contents in a hearty swallow and, after heaving a sigh of contentment, sat back comfortably in her seat.

"As for Lulya," she said, "she might not even turn up. Do you remember, Lisa, the time we were supposed to go on a trip with her? She never showed up and later said that she missed the train. Maybe we will be lucky this time, too, and she will miss the train again. We will be better off without her."

"Well," said Lisa, in a voice full of promising information, "do you know that she called me last night and said that she was not going to return with us, as she had received instructions from the Botanical Institute to go to Kursk to research certain field plants, endemic to the region. So she got a paid trip with an official posting, all expenses paid."

Elena laughed loudly as she popped another can. "The Institute! We all know what institute that is. Crazy Lulya has been with the KGB for years and we all know it. Tell me, why does the Moscow Institute of Botany need to send a seventy-year-old *babushka* to Kursk to study field flowers? The truth is that the KGB still wants to shove its nose into our free society, and also to sniff out why a daughter of an avowed anti-Communist would decide to visit Russia after all these years. No, she is lying and I am glad that she missed the train again."

Well, well, I thought. *This is going to be an interesting trip. It seems I am getting to know my cousins better and better with every passing moment.*

As the train started moving slowly, the door of our compartment opened and there stood Lulya. She had obviously been hurrying and her hair was in disarray. As she clutched several packages in her arms, her backpack was seemingly bursting at the seams.

She was smiling slyly as she said to her two cousins: "You see, I didn't miss the train this time. I bet you thought I wouldn't come, but here I am. I am late because I cleaned out my refrigerator of absolutely everything. Some of the food had been there for a long time and I decided that it would be a good idea to take it with me." That said, she proceeded to unload dozens of paper packages and some glass jars with gray-colored leftovers. "There is plenty for everyone."

Rather surprised that no one was hungry, she proceeded to open every package, saying, "Please help yourselves, as I suspect that some of this food will turn bad if we leave it until tomorrow."

Elena, who, I found out, was more direct and outspoken than Lisa, said, "Here, Lulya, I have this plastic bag where we put our garbage, and when you are through eating, I will help you empty all those containers, unless you want to keep them for future use."

While Lulya was absorbed in fishing out, with her fingers, some tasty morsel from a foggy jar, Elena held her nose with her fingers in an unmistakable universal signal which Lisa and I had no trouble understanding. Our compartment soon filled with the odor of dated pickled cabbage, smoked herring and other equally unappetizing aromas. Elena, who turned out to be a heavy smoker, tried to light up, but Lisa and I instantly banished her from our compartment. Annoyed, she rushed out, banging the sliding door to show her displeasure.

As soon as the door closed, Lisa and Lulya joined together in complaining about Elena. "She is killing herself," said Lulya. "But, of course, in her case it is understandable. Look at her size."

"What a pity," said Lisa. "She drinks and smokes in front of her five-year-old granddaughter, who adores her. What example is she giving the child? Do you know that some of the first words little Sonia learned were 'gin and tonic'? I suppose this is a good introduction to English. Elena says her grandchild will be a linguist."

Thus I was entertained for twenty minutes by hearing about the shortcomings of our smoking and drinking cousin. I was promised to learn later "plenty of other details" about Elena, and I had a feeling that I was going to learn much more than I bargained for or needed to know.

The Kursk sleeper train, called the "Kursk Nightingale," was somewhat better than the St. Petersburg train. We were given linen sheets, a blanket and two pillows, probably stuffed with rocks. Elena and I occupied the lower bunks while Lisa and Lulya climbed the perilous hanging ladders not designed for ladies in their golden years.

Once Lulya's "banquet" was cleared up, we made sure there were no leftovers by deftly disposing of them while Lulya was in the bathroom. We were ready for bed. Lulya's bunk bed was above mine and for some time she could not settle down, asking us to hand her a bottle of water; then handing me some forgotten food package from above. She hung upside down trying to reach me. "You just have to taste this," she whispered. "It was given to me by my neighbor only last week and the sausage is very tasty. Don't eat what's on top, as it might not be good anymore." After a stunned silence on my part, she added, "I was saving it all this time so that you could enjoy the real Russian food after all the artificial stuff they feed you in the States." I could hear Lisa hiss some warning to me, but decided to accept the gourmet gift, which made it necessary for me, later on, to take another trip down the dimly-lit, swaying corridor in search of a garbage can.

By morning I was a physical wreck, since I was not used to sleeping on Russian trains, and welcomed the hot morning tea. My companions said they all had a good night. Through the windows, we could see the lush green Russian countryside flashing by; although it was June, the skies were cloudy and it was drizzling, which apparently was often the case.

No modern buildings or large houses, just tiny huts with small vegetable gardens. My heart contracted with pity for the long-suffering

Russian peasants, as they always remained poor in spite of changing governments.

In retrospect, I can say now that from then on, all my impressions of Russia contradicted the sometimes negative and not-too-favorable impression that I had received upon my arrival in Russia ten days before. With the exception of the warm welcome given to me by Sergey and Tanya, and visits to some beautiful ancient buildings and churches, I could have labeled my trip to the Motherland as a complete disaster. In big cities, the people were not very friendly, sometimes very rude, and never smiled at strangers, but this was going to change when we reached Kursk. At that time, I was hoping that my impression of Lulya was going to improve; but alas, some things do not change.

At seven o'clock in the morning, the big vaulted station at Kursk was quite deserted, and most businesses catering to the travelers were closed with iron grills. We made our way to the exit, where a pleasant man in his forties met us with a big smile that sported bad teeth.

He introduced himself as Nikolai Stepanovich. "I was sent by the director of the Cheremisinovski region to meet you and am delighted to welcome you, for we get few visitors from out of town."

We bundled into the rickety Volga and were soon driving through fields. A fine rain was misting the windshield as I gazed at the endless green horizon, which had been the delight of my father when he was a young boy. I was so absorbed by my surroundings that I didn't stop to wonder why we had been met in such a grand fashion. I had imagined that we would be staying at a nearby hotel, rent a taxi and visit what was left of my family estate. I concluded that Sergey had arranged transportation for us, and my heart warmed up to him for his thoughtfulness. The three cousins in the back seat did not say anything and I did not want to ask in front of the driver. Maybe it was just as well, as I hardly would have believed them had they told me about what was going to happen.

Sitting in front, I could still catch more than a whiff of my cousin Lulya, and I felt sorry for Elena and Lisa, stoically enduring her close proximity, all in the name of family history.

After about forty minutes through the countryside, we approached a small village with scattered small houses. There were no fences between them. Gaggles of geese with goslings enjoyed the rain, sitting family style in the puddles along the country road. A single cow or goat testified that it was a dying village. A lonely bakery and a dry goods store, both closed, represented the center of commercial activities. Nobody was out doing any chores, and although some houses had small vegetable patches, it all looked pretty dismal.

At last, our Volga stopped in front of a group of nondescript two-story buildings, and Nikolai Stepanovich gallantly opened our doors.

"The director is waiting for you," he said. As we got out of the car, a middle-aged woman came out of the building. She ran to us, her face wreathed in smiles.

"Hello," she said. "I am Olga Petrovna, the secretary of the director, and I welcome you to Cheremisinov. We are very proud to receive the descendants of the Markov family."

I was stunned, to say the least. My three cousins enjoyed my surprise and smiled broadly, as they seemed to know Olga Petrovna, who greeted them as old acquaintances.

There was no time for further talk or questions and we were ushered towards the stairs leading to the second floor. Olga Petrovna deftly supported me as I heaved myself up the old steps, clinging to the damp rail with one hand and hoping not to drop my precious antique cane in my other hand. On the second floor, we were shown into an apartment, which was apparently the Civic Center.

The director, Youri Vassilievich, rose from his desk to greet us. He seated us at a long conference table, giving me the place of honor at his right hand, and launched into a welcoming speech.

"I am proud and honored," he said, "to be able to meet the last descendent of a family that had, for centuries, been a part of this corner of Russia. We want you to know that we are aware of the unfortunate circumstances that made your family flee our country in 1920. Your father had not forgotten his roots and, through his literary works, remained in close contact with his birthplace. Your great-grandfather, who was a well-known writer and benefactor of this area, had put us on the map of Russia, and we are proud and grateful that the Markov family is a part of our history.

"In spite of the destructive Communist regime, which had, for seventy cruel years, tried to abolish all that was good and sacred in our country, we want to remember and honor those who helped us to grow and prosper. You are the descendant of those noble and kind people who developed this area. Your father was a young man in his early twenties when he fought as an officer in World War I, serving his country and, later on, in the Civil War. Even after he was obliged to leave Russia, he fought with his pen for the ideals he believed in. Today his books are read in our schools and we consider him a national writer and a Russian patriot.

"Let me present you with a book about our area, together with a recording of our famous nightingales, for which the city of Kursk is famous."

I had a difficult time holding back tears as I thanked him. I wished I could have prepared a suitable speech, but probably after a quick look at my red eyes, he must have understood my state of mind.

At that moment, Olga Petrovna entered with a tray of champagne and candy. She filled our glasses and Youri Vassilievich toasted us in grand style. To tell the truth, by now I was desperately hungry, since we did not have any breakfast, and I could tell that my cousins were also hoping to have something more substantial to eat, but we drank a couple of toasts like real troopers. As we filed out of the room and made our way downstairs to the waiting car, Lisa whispered in my ear, "Don't worry, my dear. I know you are also hungry, but I am sure that they will feed us superbly. When we visited this region before, they plied us with food and drink. You will be surprised."

These rather vague and mysterious words led me to wonder what was yet in store for me. I was not told anything about where we were going next, but the three cousins seemed to know.

When we climbed into the Volga, Olga Petrovna came with us, but we had a different driver. He said his name was Pavel Ivanovich and to me, he looked very much like his predecessor, but this one was chattier. After we drove a block, he stopped the car near a group of older houses. We entered a large yard and stopped before a small church. We could see a group of people with a priest in church vestments standing in front, watching something that was going on.

Five

Olga Petrovna explained that this was the village church, which had just received a long-awaited cupola. This golden globe, topped with a cross, was, at that moment, lifted by a winch from the truck that had carried it to the roof of the small church building. Three athletic-looking men were on the roof, ready to receive it.

We got out of the car and watched as the gleaming sphere gently swung in the air. A fine drizzle fell upon the small, silent crowd of villagers who gathered around the priest, but no one seemed to mind the rain. The priest held a cross in his right hand and a small birch branch in the other. He intoned a prayer, and everyone responded softly, crossing themselves, their eyes turned towards the cupola in its uneven trajectory to the roof. The priest looked up and blessed its ascension to the waiting arms of the men above. He dipped the birch branch in holy water and sprinkled the still morning air. After this blessing, he lifted his right arm with the gleaming cross towards the sky. "In the name of the Father, the Son and the Holy Ghost," he prayed. "Thank you, O Lord, for fulfilling our prayers that we may now gather freely to pray in a consecrated church according to our ancient traditions, of which we have been deprived for many years."

Then, one of the women sang the first line of a prayer. Immediately, a chorus of voices joined her, and I could see tears running down the faces of some women. My throat constricted with emotion as I watched this scene. I felt humbled by the show of faith and joy that the villagers felt to have a beautiful cupola with a cross on their tiny church.

Out of the corner of my eye, I saw that the director had joined the little crowd and was singing with the rest, his face glowing with happiness.

A sigh of relief rustled as the three men on the roof caught the unsteady cupola with their outstretched hands and deftly eased it in place. Everybody laughed and applauded, and the young men on the roof clowned among themselves, to the delight of the onlookers.

Youri Vassilievich approached us and explained that the villagers had saved their money over two years to see this long awaited moment.

"Of course," he said, "the cupola is not covered with gold leaf, nor is the cross, but nowadays, few churches have real gold leaf. Now that we are allowed to worship, we are very happy that we can again pray to God in a church crowned with a cross."

Taking advantage of the milling crowd, I slipped quietly into the church, where a faint fragrance of incense hung in the air. In the semi-darkness, Byzantine-style icons of saints in gold and silver frames, hanging on all the walls, looked gravely upon me. The tiny red icon-lamps glowed like jewels as I approached the central pedestal with the image of the Holy Mother of Kursk. Every church in Russia had a copy of this famous icon, said to be miraculous, but the original had been taken out of Russia in 1920. It had been secretly absconded with by the faithful monks, with peril to their lives, so as not to permit it to fall into the sacrilegious hands of the Bolsheviks. Today, it is in a monastery near New York, but every year, a group of dedicated priests carry the icon to visit every Russian church in the United States. Since the fall of Communism, there were talks about bringing the icon back to its home in Kursk, but nothing definite had yet been decided.

As I was about to turn away from the icon, a gentle hand stopped me. It was the village priest. He was surprisingly young, with a bright red beard framing his kind face.

"I hear that you are from America," he said, "visiting your family's birthplace. You are welcome in our humble little church. You must know that you are here at home and that God is with you. Here is a gift for you to remind you to come back someday." He handed me a small icon of the Virgin Mary and I was stunned by his kindness. When I attempted to give him something for the church, he stopped me. "Just pray for me and our village," he said. He turned away and I stayed a little longer, savoring the peace in my heart. I realized that I was just discovering the real Russia: that here in this small village, I had finally encountered what it was to come back to my roots. It was an unadulterated feeling of belonging, after a lifetime of living in various countries, wonderful maybe, but not my own.

We got back into our car and continued our planned itinerary, apparently to the local school. It was a short ride and we arrived at an ugly stone building, probably dating back to the fifties.

"This is our village school," announced Olga Petrovna. We crossed the large recreation yard and entered a spacious lobby. The principal, a big-boned, blond woman, met us at the door. She welcomed us informally and immediately led us down a long corridor. As she opened a door, my ears were assaulted by the familiar sound of a crowded school auditorium. *Students,* I thought with pleasure. *I will have the opportunity to see Russian students and maybe speak with them. This is going to be fun.*

The principal interrupted my thoughts as she ushered us into the auditorium. All the chatter and din stopped at once. The large hall was packed with high school children and teachers, and they were all looking at us expectantly. The principal led us, by a short flight of steps, onto the stage, where a long table was set, covered with red cloth. I did not expect this at all and wanted to hang back, but was rewarded by a nudge from behind, courtesy of Elena.

A feeling of panic rose in my throat as I was given the central seat at the table, flanked by my three relatives. Olga Petrovna sat modestly on the side. The principal approached the podium and started speaking. *Oh my God,* I thought, *I will certainly be asked to say something, and what shall I say?* In fact, I was never much of a speech-maker. As much as I was at home with my students at the school where I taught, I invariably got stage fright when I had to address the parents at the yearly meetings.

As I was mentally floundering, with a deep urge to run off the stage, the principal finished her speech, saying, "And today, we have the honor of welcoming the daughter of our beloved émigré Russian writer, Anatoli Markov. Children and teachers, I want you to give a good hand to Victoria Anatolevna Markov Surovtsov, all the way from the United States of America."

I got up and faced a sea of expectant faces of children, who were applauding loudly, probably giving vent to the boredom of sitting in one place for who knows how long.

I could see Lulya grinning maliciously at me, enjoying my discomfort, and the friendly faces of Elena and Lisa, winking and trying to give me courage. The principal, her face friendly and expectant, was turned towards me. My mind went blank.

Here goes, I thought. *Father, wherever you are, help me!*

"Teachers, administrators and students," I began. "This is my first time in Russia, and I am very happy to be here, the cradle of my family. All my life, I heard about this part of Russia from my dear father, and although he died before he was able to see his beloved homeland again, I am here today, fulfilling his greatest wish.

"I plan to visit all the places where my ancestors lived, and this afternoon, I will start at the Pokrovskoye." Then my mind stopped working.

As I hesitated, a young voice asked, "Where were you born, and how come you speak such good Russian?"

Halleluiah! I thought. *Bless him.* I could certainly talk about that.

"Well," I started, "I was born in a tent in Egypt." An incredulous gasp went up from the audience. "The tent was a military hospital, because my parents, together with other Russian émigrés, lived temporarily in a military camp. You may know that my parents were political refugees, participants of the Russian White Army, who could not accept the Bolshevik regime, and therefore left Russia forever in 1920.

"King Fouad of Egypt was kind enough to shelter the homeless Russian refugees and gave us unconditional permission to remain in his country as long as we wished. So Egypt was the only country I knew as I grew up. We were provided with official papers that guaranteed our protection by the Egyptian government, and these documents allowed us to travel freely to other countries for study or pleasure.

"In 1958, mainly for political reasons, we applied for an immigration visa to the United States and were accepted almost immediately, so that is where I live now with my husband. My parents died in 1961. I will be happy to answer any questions that you may have."

I started to enjoy myself. Here was an audience of kids, not much different from the ones I had taught and nurtured in the United States. I could put myself at their level, and I felt I was still in my beloved school in California, from where I had retired some years before. As the questions showered, I was able to tell them about my profession, that I was married, that I had no children. They asked if the American kids took Russian lessons. And was Disneyland far from where I lived in Santa Rosa?

Seeing that the principal was getting antsy, and Lulya was heaving sighs of impatience, I had the good sense to end the question-and-answer session by passing my place at the podium to the principal, who, no doubt, had her own agenda to follow.

Holding up an imperious hand to halt the students' applause, she introduced Lulya, who, she said, would tell them herself about her connection to the Markov family.

Lulya gave her best imitation of amiability as she spoke. "I am related to the Markov family through my grandmother. She had three sons and, although the two elder sons decided not to live in the Soviet Union, my father, Eugene, had distinguished himself during our glorious revolution and instilled in me the noble principles of world communism. So, following in his footsteps, I have devoted my life in serving the State and being an instrument of social welfare."

An audible "boo" was heard, but Lulya was on a roll as she continued, unabashed. "I have the distinction of being a leading botanist in my field, and I am proud that my father did not leave his country when it was time for the reconstruction of old useless values."

A young voice shouted from the back of the auditorium, "Down with Communism, Grandmother. Go and join Lenin at the mausoleum!"

Lulya remained unfazed. She called back, "You want to argue the point, young pup? Communism has not said its last word yet and one day, you will be sorry you opened your mouth."

Several young voices called out in protest, and a girl of around sixteen stood up. Her face was flushed and she was trying to keep her voice steady. She said, "Comrade, whatever your name is, please do not give us any more of that talk which was fed to our people since 1920. Today, this is no longer the Soviet Union. This is Russia, my Russia, our Russia, and we reject everything that even slightly suggests the dictatorship and terror, which our people had to endure for seventy years. You are trying to keep alive a lie which held us in bondage for all these years, but today we have freedom of speech and we are not afraid to tell you the truth. We want the prerevolution past back, which was denied to my parents, and we want to tell the American descendent of the family we are honoring today that we are the new Russia, which needs to learn about its true history and traditions."

Lulya was taken aback, and showed all the signs of wanting to argue and impress the students, but the principal moved forward and laid a commanding hand on Lulya's shoulder.

"Thank you for your input, dear friend," she said. "We will now give the word to our next speaker, Lisa Kalinsushkina, who has some interesting things to tell us."

Lisa approached the podium with a friendly smile at the children, and won them over immediately with her informal speech. She said, "I, too, am not directly related to my cousin Vicka, since I have come down from a branch of the family through a grandmother more than three generations ago. However, I am interested in genealogy and have been collecting dates and documents for a long time. Thanks to written documents compiled by Anatoli Markov, who kept detailed records, today I am able to publish a book about our family, which dates back to the fifteenth century. I hope that his daughter Vicka, present today with us, will continue the work that her father had begun and will write about her ancestors and her life in Egypt, when she gets back to her home in the United States.

"Now let me tell you about myself. I am a communication engineer with the telephone company. I am married and have two sons, both of whom are married with children. It has been a pleasure to see you all, and I thank you for giving us such a warm welcome."

Then it was Elena's turn. She introduced herself as my nearest blood cousin, but soon lost the audience by talking mostly about her granddaughter, whom she adored, and the students looked bored. The principal interrupted by reminding everybody that there was yet another item on the program.

A blushing student, about seventeen years old, stood up. There was sudden silence as he began to address me. He said, "My name is Boris Loukianov. Dear Madam, I would like to offer you a copy of the dissertation that I wrote on the latest book of your dear father, *The Nests of Homeland*. His love of our peasants and the rich nature of Kursk have inspired me to chose his work for my thesis." He went on stage and handed me a bound, typed copy of his work.

I was too moved for words, so I put my arms around him and hugged him. The audience exploded in applause and cheers.

When there was silence this time, I had no difficulty to express my thoughts. I said, "Dear Boris. My father left Russia when he was only a few years older than you. While in exile, he had not, for a single day, forgotten where he came from. All his writings and his dreams were about this part of Russia and the wonderful people he had known as a boy. Although he was from a wealthy family, his best friends were the village boys who taught him all about life in the country, the seasons, the animals and the birds. Although my father died in 1961, his books are now being read in Russia, and I can now say for certain that he has finally returned to his homeland, welcomed by you all."

The principal rose and led us down the steps from the stage, showing us the way to the dining room.

The long table was attractively set up to accommodate about twenty people, including some teachers and administrators. No children were present. Bottles of vodka and champagne stood among enticing dishes of smoked herring, with slices of hard-boiled eggs, pork aspic, sausages and cold cuts. Small dishes of red caviar and platters of smoked salmon were tastefully placed along the center of the table, and pickled cucumbers and slices of boiled potatoes completed the picture. Apparently, in Russia, vodka is served with every meal, and I remembered with a smile Elena's remark during our trip, when she said, "Only beggars don't have vodka with soup."

The lunch lasted for over two hours, during which time many toasts were made honoring everybody, and I was asked many questions, especially by the women, while the men sent me friendly smiles and gallant toasts. I was still in a happy haze when Lisa and Olga Petrovna took me aside.

Lisa spoke softly and confidentially. "Vicka, I have a suggestion to make. This afternoon, we have planned a visit to your father's family estate, or rather what is left of it. I have spoken with Olga Petrovna and she agrees with me that you do not need to have us three long-distance cousins with you. What you need is someone who is familiar with the area and its history, and we have chosen for you two such persons. One of them is Marina Kholodova, an architect specializing in the history of old estates of the Kursk region. She is the author of two books on the subject. The other person is Galina Korostina, who is preparing her doctorate in literary history on Russian writers of the Kursk region, and her subject is your great-grandfather, Evgeni Markov, the writer.

"Galina has a van at her disposal and she will be traveling with you until the time you have to go back. Olga Petrovna will stay with us here in the village, and tomorrow morning, we will all go in Galina's van to Kursk, where her mother has kindly invited us to spend the night at her house."

This arrangement seemed very attractive to me and I readily agreed. Elena and Lulya left with Lisa and Olga Petrovna in the car in which we came. It was not difficult to predict that they were going to continue partying, wherever that was.

Marina Kholodova and Galina Korostina had arrived by this time. They each were in their early thirties and I immediately felt at home with both of them. They seemed to have a wealth of information about the area, which we were about to visit the next day.

Marina said, "I know how impatient you are to visit Pokrovskoye now that you are here, but I would like to warn you that there is not much left of your family estate. Do not be disappointed that there is only the foundation and broken stones left where the house once stood, but you will be able to see the outline of the house, whose spirit still lives." She handed me a book. "I have just published a book I have been working on for a few years. This is *Historical Estates of the Kursk Province before the Revolution.* By digging in the libraries, I have been able to reconstruct the plans of the estates that were demolished during the 1920s and surprisingly enough, I have been very successful in that respect. Many documents could not be recovered, but everyone was very cooperative and I was able to include the building plans of many of the estates in my book. Fortunately, Pokrovskoye had been one of the estates whose plans I had been able to salvage from the archives of the Kursk library, and I am sure that you will want to see them. We'll set out immediately because we want to show you some interesting places before we reach Pokrovskoye."

Galina was already at the wheel of a small van and I said good-bye to the principal and the teachers, while the students poured out of the doors, laughing and waving hands. I was finally going to see Pokrovskoye.

Six

When in my dreams I return to Pokrovskoye, my mind immediately conjures up the view from the hill where I sat that afternoon, among the ruins of the mansion. I can still feel the warmth of the polished stones, which, I imagined, were once part of the vast entrance hall described in my father's diary.

For centuries, the big house stood overlooking endless fields of green, stretching from the banks of the River Tim at the foot of the hill. It was accessible from the house by winding paths down on gentle slopes, covered with lilac bushes.

When my father was just a boy, festivities were held on a circular clearing on the lower terrace of the slope, surrounded by an alley of birch trees. There, my grandmother Victoria presided over so many parties when the hill was alive with young voices, music and happy sounds of laughter. Those sounds stayed forever in my father's memory during the long years of his exile from his beloved country.

As a little girl, before I went to sleep on the hot nights in Alexandria, I often heard the quiet click of my father's antiquated typewriter as he tried to recapture every event, every mood of his life in Russia, so as not to lose touch with what was lost to him forever. He spoke of green fields in the summer and the graceful birches with damp buds in the spring. He remembered the winter snows softly covering the world around him and the fragrance of smoke coming from the numerous chimneys, snaking upwards into frosty air. Every so often he shared, with my mother and me, memories of his past life as we listened to him around the dining room table. The overhead fan whirled softly as he read in the circle of the yellow light to the accompanying sound of rustling pages and the insistence of flying bugs. His voice, saturated with nostalgic overtones, stays indelibly in my mind, and the details of his happy childhood life at the Pokrovskoye estate is one of the reasons for writing this memoir.

Growing up, I learned about the tragic destiny of his beautiful mother. My eyes filled with tears as Father would reminisce about her, but no matter how hard I tried, I could not feel any warmth towards her unfaithful husband, my grandfather Leo. I disliked him in all his photographs: in a military uniform, in the company of his friends or on a hunting party. As a young man, Leo was handsome. His clear, arrogant eyes spoke of a person used to being obeyed without any protest, while full-curved lips betrayed his sensuous nature. In his mature years, he gave the impression of a self-possessed man, confident of himself, sporting a fashionable, thick moustache and a receding hairline. Much later, while in exile in Yugoslavia, he sent us, from time to time, short letters devoid of kind words or feelings. He was always complaining of the circumstances that put him in exile, but my heart hardened against him as I remembered only what I knew then: that my lovely grandmother died shortly after she found out that Leo had a liaison with a woman she trusted. When I finally met him in person, I still could not bring myself to like him. I was then fifteen years old and was instructed by Mother to be on my best behavior. Probably the feeling was mutual, as he only addressed me to harp on some of my shortcomings. The truth, as I see it today, was that I was a brat and, very likely, quite insufferable. He was already very sick and lasted only three more months. His painful end and the funeral left an unpleasant memory in my mind. It was the first death in my young life and I was frightened and felt guilty at not being sorry to see him go.

Only much later did I discover more about him, which did much to change my negative attitude toward him. What I learned then about my grandparents gave me a new understanding of Leo and helped soften my unforgiving attitude towards him—but I will speak of that later.

As much as I disliked my grandfather, my grandmother Victoria fascinated me. Love and compassion flowed through my whole being as I examined her photograph. Smoldering dark eyes looked at me from her oval face. This was her wedding photograph, taken at some fancy studio in Kursk. The sepia colors only enhanced her loveliness and she seemed to me like a bird poised for a moment, and impatient to start her married life. The elaborate lace gown showed off her slender figure, her white hand resting on a small column, boasting her brand new wedding band.

Now, a hundred years later, I sat among the ruins of what once was home to her, her husband and her four children.

Weeds pushed among the broken stones, but still I was able to make out the outlines of the large house, which appeared to have been built on the slope going down towards the attractive creek flowing at the bottom of the hill.

I knew that later I would be going back after examining the plans detailed in Marina's book, but for the present I just let the nostalgic feeling of the past wash over me, filling my heart with memories passed on to me by my father.

Built in the first half of the nineteenth century, this house was home to many ancestors, but as I walked among the ruins, I could only think of my grandparents living there, Leo and Victoria. I had brought my father's diary with me to Russia, in which he faithfully recorded the events of his family life at Pokrovskoye, and my imagination was actively reconstructing different phases of his life there. Now, gazing out of my perch overlooking the green expanse of late spring unfolding at my feet, I decided impulsively that it would be right for me to show the dairy to Marina and Galina, so that they could perhaps publish it in Russia.

The two women interrupted my reverie. When we first arrived, they had discreetly wandered off, leaving me alone to walk among the uneven stones and broken foundations.

Galina was greeting a small group of women accompanied by a young man who was dressed in the simple robe of a postulate. The women wore simple cotton skirts and loose shirts. She introduced them to me.

"These are the nuns of the Skit [a small hermitage], which was built here a few years ago. Meet Mother Agafia," she said, and a strong working hand gripped mine, while merry blue eyes smiled their pleasure at seeing me.

"Welcome to our small Skit," said Mother Agafia. "I just heard that you have come to visit us from a very distant land to honor the remains of your family's nest. May God bless you for not forgetting your forefathers, and may you find peace and forgiveness in your heart for those who did not know what they were doing. We are here to pray for all those who suffered and to send enlightenment to those who have lost their way." She looked fondly at the nun standing next to her. "This is Mother Aksinia. Together with her, we run the Skit and help the needy villagers as well as we can. We have two small rooms that are always open for wanderers who travel on foot across our land. Brother Pavel here," she nodded toward the young man in the long robe, "has just arrived from the seminary in Voronezh, and is spending a few days with us."

It was then that I took a good look at the Skit: a couple of small log houses built in the traditional Russian peasant style, with a picket fence around them. Near the gates stood a wooden belfry with small bells spaced at irregular intervals. Mother Agafia asked me, "What is your given name, sister?"

"My name is Victoria," I answered. "Victoria Anatolyevna."

"Of course," cried Mother Aksinia. "You must be the granddaughter to our own Victoria Vechislavovna, who is remembered always in this part of the county. She was an angel on earth who helped the orphan village children, and in our village church, her name is always mentioned when we pray for the departed souls at the end of our Sunday service.

"What a shame that our old village priest just passed away last summer. He was one hundred ten years old and he remembered your grandmother, who always came to the church on Sundays. He said that she was so young and beautiful, accompanied by her four children. Why, your father must have been one of the young boys with her!"

This was more than I expected and I hungrily waited for her to tell me more, but she walked a few paces ahead and asked me to sit on some stones.

"We will sing for you," she said. "This is our way to leave a part of us in your heart. When you have gone back to that far-away country beyond the seas, you will maybe remember us."

I valiantly tried to suppress the emotion that filled me and fought to control myself. I failed, miserably, and let tears flow unchecked down my face. The nuns sang, their voices, mingling and separating, beautiful in the silent afternoon. Their kind eyes showed no surprise at my tears, but understanding and encouragement. They stood close to each other, and the slanting rays of the afternoon sun lit their suntanned country faces, wrapped in homespun linen kerchiefs. They went from one song to another, obviously used to singing together. These ancient church melodies bore a startling resemblance to the folk songs that were so popular in Kursk, and had been sung for centuries in that part of

Russia. Now they were singing to *me*, a prodigal daughter home at last, reminding me about my roots deeply buried in the ground on which I sat.

The light rain had stopped, and as the sun appeared through the receding clouds, the meadow around us exploded in zillions of raindrops clinging to the tall grass. Field flowers, poppies, forget-me-nots and wild strawberries were everywhere. A fragrance of crushed green grass assailed my senses while tiny birds darted and sang their hymn to the sun. *This is a magic moment,* I thought, *which I shall treasure all my life.*

We were quiet going back to the village. I was grateful to the two young women for letting me deal in silence with the tide of impressions that filled my heart. I felt that I had, for a short while, become another person, very different from the one who had left Santa Rosa, California, a few weeks earlier. It was a new, deeply emotional experience for me, and I wanted the moment to stay with me, unbroken by distractions.

As we approached Kursk on our way to Galina's home, where we were invited to spend the night, the country landscape changed noticeably. Gone were the small village huts with geese wandering along the road. Suburban houses appeared, some neatly fenced with small vegetable gardens. When we entered the city of Kursk, with its wide streets and beautiful buildings, some dating to the last century, I was pleasantly surprised by the many wide streets and bridges on which traffic was proceeding in an orderly fashion. This was a weekday, a little after five, when buses and trolleys were filled with commuters. Marina asked to be let out, as she wanted to return home in time to prepare dinner for her family. Galina and I continued on our way.

I inquired about my three cousins, and Galina said that they were also invited to spend the night at her mother's, and would join us later. I asked Galina, "Would it not be too much of an imposition on your mother to have four unexpected guests for the night? I am sure that this could not have been planned before."

Galina just laughed. "You don't know my mother. Her heart is as big as her hospitality, and I did call her from the school where we had lunch. She is delighted to have you spend the night in her house. Here we are, the second house on the right."

The van stopped in front of a small house, wedged between two others on the unpaved street. A wrought-iron door in the tall wall

271

opened, and Lydia Maximovna emerged. Tall, of pleasantly generous proportions, she exuded energy from the top of her curly blond hair to the tip of her American Nikes. Her tight-fitting jeans and summer blouse hid very little of her well-shaped anatomy, while her make-up, expertly applied, spoke of a woman who was not ready to be relegated to the status of a *babushka*.

She presented a glaring contrast to her daughter, Galina, whose face bore no sign of any cosmetics, but who was very pretty in spite of large, dark-framed eyeglasses.

"Welcome, welcome," said Lydia Maximovna, grabbing my carry-on and embracing me at the same time. "You are just in time, for I am dying to have some decent refreshments. Galina, show our guest to her bedroom. Call your sister and tell her you are going to be late picking up your child. We are going to have a party tonight. Dinner will be in the gazebo in the garden, and I want you to find some warm jackets and shawls for our guests. It will be chilly for them. When the rest of our guests arrive, we'll start celebrating. My friend Sasha is already here. Also, when you are in the house, grab my cellular and bring it here, along with the potato salad that is in the refrigerator. I have to feed the dogs or they will not stop howling." She machine-gunned her instructions at her daughter, who only smiled and said, "O.K."

Galina ushered me inside the house. It was small, with a tiny covered porch where we were invited to take off our shoes. Since this was what I had to do in Sergey's apartment, I was not surprised. This done, I was led through a number of tiny connecting rooms. Each room had sleeping accommodations: narrow beds or couches covered with handmade woolen blankets, and walls and floors covered with colorful Eastern carpets which gave the impression of the interior of a yurt. The windows were very small and double-paned. A fragrant whiff of something delicious came from the small kitchen, mingling with the clean smell of waxed floors.

I barely had time to set my small bag on a chair when Lydia appeared. Keeping up a stream of more instructions to Galina, she propelled me in front of her to a pleasant arbor in the backyard. It was densely covered with vine leaves and creeping jasmine, although it was still early June.

A large table with a bright tablecloth was already set up for the festivities. Wooden benches could seat at least ten, and I wondered who the other guests could be. Before I could speculate further, they arrived. Cousin Lisa led, followed by Lulya and Elena, who walked across the backyard, provoking some loud barking by two large dogs, trying their best to get out from behind their enclosure. I was about to have my first party in Kursk.

Seven

I was already seated at the table, cocooned in a warm jacket two sizes too big, when my three cousins made their appearance.

Elena led the pack. She sashayed across the patch of green, zigzagging on unsteady legs. Lisa walked behind her, hands in a protective gesture, ready to prevent a humiliating tumble. Lulya, close on her heels, carried two large paper bags full of goodies. As soon as the three women appeared, the two large dogs, sequestered behind a tall iron fence, set up a barking competition, rattling the metal enclosure. Their fierce barking jerked Elena out of her mellow haze and she made a rush towards the gazebo where I sat. As in a slow-motion movie, she started to fall, while Lisa tried to support her. Lulya dropped her packages and flapped her arms like a crow, not knowing how to help.

At that moment, Lydia Maximovna came hurrying out of the house. She held a pail of food for the dogs in one hand and a dish piled high with people food in the other.

She immediately assessed the situation. Shouting "Shut up!" at the dogs, she placed the pail and the dish on the grass and ran towards the group. She put her arms around Elena and half-carried her towards the table. Then she ran back, got the pail and threw its contents to the happy dogs, over the metal fence. She picked up the dish of food and brought it to the table without spilling a drop. All this was done quickly and neatly. Smiling at my three cousins, she said, "I am so happy that you have come. Welcome to my home. Please call me Lydia."

At once I warmed to this energetic, adaptable woman, who went right to the heart of the matter, without unnecessary theatrics or words. Here she was, with hardly more than a few hours' notice, back from her work, preparing and organizing a feast for four complete strangers, and on top of that, being gracious and welcoming.

The three cousins were already seated at the table, a little rattled by Elena's near tumble. Elena, slowly trying to regain control of her wits, was safely wedged between Lisa and Lulya. The latter had her head in one of the paper bags, checking on her food supply. My guess was that the bag contained some leftover food, and apparently I was not mistaken. Since Lydia Maximovna had again rushed off, Lulya asked Lisa in a loud whisper, "Do you think I should put some of this food on the table? Since I am not coming back to Moscow with you girls, I made sure that I will not go hungry when you leave."

She was examining a greasy package, holding it close to her face, eyeballing it and sniffing. When she started to unwrap it, Lisa, one eye balefully squinting at me, shushed her with, "Put it away, Lulya. You will need it in the days to come, and it is impolite to bring your own food. Our hostess may be offended."

That settled the question, and the offering joined the "gourmet collection" in the bag under the table.

Two of Lydia's friends arrived, accompanied by a hassled-looking Galina. They were carrying dishes and bottles and we all rose to help. Lydia followed with a large basket full of ice, with more interesting bottles peeping out.

"Whew," Lydia said, finally sitting down. "I think we have brought everything. Girls, I would like you to meet Maria and her husband, Evgeni. Evgeni is an engineer, but he is also a published poet, and we are very proud of him. Maria is my close friend. We are both members of the Kursk Folk Chorale group with Sasha, whom you are about to meet. Sasha is the lead singer in our group."

"Dear friends, prepare yourselves!" said Maria. "Vicka, tonight we are going to celebrate your first visit to your homeland and you will hear the ancient songs of Kursk, which were sung by our village nightingales for many generations."

I knew from my father's stories that Kursk was always famous for its nightingales, and the folk singers from Kursk villages were called the "village nightingales."

A pleasant middle-aged woman joined us. This was Sasha. Her typical peasant Russian face, with high cheekbones and upturned nose, was smiling while she examined us with her sharp blue eyes.

"I already met Elena and Lisa before," she said. "I am glad to see you again, but this new lady," she said, directing her gaze upon me. "You must be the visitor from America. You are my first *Americanka* [American]," she said to me. "Welcome to Kursk. I am particularly happy to meet you because my parents and grandparents were born in the village of Ozerki, attached to your family's Pokrovskoye estate. Welcome home! I hope that we will make your stay so pleasant that you will want to return back soon."

I was overjoyed to see Sasha as the descendant of those peasants whom my father loved deeply, and with whose children he played during the long summer holidays.

Lydia was busy arranging the dishes on the table. While keeping up an incessant flow of talk, she deftly placed several chilled bottles of vodka on the table, followed by some brandy in fancy bottles with Russian names, and took the plastic covers off the dishes. This was a wonderful array of home-cooked Russian food. There were two kinds of the *pirogi* (Russian pies): one with meat and one with cabbage filling. A baked potato pudding, *forshmak,* was dotted with small pieces of meat and salted herrings. Red beets nestled in sliced onions with sour cream dressing, and fried marinated fish and pigs' feet in aspic tempted the eye. A fragrant loaf of rye bread and a platter of *zakuski* (hors d'oeuvres) occupied the center of the table, and I suddenly realized that I was very hungry.

"First of all," said Lydia, "let's have a toast to our guests. I propose a toast to Vicka, who has come to us from America, and of course to our local Russian guests from Moscow." Our glasses were quickly filled with vodka, and there was a general rush for the hors d'oeuvres.

"Za vashe zdorovie [Your health]!" Lydia exclaimed and swallowed her large shot glass with lightning speed, signaling the start of the banquet. The celebration had begun!

As the evening progressed, many toasts were drunk. Nobody was forgotten, and when everybody's health was toasted, our imaginations took over and we seemed to be drinking to everyone's health south of Moscow. However, nobody was drunk because we were giving our due to the tasty succulent food prepared by our hostess. As for me, I was mesmerized by the quantity of food and drinks enjoyed by everybody. After a while, I stopped eating and drinking and silently marveled at the amount of food consumed by the company. Upon announcement of a new toast, I would lift my glass with soda water, hoping that my ruse would go unnoticed. However, Lydia's sharp eye did not miss anything, and she only smiled conspiratorially and toasted me silently, as a sign of understanding.

The sun had already set over the gazebo and Galina ran to get some candles. An aroma of lilacs in bloom and honeysuckle rose from the surrounding gardens. There was no wind and I felt warm and cozy in my borrowed jacket. The candles shed a mellow light on the faces of our little group. There was a lull in the conversations around the table and Lydia Maximovna rose.

"Well, Sasha, Maria, are you ready? Shall we show our friend from America what we do best? I am ready. Are you?"

"We are ready, Lidochka," said Sasha. "Just move your tight American jeans next to us, and we can start."

Glasses were refilled and we settled down in anticipation of the promised treat.

Sasha's voice rose in the quiet evening. She had a low, powerful voice, which sounded like a cello solo. It was a plaintive song of sorrow and pain. It was not a story but an appeal to one's fate; an acceptance of a destiny that could not be changed. It must have been sung by women of generations long gone, passed on from mothers to daughters in long winters sitting around the family hearth.

After the first two lines of the song, another voice joined in. It was Maria. The two voices blended and separated in a dialogue, where every word seemed to echo the other's pain and hopelessness, lending sadness to the unspoken words. I could feel the loneliness, the cold inescapable destiny in the simple melody of the folk song. It was the song of Russian women throughout centuries, living through the Tartar occupation, many wars, German occupation, famine and poverty. Running through the song like a red thread was the humble acceptance of their suffering.

There was silence at the end of the song. We all sat, sharing the feeling of oneness with the song and each other; our hearts aching for those sisters of ours long gone.

Then Lydia called out, "Sasha, how about a lively song?" Lydia started singing a familiar Russian dance song, one of those fast songs which everyone knew, and we all joined in. The quick tempo of the song was infectious and we clapped to accompany the singers. Lydia's voice had a metallic quality and at one point, she started beating on a small drum she had hidden behind her. Not only did she give a new direction to the lively song, but started a syncopated beat, ending each verse with

"Tarara-bam, tarara-bam, bam bam, bam bam!" She was imitating the American jazz singers and it was very funny to hear her transform a Russian folk song into a jazzy rhythm.

After a couple of folk songs, we heard a ballad, this time sung by Sasha and Lydia in unison, typical of the Kursk region when the village women would gather together in the evening, singing, their fingers busy sewing and embroidering. Then Evgeni and Maria joined in softly. It was obvious that the women were accustomed to singing together, and I found out later that they were part of a very well-known choir which traveled once a year to various Russian cities, giving concerts.

At times, Galina joined in the singing, but more in a supportive fashion. Sitting next to me, she whispered that she and Marina had interesting plans for me for the next day, and promised to speak of that later on.

As one song followed another, my eyes started to close and, profiting from an interval, I slipped quietly into the house and found the little room where I was to spend the night.

A small pillow embroidered with sequins lay invitingly on the bed and once again, I thanked the foresight which made me bring along my little squishy pillow. I got under the cozy comforter and went right to sleep. In the night I woke up once or twice and could hear the singing in the garden, frequently interrupted by laughs and loud toasts, the voice of our energetic hostess dominating the others.

At five in the morning, I woke up and saw light under the door. I tiptoed and peeped out. Lydia was in the kitchen cleaning up after the party. She quietly put everything in place and went to the closed porch. There she stretched out in on an open sleeping bag, and I realized in confusion and guilt that she had given me her bedroom for the night.

Breakfast was late, but no one complained as we sat at a round table loaded with a typical Russian breakfast. Kasha (groats) was served with a choice of yogurt, *koumis* (mare's milk), honey, fruit and plenty of that wonderful Russian rye bread, cut in large slices. No eggs or bacon. Generally, the Russian families I met did not eat eggs for breakfast, and when they did, they were usually served hard-boiled.

Galina had gone home after the celebration, but appeared after breakfast with a little girl of four, her daughter, Nina. While my three cousins went picking cherries from the large tree in the front yard, Galina and I discussed the plans for the day.

"I think you will enjoy the schedule for the day," Galina said. "This morning Marina and I arranged for us to visit the cemetery near Pokrovskoye and we also wanted to show you a very holy place. This is a place of worship where the waters of a healing spring mark the place where a Russian hermit lived centuries ago. A beautiful monument of the saint, just completed by our famous sculptor, Klikov, was inaugurated last month, and it is something that you will really want to see.

"Then later on, we will drive to the church where the icon of the Holy Virgin of Kursk was, before it was taken to safety out of Russia during the 1917 Revolution in 1920. This is another place where the pilgrims congregate once a year and we only hope that it will not continue to rain today. There is a museum adjacent to the church and the curator and his wife live there. My mother asked them to provide us with a late lunch when we get there, as it will be a long drive.

"My friend Ilya Tarnovski will join us for the trip. He is the historian I told you about. He is looking forward to meeting you very much. For the past two years, he has been researching the history of families of the Kursk region, and hopes you can provide additional material about your family."

Ilya joined us after breakfast. He turned out to be a shy young man, tall, with curly blond hair, badly in need of a haircut. He was carrying an attaché case, and a small bunch of flowers for me. We hardly had time for small talk as we were summoned by Lydia, telling us that the van in which we were to travel had arrived. It was then that I learned that Lydia Maximovna was the director of the well-known "Dvorets [palace] of Young Russia." This was now a center of all kinds of activities for teenagers. This center had formerly been the "Dvorets of Russian Pioneers," a Communist version of the Boy Scouts. In addition to that, she was one of the supervisors in the governing body of Kursk. It all came out when she said that she was commandeering the van to be put at our disposal, which she considered to be quite normal, since I was on a nostalgic pilgrimage to ancestral sites and entitled to such benefits, as an honored guest of the city. The van with a driver was large enough to accommodate our hostess, the three cousins, Marina, Galina, Ilya and myself.

Before starting on our journey, we stopped at the Dvorets, where Lydia wanted us to sign the visitors' book, and invited us in. I was astounded at the size and the symmetry of the palace, probably built at the beginning of the twentieth century. The two-story building occupied half of the city block, with wide steps leading to an imposing double door, badly scarred in places by German bombers during World War II. We all followed Lydia as she led us up the marble steps to her office. The Dvorets was buzzing with activity. A group of teenagers was running down the steps, talking and laughing among themselves. When they noticed our hostess, they sang out: "Good morning, Lydia Maximovna!" which she acknowledged with a happy smile.

On the next landing, we all trooped to the bathrooms. To my surprise there were common bathrooms for boys and girls, but what shocked me more was that behind the swinging doors of each cubicle, there were no commodes—but just a round hole in the floor, with ribbed tiles on both sides, probably to prevent skidding. I wondered briefly if these sanitary appointments were left over from the Tartar occupation in the fifteenth century, but remembered that I was told that they were built in the 1930s by the "progressive" Soviet government.

On the second floor, we crossed a reception room, empty except for two secretaries, and were ushered into Lydia's office. A large oak desk was piled with files and papers, with an old-fashioned computer on the side. A conference table dominated the room, and I shuddered with disapproval as I saw dozens of ashtrays on its polished surface. Apparently smoking prohibitions had not yet reached the province of Kursk.

Lydia excused herself and disappeared while our little group studied the photographs and framed documents on the walls. These were official photographs of the life of the Dvorets, with Lydia in most of them; some were with a much younger-looking Lydia, and one particularly drew my attention, in which she was standing close to an attractive man, with his arm around her.

Approached me, Galina said, "This is my father, Andrei Ivanovich. Together with Mother, they were very much involved in the Dvorets activities since 1992."

I remarked, "What a handsome man. He must have been very athletic?"

"Yes," said Galina. "This photograph was taken before he became ill. Five years ago, we lost him to cancer. He was very courageous until the very end, and we miss him terribly in all aspects of our lives."

Lydia Maximovna erupted into the room again. A woman with a tray of cups and a steaming tea kettle accompanied her. Tea was served on a small table in front of the couch while we signed the guest book at the conference table.

I sipped my tea and watched Lydia in admiration. She asked her secretary to hold the calls, but I noticed that once or twice she did take some apparently important ones. I decided that this time, I would take the initiative and suggest that we be on our way, having already taken too much of this busy woman's time.

Eight

A fine rain started as we set off on the first leg to visit the holy Spring of St. Seraphim of Sarovski. Marina joined us and we took an alternate route from the one traveled the day before on our visit to Pokrovskoye. The bumpy country road led along fields of rippling rye, shimmering in the morning breeze. I felt all tension seep from my body, dissolving in the fragrant air. From time to time, the sun peeped through the torn tumultuous clouds, promising a warmer day. There was hardly any traffic on the road, with the exception of a few unhurried horse carts.

The van turned onto an unpaved road, going slightly uphill. We entered a grove of birch trees, their low branches parting like a curtain. Tender buds and leaves of early June attracted gaily-buzzing insects. The sweet chirping of birds assailed our ears as we got out of the bus. This was the entrance to the Spring of St. Seraphim. A small log cabin was built over the spring, and we could see a flight of stone steps leading below to a cave. Near the door were several framed photographs and icons depicting St. Seraphim and his life.

There was only one attendant, an old monk. He quietly welcomed us and went back to his seat by the door of the hut.

A barrier, surrounding an opening in the ground, guarded the entrance to the spring. A number of steps led into the cave below. As I stepped down into the small cave, I could almost feel the silence wrap around me like a damp cloak. The kerosene lamp standing in the corner threw intricate shadows on the rough-hewn walls. It was quiet and serene in the semi-darkness of the cave. The well was in the corner of the cave and a tin cup on a string could be lowered down the well for a sample of holy water. I thought about the lonely monk who had lived here for many years and wondered at the powerful urge of faith he must have had in his heart, to be able to survive such an existence. My companions must have felt the same. We spoke in whispers, respecting the ancient holy place.

The water was good-tasting and ice-cold. Marina, who came equipped with several small bottles, filled one for me, and told me to wash my face and my eyes with the holy water.

"This is to protect you from any illness or accidents," she said. "Take a few sips of the holy water, for it is said to be miraculous." She gave me a small bottle to take with me to Moscow, for Sergey and Tanya.

Loaded with holy water, we climbed up the precarious steps. The friendly monk took us to the back of the hut and showed us the path to the recently inaugurated statue of St. Seraphim, standing on a terraced hilltop.

We gazed in awe at the artistic interpretation of the artist. Larger than life-size, St. Seraphim was kneeling in prayer. The morning light illuminated his bowed head and shone in the raindrops left from the recent rain. Behind and around the statue, a high slender arch outlining the shape of the Holy Virgin was placed in such a way that she seemed to bless and protect the praying figure with her outstretched hands.

The talented artist, Klikov, a well-known sculptor, had infused his masterpiece with an aura of simple faith, which seemed to radiate outwards from the kneeling monk.

We stood quietly, contemplating St. Seraphim; then one by one, we slowly returned to the bus.

"Our next visit will be to the Pokrovskoye cemetery," announced Marina. "Not much is left of it. It was vandalized and the chapel destroyed during the revolution, but there is something that you will be very interested to see, especially you, Vicka. This is the headstone at the grave of the old *Niania* [Nanny] who took care of several generations of your family. She died before the revolution, but as she was from the village nearby, her grave was left untouched. The rain has stopped, so we can walk there without getting drenched."

After half an hour, we arrived at a grove of trees by the side of the road. My cousins, Ilya and Galina walked in Indian file, led by Elena, through the trees into a small clearing. The old cemetery was half hidden by low branches and juicy spring weeds. There were crooked crosses on the graves with unreadable names, long forgotten and untended. It was obviously an ancient cemetery, and I wondered how Marina had discovered it. After wandering about for a while, she finally stopped. "Here it is!" she exclaimed.

She read the inscription on an old headstone. "Marfa Fomichna from Pokrovskoye village." She looked closer and cried, "Look, there is something else written here. It's pretty much obliterated, but we'll try to decipher it."

We read together, "In memory of our beloved *Niania* [nurse] Marfa, who loved and nurtured three generations of our family. We are forever grateful. The Markov family. 1908."

Tears welled in my eyes as I remembered my father's tales of the old nurse, Marfusha, who died when she was nearly a hundred years old. She came to live with the family as a very young girl and remained as a nurse for three generations of children, starting with my grandfather Leo, when he was still a baby.

We walked around the old graves, trying to read the names, and Marina told us what she knew about the cemetery.

"In 1919, when the Red Army ransacked the countryside, pursuing and killing the families of noblemen, the soldiers reached the estate and village of Pokrovskoye. Your grandfather Leo was arrested and put in jail for crimes against the people. Pokrovskoye was burnt to the ground. A commissar was appointed to leach out wealthy villagers and people sympathizing with the nobles. The village church was burned and so was the chapel of the cemetery. The graves of your ancestors were vandalized and their remains thrown out. However, at night, the villagers, armed with shovels, collected the remains of the dead, and buried them in unmarked graves nearby. Therefore, it is possible that today, we are walking on their graves. Your grandfather, the writer Evgeni Markov, is also, no doubt, somewhere here also, along with his two wives."

We bundled in the van again and drove off to our last destination, which took us along a well-maintained road to the monastery of the Holy Virgin of Kursk. The trip took about two hours, during which time Lulya argued with Elena about the merits of the Communist five-year plan, which had failed some thirty years before. I drifted in and out of a drowsy state, and finally fell asleep.

We arrived at the monastery in pouring rain. There were several buildings in the compound, grouped around an ancient church, which bore signs of recent repairs. I looked in dismay at the steep steps, which led to the imposing entrance to the church, hoping that there would be an elevator hidden somewhere on the premises.

As we got off the van, a man with a large umbrella scurried down the stairs and greeted Galina and Marina by their names. We were obviously expected. I suspected that Lydia Maximovna had arranged that welcome as well, in spite of her busy schedule.

Fortunately, we did not have to go up the slippery wet steps. The individual with the umbrella, who turned out to be the resident docent of the church museum, took us to a nearby low building. Dripping with rain, we trooped into a small hall, where the docent's wife met us. She shepherded us to a restroom where we tried to clean up our wet feathers, which proved to be a challenge. Then we emerged, smiling and hungry, into the nearby dining room, where a Russian feast awaited us. Iced vodka was in sparkling evidence, surrounded by dishes of tasty accompaniments of smoked tongue, herring and pickled cucumbers. I started to really like being a pilgrim in Russia.

The docent, Mikhail Alexandrovich, sat next to me. He told me how in 1995, he and his wife, Varvara Ivanovna, took on the project of renovating and rebuilding the church of the Holy Virgin of Kursk. With the help of donated money and community skills, they were able to restore what was left of the monastery compound. Even before the project was finished, thousands of pilgrims would visit the holy site, and that brought in additional funds. As a result, he was able to put together a museum of church art, and restored textile art depicting Russian Orthodox saints.

Many toasts were drunk, and before we took our leave, we parted as good friends. Mikhail Alexandrovich gave me a gift—a book he wrote about the monastery, which he signed with a friendly dedication. To my pleasant surprise, he also produced my father's book *The Nests of Homeland*, which he asked me to sign for him, as the daughter of the author. I was very touched by this gesture, and wished we could remain longer, as I wanted to talk more with his wife, who also was skilled in iconography.

The rain stopped. I joked with Galina as to whether her mother had arranged that too. Then we all went to visit the monastery and the church.

Elena, who was in a vodka-induced uplifted mood, picked on Lulya, asking her, "Tell me, Lulya, didn't you go to a *komsomol* school that taught that religion was the opium of people? How come you want to visit the church? I also noticed you took a bottle of holy water with you. Is it to water the cactus you smuggled from Mexico?"

Lulya snarled back at her, "I am too evolved to believe in this religious nonsense. I only play along so that I won't be bothered with silly questions from fanatics like you!"

"What a liar you are, Lulya," said Lisa with a placid smile. "I saw you cross yourself when you thought nobody was looking. Don't worry, Comrade Ludmilla, we have no spies here to report you to your Communist Party members, so you need not pretend you are an atheist. Moreover, if I am not mistaken, I saw you in the Cathedral of Christ the Savior during last Lent. Were you there perhaps on a party assignment?"

"Leave her alone, Lisa," said Elena. "She thinks that the Communist regime is coming back and she wants to be in their good books. Now that we are going to visit the church, let's ask God to bring her to her senses.

"Moreover, it is not Christian to be criticizing everybody," added Elena, determined to have the last word.

The church was empty when our small group came in, with the exception of an old monk who was snuffing out some of the candles. The rain had stopped for a while and daylight was streaming through the multicolored glass windows on both sides of the walls. An imposing altar with closed gates dominated the far end. Icons of Christ, the Virgin Mary and the saints were painted on the panels of the altar gate. Large gilded Bibles lay on pedestals and a large replica of the Holy Virgin of Kursk reposed on a central high table. The icon glowed with silver and turquoise stones, which covered the whole surface of the holy image, from which only the grieving face of the Virgin Mary looked back at me.

We stayed at the church a short while and tiptoed out silently.

At dusk, we returned to our van for our trip back to Kursk. We were all tired after our busy day. Elena and Lulya were sleeping, leaning against each other like two loving sisters.

That evening, after dinner, Ilya, Marina, Galina and I planned to share information about my ancestors, and I was glad that Lulya would not be attending that meeting, since Lydia Maximovna diplomatically promised to take the three cousins to a performance of the Tula folk dancing group.

Nine

Night had fallen. After dinner, Galina, Marina and Ilya joined me in one of the small rooms put at our disposal by our gracious hostess. Galina was taking notes. She adjusted the lampshade just enough to illuminate her notebook, while Ilya fiddled with a tiny tape recorder. I made myself comfortable on a small sofa covered with colorful tapestries, while the three young people sat on the carpeted floor. They were barefoot, having shed their shoes at the front porch, Russian-style.

I watched their expectant young faces, and marveled at the intensity of their interest as they prepared to listen to me. *How unspoiled and dedicated they are*, I thought. How much work and effort Marina had put into her published work about the architecture of old estates of the region; and dear Galina, who spent long hours at libraries and bookstores in the hopes of salvaging treasures lost during the terrible years of bondage and ignorance.

Ilya looked up. "I have collected a great deal of material about your family," he said, "but I would like to have more information as to the origins of the Markov family. I brought with me your family crest, which I copied from the heraldic book at the library. Maybe you could interpret some of its symbols for me?"

"I'll be glad to do it," I said. "When I was still a little girl, Father had a copy made by a graphic artist and I am familiar with the historical meaning of our crest. Let's start first with any questions that you may have, and we'll go on from there."

"Do you have," asked Ilya, "a genealogical tree showing names and dates of the descendants?" Then with a sly smile he asked, "Could you tell us some spicy anecdotes and stories to liven up the dry facts about any of your ancestors—the kind that is known only to the family?"

I chuckled with pleasure. Here was someone with a sense of humor. I hoped his historical accounts would be peppered with comical or racy facts. Many historians tend to be too stiff and serious, to my taste, when they stick strictly to events and dates, putting the patient reader to sleep.

"Yes, indeed, Ilya," I said. "I have with me a copy of our family tree, which I will be happy to give you. In addition, I will be glad to share with you some titillating stories of family skeletons. As a matter of fact, I can tell you about two of my ancestors who were colorful historical figures, plus some family gossip, not mentioned in the history books, which my father told me he heard from his great-grandfather."

"This is fabulous," said Ilya. "That is exactly what I am looking for. I am so lucky to be able to glean such privileged information from a member of the family that I am researching."

"Most of my ancestors," I began, "I knew only through official documents, family albums and portraits. I thought they were a dreary collection of individuals in starched shirts. A number of portraits were of military men in uniform with decorations from the numerous wars which old Russia fought with her neighbors. However, there were exceptions.

"I am the last descendant of an ancient family, the Markovs, whose members, from the year 1073, faithfully served their Tsar and country. They were mainly soldiers, bankers and writers, whose sense of duty matched a fierce and unshakable faith in God. This faith challenged them to be the best among their equals to serve their less-privileged countrymen. Were they all paragons of virtue? The answer to that lies in the tumultuous history of Russia, where some founders of our family had the dubious honor of being adventurers, highway robbers and despots, owning entire villages of serfs, whom they could dispose of in any way they chose. These were strong people who had their part in building the Russian Empire and an important place in the saga of our family.

"They shared in the enlightened ideas of the Russian Renaissance during the reign of Peter the Great and Catherine II, who had made significant strides to catch up with the rest of Europe. Russia was still recovering from the Tartar occupation that held its people in bondage for two hundred years, and it took some doing on the part of Peter the Great to convert the caftan-robed noblemen into European diplomats. As for Catherine the Great, besides numerous other innovations, she introduced the monetary system in Russia."

Galina said, "But I understand that your family dates back to the fifteenth century, long before the Russian Renaissance. Am I wrong?"

"No," I said. "You are correct in that respect. Mark Tolmach Volshenin gave our family its start in 1473. He was a talented man, at the court of Prince Ivan III of Moscow, the first ruler of the newly created Russian Empire. As a reward for his distinguished services, Mark was appointed as Ambassador to the court of Shah Hussein Hassan of Persia. Mark Tolmach was a linguist and the history books describe him as being fluent in various Tartar dialects. This particular knowledge was instrumental in his extraordinary adventures, which were documented in a book *Il Fantastico Viagge de Ambrogio Cantarini* [The Fantastic Voyage of Ambrogio Cantarini], written by the Ambassador of the Republic of Venice to Persia, Ambrogio Cantarini."

"How exciting," said Marina. "Although it does make sense that he could communicate with the Tarters, since they still occupied the Russian territory at that time. It speaks volumes for Mark Tolmach that he was singled out to be appointed Ambassador to Persia."

"Persia was always a friend to Russia," I went on. "They have a historical friendship. They have never been at war with each other, and even today the two governments maintain a neighborly attitude. That said, I'll go back to my story.

"In this book, the author, Ambrogio Cantarini, spins an incredible tale of how he and Mark Tolmach, also known as Marko Ross, because of his Russian origin, were traveling companions in the year 1476.

"According to Cantarini, the two envoys were returning to their respective countries, when the Venetian diplomat received word that a warring Tartar tribe had cut off the merchant route by which he was planning to travel. Mark Tolmach invited him to travel with him to Russia. Together with their retinues, they had to cross vast uninhabited areas, teeming with nomadic bands, and only the knowledge of the Tartar dialects and the quick wit of Mark Tolmach saved them from certain death. Returned safely to Russia, Mark Tolmach and Cantarini were warmly welcomed by Prince Ivan III. Cantarini spent a few months in Moscow, and then returned to Venice by land and sea."

"Who," asked Ilya, "found out about Cantarini's book? Surely it could not have been translated into Russian in those early times?"

"Indeed, no. Four centuries later, in the year 1830, my great-grandfather, the writer Evgeni Markov, discovered by chance the translation of Cantarini's book into French when he visited the Vatican library."

"Yes," Galina said. "In my thesis on your great-grandfather Evgeni, I have included this particular discovery. I was amazed at the time when I read how he was looking for some ties between the Venetian Republic and early Russia, and it was by sheer accident that he discovered Cantarini's book. But I am interrupting. Please go on."

I continued, "When Prince Ivan became Tsar Ivan I of Russia, he united scattered princedoms into a Russian Empire. He generously endowed Mark Tolmach with honors and land in the fertile region south of Moscow, and bestowed upon him the title of *Stolbovoy Dvorianin* [Founder Nobleman] for valuable services to the Tsar."

"How does that show in your family crest?" asked Marina. She smoothed the rolled-up parchment, and they examined the colorful emblem divided into four parts.

"Well," I said, "in the upper left corner appears the Lion of St. Mark holding a cross, which represents Mark Tolmach's service to the Venetian Republic, earning him the name of Marco Ross [Marko the Russian]. The upper right shows the half-moon and star as a symbol of his diplomatic career in Persia. In the lower left is a castle, symbolizing land ownership granted by the first ruler of Russia, and in the lower right, a mounted courier representing a diplomatic mission."

Ilya laughed. "I bet that Marco Ross was an outgoing person and fond of adventures."

"I am sure that he was. The family lore, passed on from one generation to the next, portrayed Marco Ross as a fun-loving character with a roving eye for whatever beauty crossed his path. His adventures at the Persian court were probably coincidental with his departure back to Russia, although Cantarini does not mention that in his book.

"In Russia, he was the happy father of ten children. The annals do not mention how many wives he had. Only two of his children survived. One of them, Andrei, succeeded his father as head of the family and fathered seven children. His eldest son was the legendary Kildiar, also known as Koudiar in the Russian folklore. Even today, when Russians gather together and fondly sing ancient songs, they sing the legend of the Twelve Robbers, who, with their leader Koudiar, robbed the rich and shared his booty with the poor. The song says that they lived in dense woods and terrorized wealthy travelers riding the highways. The song goes on to tell how one day, this Russian-style Robin Hood had a revelation from God. As a result, he left his companions and entered a monastery under the name Pitirim, to serve God and men."

My three friends laughed and Marina hummed the first line of the song.

"We all know that," said Ilya, "but is there any truth to that legend? There are colorful additions to the truth, and Russians have long admired folk heroes, especially those who helped the poor. The song 'Volga' is also about the famous bandit Stenka Razin, who terrorized the river country, and although he is immortalized by many folk songs, he must have been a particularly nasty number."

"Quite true, Ilya," I said. "But in the case of Koudiar, there is an amazing story, which happens to be true. It has remained intact in our family history, and my great-grandfather Evgeni has mentioned it in his manuscripts. I am sure that Galina has already researched this."

"I just skimmed the surface of that event," said Galina. "I found documents saying that Kildiar was the son of Andrei, and that he was one of the close counselors of Ivan the Terrible. Kildiar was sent to Poland to negotiate some disputed territory between Poland and Russia, and shortly after his return he fell into disfavor with Ivan. That's as much as I found out, but I am sure there is more to that story."

"Oh, yes," I said. "At first, Ivan the Terrible favored Kildiar and showered him with gifts and honors. Kildiar, in his turn, adored the Tsar and was very loyal to him. Kildiar was married to a very beautiful woman who attended the court festivities with him, and the emperor's lustful eye singled her out as a possible favorite. To get rid of Kildiar, he sent him off to Poland on an official mission, but in a secret dispatch, asked the Polish king to assassinate the young nobleman. This plan did not work out, as the king of Poland, planning to start yet another war with Russia, took Kildiar into his confidence and told him about the plot. Kildiar did not believe him and rushed back to Russia to denounce what he believed to be the treachery of the Polish king. In the meantime, Ivan the Terrible had made his move to seduce Kildiar's wife.

"Apparently, she was not accommodating and the humiliated Tsar had the young woman killed. When Kildiar arrived back from Poland, he was rewarded with a banquet at which he was served a broth in which floated his wife's fingers."

The three young people gasped with horror, but did not interrupt my story. I went on. "Ivan threw Kildiar into a dungeon from which he somehow managed to escape. Vowing revenge, he gathered around him a band of unhappy noblemen, who had their own axes to grind with the unpopular Tsar. Together, they began to attack the highway on which the valuables and gold destined for the Tsar's treasury were transported. They were very efficient and mercilessly killed the couriers who accompanied the transports. They were never caught, and thus Kildiar got his revenge on the cruel ruler. Upon the death of Ivan the Terrible, Koudiar, as he was then named, entered a monastery to expiate his sins and to pray for his wife's soul. He took on the name of Father Pitirim."

I stopped and looked at my three friends. "Is this enough family lore for you?" I asked. "It is getting late and I have to pack my little suitcase. We will be leaving tomorrow."

"Will there be time for you to tell us about your own life?" asked Galina. "We would like to know the circumstances just before the revolution when your grandparents still lived in Pokrovskoye. What happened in 1914 when the First World War broke out? Your father must have been just out of the Officers' Academy. Did he participate in the war? How about your mother? I understand that your grandmother died when still young. I saw her photograph. She was very beautiful. Can you tell us something about her?"

Ilya joined in. "You were born in Egypt, so how did you feel being Russian in Egypt? Did you feel exiled like your parents? Were you happy growing up?"

I sighed. "I was thinking of writing an account of the events dating from the beginning of the century, using my father's diaries of those years, including the First World War and the Russian revolution. I think that an important part of the memoir will be about our life in Egypt. This is a page in history that encompasses about thirty-five years, when a group of Russian exiles arrived in that hospitable country, where they could remain under Egypt's protection. It is curious to note that they all came in 1920, and all but a few left between the years of 1957 and 1959. I doubt whether this has been documented elsewhere. I shall research the matter upon my return. I will have plenty of time on my flight home to think about that, and I will keep in touch with all of you as to any progress in that respect.

"I'll say good-bye to you now, dear friends, and hopefully, we will see each other again. I'll be constantly in touch with you, as I feel that I have made real friends in Russia," I said, holding back my tears.

As I lay on my narrow cot, I thought about Ilya's questions about Egypt. I was born there, so was I ever really an exile? Did I ever feel I was an exile? I closed my eyes and filled my being with images of my childhood. Images of the land where I was born; where the incredible blue sky merged on the horizon with the warm Mediterranean; where half-forgotten brown faces with shining kind eyes and white teeth laughed with me. Learning how to chew the sugar cane in a Bedouin tent and running freely in the sand, playing ball with Ratiba's children. Other images flashed through my mind in a kaleidoscope and before I knew it, I was asleep.

Ten

The next day, Lydia Maximovna prepared a basket containing meat piroshki and fruit for us to take along, and bundled us all into the van. I was relieved that Lulya was not to return to Moscow with us, supposedly because of her botanical assignment. She still managed to stick with us and declared that she would accompany us to the station. I decided to grin and bear it.

A few blocks down the road, the van stopped and we picked up Sasha, Maria and Evgeni. Sasha smiled and said conspiratorially, "We are going to give you a real Russian send-off," as she settled down beside me, which left me wondering what else Lydia Maximovna had up her sleeve.

By then, my knee had healed enough for me to walk normally to our train. The driver took care of our suitcases and shepherded us to our car. It was the same train car we had when we arrived a week before, dark green with gold lettering with the name the "Kursk Nightingale." A helpful young woman in uniform showed us to our compartment. This was the night train and most of the passengers were already aboard. We still had time before the departure, and Elena, Lisa and I stood on the narrow platform in the open door, chatting with our friends, promising to call and to write.

"Give me a call when you get to Moscow," said Lydia Maximovna. "I will still be at home and you can then tell me how your trip went."

"Yes," said Lulya. "You must let me know how Tanya is planning to organize your good-bye celebration. I bet she will invite a lot of people. I am sorry I won't be there."

I was about to mumble that we would miss her, when Elena nudged me to silence and said, "Surely, Lulya, you will be working on your assignment in some field, or do you intend to stay longer with Lydia Maximovna?"

That provoked a peal of laughter from Lisa, while everyone smiled, pretending it was a joke.

There was a lull in our good-byes, when all of a sudden, Sasha said: "Let's begin!" and the four of them broke into a lively song—a catchy ballad about a pair of lovers saying good-bye at a railway station. It was quite modern in tune and words, which were simple and touching. The gist of it was that they were begging the conductor to delay the train so that they could say farewell one more time.

We laughed and clapped. The young attendant in uniform joined us, and people appeared from the farther ends of the pier, curious to see what was happening.

Encouraged by our support, the small chorus started another song. This time it was an old folk song about friends parting. Sasha, the leading singer, was in her element, seconded by Lydia in her rhythmic accompaniment of "Tam, tarararam"; even Lulya joined Maria and Evgeni in another song that we all knew.

The third train whistle went off, but the songs continued. The attendant did not close the door, so we could stand and wave from the train as it smoothly glided away from our singing friends. When we lost sight of them, I was swallowing tears at the unexpected and touching performance. Lisa and Elena were also deeply affected by this show of goodwill; Elena blew her nose with gusto, and Lisa was teary-eyed.

We trudged to our compartment and were surprised to see a young man of about twenty-five years of age occupying the corner seat. He said, "Hello, I will be sharing your compartment. Do you mind if I use the upper bunk? My name is Alexei."

"You are certainly welcome," said Lisa. "My name is Lisa and this is our cousin Vicka from the United States. The person next to you is our cousin Elena and she is a Muscovite." We sat chatting until the attendant brought us clean sheets, pillows and blankets for the night.

The lights were turned off and I lay sleepless. I watched the sudden flashes of light as we sped by nameless stations, illuminating our compartment for a moment. As the train rattled over a bridge or negotiated a curve, I would dreamily wonder where we were. My mind was too tired to dwell on the last few days, so I let my thoughts drift.

I awoke up with a start when the loudspeaker announced that we would arrive in Moscow in an hour. It was five o'clock in the morning. A heavy fog shrouded the world outside, and not a light appeared in any of the tiny houses as we flashed by.

Elena managed to climb down without falling and wished us all a grumpy good morning before disappearing for a smoke. There was a general rush to the bathrooms and a sleepy attendant brought us some hot tea.

We shared our food with Alexei, who joined us from his upper berth. He had a quiet manner of speaking and finally, his shyness wore off.

"Are you a student?" I asked him.

"No," he said. "I started working in a shoe factory six months ago. My parents wanted me to study, but I was anxious to start earning money as soon as possible."

"But surely," I said, "you could still study in a night school?"

"That is easy to say," said Alexei. "I get off work at five o'clock and by the time I arrive at home, it is past six o'clock. That does not give me much time to rest, get organized and go out to school again."

"I am very interested," I said, "to learn about the working conditions in your new democracy."

"There is not much to say. We don't have much hope for the future. Before democracy, we all ate well and were guaranteed to have some kind of a job. Food was cheap, even if we had to wait in lines. Now, in our work, we have to prove that we are better than the other guy, and if we work harder, we can advance. Before, it was not that difficult. Now we have plenty of food, but it is more expensive. Besides, now I have to get up really early to get to work on time and I have to commute by the metro, which is always crowded. It is not like you have it in the U.S.A. You are all rich there."

I asked, "What time do you start work, Alexei?"

"At nine o'clock in the morning," he said, "and we only have an hour for lunch."

"Well, Alexei," I said, "did you know that our factory workers in America start their day at eight o'clock, and often work night shifts? I was a teacher and I had to be at school at eight in the morning and we, too, had only one hour for lunch. My husband and I woke up at five in the morning to get ready for work. Most Americans, whether blue or white collar, have the same schedule."

"But you are getting paid a lot of money," said Alexei.

"Not really," I said. "I taught in a private school. I received a small salary, but plenty of responsibility. As to competition in work, this is what keeps the ball rolling. If you prove that your work is better than that of others, you will be promoted in your line of business. If you just do the minimum, you will probably not advance, for there are always those who are more ambitious."

"What about those who are not capable of doing better work, or those who are not smart enough?" asked Alexei, getting red-faced. "Do they have to starve?"

"In a democracy, Alexei, we have the free will to improve ourselves through study and hard work, and we are judged by our performance. Those who are not capable of improving themselves in a particular line of work usually seek another job at which they can excel. We have many night schools and trade schools. Many companies have training classes for their employees. We have a saying in the States that there is no such thing as a free lunch."

Alexei shrugged. "This is a typical capitalistic idea for exploiting workers," he said derisively. "But do go on. I am also interested to hear your views."

I went on. "We have to be responsible for our families and ourselves. The democratic countries expect their citizens to earn their salaries by working hard."

"In our socialistic system," said Alexei, "we did not have unfair laws like that. My father said that he was better off before 1991. He was getting paid and received increases regularly whether he produced a lot of work or was unable to put out his production quota."

Lisa listened attentively to our discussion. She was ready to interrupt several times, but kept silent. Alexei's last remark provoked her to raise her voice. She said, "That's why, young man, your socialistic system went bankrupt. We were promised that Communism would rule the world, but the sad fact is that it set Russia back a hundred years. Obviously, your father is too old to adapt to a new system, but you are young enough to reap the benefits of a democratic way of life. Change is painful and we are all hurting, but we have already made great strides. I pray that God grants us honest and capable leaders."

There was silence in our compartment. I wanted to hug Lisa for speaking so frankly to Alexei, and I hoped that he would think about what she said. I knew that there were still die-hard Communists in Russia, and that only time would heal this long-suffering country.

Sergey was waiting for us at the station. His welcome and kindness made me feel that I was part of his family.

A lanky young man who turned out to be Pavel, Elena's son, came with him. After a brief introduction, Pavel loaded Lisa and Elena's bags onto a cart and hurried them off to the parking lot.

"Do you know, Vikulia," he said, "why don't you extend your visit for another month? You only spent two weeks with us and then you went to Kursk. I know a fellow in the foreign visa department who could fix you up with a one-month extension visa."

Without waiting for my response, my forceful cousin quickly gathered my belongings and led me towards the exit.

"Let's hurry and go to the visa department at once," he said, maneuvering his large frame with agility into the busy street outside the station.

"Whoa, Sergey," I said. "Not so fast. I really have to leave tomorrow morning. I would love to stay, but George is expecting me. As soon as I get back, I will start on my memoir. Today, I will tell you and Tanya about my wonderful visit to Kursk. I don't know how I could ever repay you for the wonderful opportunity you have given me to visit Kursk. I am sure that you didn't even suspect what a treasure of memories you have given me when you were arranging my trip."

"Well," said Sergey, "that means that Tanya and I will have to visit you again soon. Maybe next summer, when Tanya will be on her summer vacation."

After arriving at the apartment, I was able to tell them all about my experiences in Kursk. Tanya was preparing a farewell feast for me and listened while standing at the stove, armed with a spoon.

"We have a surprise for you tonight," said Sergey. "We called the sculptor Klikov, who promised to come and meet you. He is not coming alone. His girlfriend is Nadia Krigina, the famous folk singer. They are both from Kursk. Klikov is particularly interested to meet you because he is a fervent admirer of your great-grand-uncle, Nicholas Markov, who was the renowned right-wing member of the Russian Duma [Parliament] just before the revolution."

"Dear old Grand-Uncle Nicholas," I said. "It is amazing how many enemies he created because of his views. He was very outspoken during his stint with the Duma. I heard that he had a real fight with the liberal member from his district."

"That may be so," said Sergey, "but Klikov is very active in conservative circles today, and even wants to honor the old boy with a monument at the site of his Alexandrovka estate."

"That will be the day," said Tanya. "But to tell you truth, there is a big movement towards nationalism today. I am afraid that Russia again will have more political parties than they have citizens."

On that note, we all had a drink.

My last night in Moscow was a suitable ending to a fantastic adventure. All that remains in my memory are friendly, loving faces, lots of good food and many, many toasts. Klikov, the sculptor, sat next to me and spoke about his childhood in a small village near Pokrovskoye. There were no highways then and he had to walk to his village school in spite of the snow. I can still feel Klikov's strong handshake and kind words, and hear the unforgettable voice of Nadia Krigina, who serenaded us until the wee hours of the morning.

* * *

On a sad note, I have to mention that a month after I returned from Russia, I learned that Klikov passed away, losing his battle with cancer. (He never mentioned to his friends that he was terminally ill.)

* * *

I boarded my early plane too exhausted after the party. I was still groggy and as soon as I reached my seat, I buckled up and went to sleep. I would never forget my experiences in Russia, nor the wonderful cousins and friends who now would be part of my life forever.

I knew that on my return home, I would write about my visit to Russia. I did not forget my promise to Ilya, Galina and Marina that I would also include an account of my life in Egypt. Drifting in and out of sleep, I felt a surge of happiness. I was returning home to George, our lovely garden and my friend Misha, with the blue eyes and an incredible fluffy tail.

I woke up several times, smiling, remembering my Russian friends. I also remembered the serious look of Sergey, when he asked whether in my heart I was Russian, Egyptian or American. I said then, as gently as I could, for I knew that my answer would disappoint him.

"Sergey, my friend, I was born in Egypt, but I was never assimilated into the Egyptian society. I never attended Arab schools, and my spoken Arabic was the colloquial lingo spoken by everybody, but very different from literary written and spoken Arabic. I never asked and was never issued papers of Egyptian citizenship. I was not alone in that respect, for the rest of the White Russian community followed the same pattern.

"I loved Egypt and the Egyptians, but we were always considered foreigners, and as part of a foreign colony, there was little interaction between the Egyptian population and various European colonies, mainly because of the low level of education of the Egyptian middle and lower classes.

"I was brought up in a Russian family, with conservative values my parents inherited from their forefathers. They proudly declared themselves true Russians, although Russia had by that time transformed itself into the Soviet Union. I was taught to respect the white, blue and red Tsarist flag that was reverently put away, folded by the holy Icons, until the time when the Russian people would have the sense to overturn the communist regime.

"So in the meantime, while I thought I was Russian, there was no Russia, but it was there in my parents' mind, and I learned to love their memories since I had none myself.

"When I became an American citizen in 1963, I realized for the first time what it was to really belong to a country, and to have a passport which protected me in other countries. But most of all, the ideas behind the words of the American constitution changed my way of thinking. I knew I wanted to live in a country where I was considered equal to everybody else, where I did not fear political terror and injustice, and I was free to think and to speak my mind.

"My pilgrimage to Russia did not change my attitude. Although my visit was wonderful, still this was not the Russia of my parents' time, and neither it was mine. My loyalty and appreciation for American values are now so ingrained in me they will remain with me until the end of my days. However, Russian traditions, history and folk-lore will always be a part of me, as a gift from my parents and my ancestors."

I believe Sergey understood me, for he put his arms around me and kissed my forehead. At that memory I closed my eyes and went to sleep, knowing I was going home where I belonged.

And that is what I did. I went home to my dear George who had missed me for the three weeks I was away. Seeing his eyes shine with pleasure when I returned was the greatest gift of all. Once more our life resumed its serene pattern, which I thought would never end.

But it did end, too soon. Two years later, George went to sleep in my arms for the last time, leaving me with a wealth of wonderful memories of our life together. He is still with me, at my side, wherever I go, and we still share very special moments when we are alone.

The End